The Art of a Salesman:
The Life of Sir Merton Russell-Cotes

Paul Whittaker

Copyright © 2019 Paul Whittaker

All rights reserved.

ISBN-13: 978-1-0720-1406-5

For Anne, Nicola and Ian

CONTENTS

	List of Illustrations	vii
	Foreword	ix
	Acknowledgements	xi
	Preface	xiii
1	Descendant	1
2	Traveller	14
3	Hotelier	30
4	Newcomer	42
5	Candidate	55
6	Commissioner	66
7	Globetrotter	77
8	Fellow	89
9	Progressive	101
10	Mayor	113
11	Exhibitor	125
12	Crusader	138
13	Donor	151
14	Recipient	162
15	Knight	172
16	Philanthropist	183
17	Benefactor	193
	Selected Bibliography	199
	Index	203

LIST OF ILLUSTRATIONS

1	Tettenhall church from the Lower Green	3
2	Grave of Samuel Cotes in Tettenhall churchyard	5
3	Merton's father, Samuel	7
4	James MacEwan, Merton's brother-in-law	10
5	Calle Piedad, Buenos Aires	16
6	Annie Clark with her father	20
7	St Vincent Crescent, Glasgow	22
8	Annie and Merton on their wedding day	23
9	Premises of John Blair & Co., Glasgow	24
10	Hanover Hotel advertisements	32
11	Anita and Lottie Cotes	36
12	Merton's mother, Elizabeth	37
13	Clara MacEwan, Merton's sister	39
14	The Bath Hotel in 1860	43
15	Albert Edward, Prince of Wales	46
16	Merton's brother, Alfred	49
17	The Royal Bath Hotel in the 1880s	52
18	Empress Eugénie	56
19	Royal Bath Hotel advertisement	58
20	Joseph Cutler	60
21	Wyndham Portal	63
22	Christopher Creeke	67
23	*SS Bournemouth*	71
24	G. Lane & Co. advertisement	73
25	Horace Dobell	74
26	The clipper *Torrens*	78
27	Merton, Annie and Bert at the Last Chance Mine, Ballarat	79
28	The White Terraces at Lake Rotomahana	81
29	Richard Tangye	83
30	Annie in plush cloak	85
31	Mont Dore and Royal Exeter hotels	91
32	Japanese Drawing Room at the Royal Bath	92
33	Invitation to the Japanese Drawing Room	93
34	Wedgwood Drawing Room at the Royal Bath	94
35	Royal Bath banquet invitation	97
36	Bournemouth's last board of improvement commissioners	103
37	Reading of Bournemouth's charter of incorporation	104
38	Merton as Norfolk Capes	107

39	Henry Newlyn	110
40	Beach amusements at Bournemouth	115
41	Merton as mayor	117
42	Lynwood, Kildare and Rothesay	118
43	Group photograph with Prince Henry of Battenberg	121
44	South Road in 1962	126
45	Plan of 'the chalet'	130
46	*The Dawn of Love*	133
47	Bust of George Washington	134
48	Bournemouth regatta, 1900	139
49	Main hall and balcony, East Cliff Hall	141
50	East Cliff Hall	142
51	East Cliff, c. 1900	145
52	Henry Irving	153
53	East Cliff from the pier, early 1900s	154
54	Building of the undercliff drive	158
55	Opening of the undercliff drive	159
56	Storm damage on the undercliff drive	163
57	*Girl Combing Her Hair*	164
58	Merton by Eustace Nash	166
59	Merton, July 1909	170
60	John Burns	175
61	Entrance to East Cliff Hall	176
62	Russell-Cotes family group	177
63	Bert Cotes	179
64	Princess Beatrice	186
65	Group photograph with Prince Albert	187
66	Diamond wedding presentation	189
67	Annie's funeral cortege	190
68	William Pickford	194
69	Russell-Cotes Art Gallery and Museum	196
70	Main hall at the Russell-Cotes Art Gallery and Museum	197

Cover image of Sir Merton and Lady Annie Russell-Cotes by Frank Richards reproduced by courtesy of BCP Council

FOREWORD

By Duncan Walker, curator of the Russell-Cotes Art Gallery and Museum

This book has been long overdue, and it is to Paul Whittaker's credit alone that he is the first to critically investigate the life of our co-founder, Sir Merton Russell-Cotes (1835–1921). Sir Merton's autobiography, *Home and Abroad*, is recognised as a difficult historical text, written in the final years of the author's life and published by his son a few months after his death. Its convoluted structure contains both valedictory diatribes, charming personal anecdotes, the archaic opinions of an older man and, for the curator, vital provenance information about items in the collections we hold. However, a curator's life is inevitably a busy one and so *Home and Abroad* went unchallenged until we decided to give Paul, then a newly recruited volunteer tour guide, the job of extracting a coherent set of facts from the book. That seed, along with relentless questions from the public around the rather mysterious source of the Russell-Cotes wealth, led Paul to do what we never had the time to do. Long-established myths and incorrect assumptions on our part have finally been settled.

A joy of Paul's book is showing how, as a product of his time and space, Sir Merton seemingly cast himself into the economic tsunami sweeping across the British Isles in pursuit of success. That Sir Merton Russell-Cotes was important to the history of Bournemouth is without doubt. Sir Merton, being Sir Merton, made sure that we all know about it. It is the period of his life he concentrates the most on in *Home and Abroad*. I am particularly grateful to Paul for uncovering our founder's pre-Bournemouth life in Scotland, Ireland and northern England, about which we had only disjointed impressions and few facts.

That Sir Merton and Lady Annie Russell-Cotes (1835–1920) decided to gift their collections and home to the people of Bournemouth is a decision for which I am very grateful. While Sir Merton's personal beliefs and opinions, especially as an older man, are not in line with my own I salute his sheer tenacity and determination to achieve his goals in a world which was a lot less forgiving than ours. He was a complex individual who loved and credited his wife as co-collector, valued the work of female artists but still virulently opposed universal suffrage. On the one hand he rants about the pace of modern life with its rapid technological change, but his travels and business activities were made possible by the telegraph, the steam engine and a global banking system.

This book reveals more about Sir Merton than we have ever known before but, tantalisingly, it often raises more questions than answers. We now know that Sir Merton made his wealth through his talents, but why he felt the need to hide his humble origins when others, such as his contemporaries Lord Leverhulme (1851–1925) and Andrew Carnegie (1835–1919), celebrated them remains unanswered. This book will, I hope, help thrust Sir Merton into the light of further scholarship and examination, where his achievements and contribution to Bournemouth and the cultural life of Britain will be recognised.

Duncan Walker, 2019

ACKNOWLEDGEMENTS

I would like to thank the following people for their help with my research for this book: Duncan Walker, the curator of the Russell-Cotes Art Gallery and Museum, gave me access to the museum's archive and shared many insights into the founders' collecting and art-buying habits; Andrew Popp, Professor of Business at the University of Liverpool's Management School, helped me to understand the role of factors in nineteenth-century commerce and allowed me to draw upon his research; John Porter, Group Archivist at Prudential PLC, carried out numerous searches in the archives of the Scottish Amicable on my behalf; Julia Hudson did a similarly thorough job in the archives of Highgate School; and Alina Silveira willingly shared her research into St Andrew's Scots School in Buenos Aires, filling a vital gap in the book's timeline. Thanks are also due to my son, Ian, and to Duncan Walker, Miranda Prescott and Helen Baggott for their feedback on my draft manuscripts. Any remaining errors in the text are entirely mine. Lastly, I must thank my wife, Anne, for her patience with what must have seemed like an endless project. With the publication of this book, she can at last get some peace.

PREFACE

The Russell-Cotes Art Gallery and Museum is Bournemouth's cultural gem. Perched on the clifftop near the pier, it is a rare surviving example of a house built to show off the art treasures and curiosities collected by its wealthy owners. The museum is not the most obvious diversion for anyone enjoying a day at the beach, but it often surprises those who take the time to discover its charms. I spent barely an hour there on my first visit, made as a newcomer to the area in the 1980s, and came away thinking it was an odd sort of place. It felt as if someone had gathered together every painting, sculpture and knick-knack they had ever taken a fancy to in their life. I left none the wiser about why it was called 'The Russell-Cotes' or how such a large and diverse collection came to be there. It was well over twenty years before I visited again, but I made more of an effort the second time around. By then, a lottery grant had brought the building back to its Edwardian prime, and it was streets ahead of how I remembered it. Looking for a challenge after redundancy, I volunteered as a conservation cleaner and later switched to tour guiding. Only then did I learn about the museum's founders, the couple known to all simply as 'Merton and Annie'. Understanding them is the key to appreciating the building and its contents. They travelled widely and collected broadly, resulting in a host of exhibits ranging from academy paintings to ethnic artefacts. To the casual observer, like me in the 1980s, it can be overwhelming.

As I took on the role of explaining the collection to the museum's visitors, I struggled to answer many of their questions about the lives of the founders. This encouraged me to read the two hefty volumes of *Home and Abroad: An Autobiography of an Octogenarian*. Written by Merton – Sir Merton Russell-Cotes, that is – the book sets out his stall at the start of volume one. 'If you do not place something of your family history on record,' he says, 'it is sometimes invented for you, and it generally does you less justice than you would do yourself.'[1] What follows is a bombastic work short on detail, about family or otherwise, and long on recording his achievements. It is an extraordinary opus, bloated by lengthy press quotes, an extensive travelogue, a rash of name-dropping and uncredited extracts from a raft of publications. The writing is very much of its time, complete with the prevailing attitudes to race, class, religion and empire that can jar with a modern audience. Of more relevance here is what the book reveals about the author. Published posthumously by his son, the final text may not be exactly as written by Merton, but it echoes much of what was said about him during the latter stages of his life. He knew how he wanted to be remembered – the traveller, the mayor, the collector and so on – and labours his points to excess.

In many ways, *Home and Abroad* is more of a eulogy to its writer than an autobiography. Merton came to prominence as the owner of Bournemouth's prestigious Royal Bath Hotel, but he reveals little about his rise through the ranks or the secrets of his business success. The story of how he and Annie gave their villa and art collection to the local council forms a key part of the narrative, as does his role in transforming the town from a genteel health resort to a haunt of the Victorian elite. His early life, by contrast, takes up just a few of the book's one thousand pages, and there is little sign of the string of controversies that punctuated the first twenty years of his life in Bournemouth. He claims to have held a senior position in the insurance industry before entering the hotel trade, but the evidence suggests he was nothing of the sort. A link to the gentry, an eminent godfather and an aborted spell at university also turn out to be suspect. These things indicate a reluctance to admit that he came from humble stock and had once led an ordinary life. Merton spent most of his twenties and thirties as a salesman and commercial traveller, a line of work that explains his knack for self-promotion. It is a paradox, then, that he manages to undersell himself in *Home and Abroad* by trying too hard to impress his readers. The book would have been enhanced by showing the downs as well as the ups, while hearing about his trials and tribulations would have placed his legacy in proper perspective.

Merton drops his guard only when writing about Annie, the woman who shared his highs and lows for more than sixty years. There is little doubt that she played a big part in his rise, a fact he acknowledged at every opportunity. For that reason, I would have preferred to give her equal billing in the title of this book, but they lived in a world where wives had to make do with a supporting role and rarely made the newspapers in their own right. While Annie fared better than most in establishing her own identity, Merton is as cagey about her as he is about himself. And yet, despite its shortcomings, the mere existence of an autobiography has discouraged research into his life. He left little by way of a personal archive to help anyone inclined to investigate, while testimonies from people who knew him are also in short supply. That said, the work carried out in the early 1990s by Shaun Garner, the museum's late curator, led to one notable exception. As part of his master's thesis, Shaun taped an interview with Phyllis Lee-Duncan, one of Merton and

Annie's six grandchildren. She portrays her grandfather as a somewhat cantankerous old man who won gratitude and respect rather than admiration and affection. While the recording contains a few snippets of family history, there is nothing to suggest that Mrs Lee-Duncan knew anything more about Merton than he was prepared to make public. Even to his relatives, it seems that he was something of an enigma.

Although he loved formality and was finicky about titles, I have chosen to refer to Merton by his first name throughout the book. Rather than being disrespectful, it is the one point of consistency for a man whose name evolved down the years to match his rising status. He was a determined social climber who courted connections with a passion and conducted his affairs with single-minded vigour. This often led to conflict, and there were some in Bournemouth who made no secret of disliking him. That changed almost overnight when he and Annie announced their intention to give away their house and its treasures. It gave them the moral high ground, a position from which Merton was able to silence his critics and hand down a rose-tinted version of his place in the town's history. *Home and Abroad*'s lopsided account of his life and achievements should surprise no one, as autobiographers have the right to present themselves however they see fit. Biographers, on the other hand, have a duty to set posterity straight. This book is my attempt to do so.

Paul Whittaker
Bournemouth, 2019

Notes:

1. This maxim first appeared in *My Life: Sixty Years' Recollections of Bohemian London* by George R. Sims. It was published in 1917, the year Merton began his autobiography.

1

DESCENDANT

In 1892, Merton Russell Cotes, as he then styled himself, wrote a speculative letter to George Augustus Sala (1828–1895), a well-known writer and journalist. Sala had recently mentioned the Royal Bath Hotel in one of his columns, and the letter sought to persuade him to experience its delights for himself. It was a typical piece of opportunism by Merton, who scoured newspapers for openings and was never afraid to be pushy in the pursuit of publicity. After all, a visit by a respected journalist might lead to a favourable write-up for the Royal Bath. Merton reminded Sala of their brief meeting in Calcutta six years earlier and name-dropped Oscar Wilde and other famous guests of the hotel. If that failed to convince him, he referred Sala to a review of Bournemouth in a guidebook called *Flying Visits* and offered him a private suite of rooms. 'You can go out and in just as you please,' he added.[1]

On this occasion, Merton's enthusiasm for promoting the Royal Bath got the better of his good judgement. Harry Furniss (1854–1925), the author of *Flying Visits*, was a cartoonist for *Punch* who relished the quirkier sides of resort life. He found 'bronchial Bournemouth' depressing and joked that no one ever laughed there because visitors could muster only one working lung between three of them.[2] His wife, who was unwell at the time of their stay, had turned down the services of the Bedroom Brigade – a group of retired military men who sang hymns for the sick and infirm. By mentioning the guidebook in his letter, Merton also risked offending the man he sought to woo. Sala had once sued Furniss for claiming he was a failed artist who drew a foot with six toes in an art school entrance exam.

For Merton, the upsides of *Flying Visits* may have outweighed these drawbacks. Although disparaging of Bournemouth, Furniss took the opposite view of the Royal Bath, which he described as a 'princely hotel' and 'a temple of art'. The latter phrase, an allusion to its wealth of paintings, murals and sculptures, cropped up a few months later in a syndicated newspaper article that waxed lyrical about the town and heaped praise upon the hotel. Merton, one assumes, was as proactive in its publication as he had been direct in his approach to Sala. A former textiles and millinery salesman, he applied the same principles to promoting the Royal Bath as he had done to the sale of fabrics and hats in his younger days. Setting himself apart from the competition was the key to his success. Newspaper reviews, eminent patrons and a regal name helped the hotel to stand out. Opulent decoration and fine art made it unique.

Merton never ceased in his quest to keep the Royal Bath at the front rank of British hotels. Nor was he ever in doubt about the value of his contribution to Bournemouth's progress as a resort. Twenty-five years on from his letter to Sala, he felt confident enough in his achievements to set them down in writing for the benefit of future generations. The intervening period had seen his personal stock rise sharply and fall spectacularly, before climbing to heights that would have been unthinkable in 1892. He had overcome controversy and conquered mistrust to emerge, triumphant, as one of the town's most celebrated benefactors. And yet, despite his reputation as a hotelier and art connoisseur, he remained a salesman at heart. *Home and Abroad*, the voluminous autobiography he began in his eighties, is proof of the point – a gilded, varnished and less-than-candid portrayal of his path to a knighthood. It was his last, and most enduring, piece of salesmanship.

Merton began the book with a minor revision to his birthplace. He was born, he says, in May 1835 in the Staffordshire village of Tettenhall. Now a suburb of Wolverhampton, it stood apart from its neighbour until well into the twentieth century. 'Here Hampton's sons in vacant hours repair, taste rural joys and breathe a purer air,' runs the poem quoted by Merton in his preamble.[3] Tettenhall's unusual features – two village greens and streams flowing in opposite directions – have helped it to keep a distinct identity. In strolling around the Lower Green, only yards from the busy A41, it is easy to imagine a time when a mile of open countryside divided the village from the town. Many wealthy businessmen made it their home, well away from the noise and grime of their factories. It was, according to *Home and Abroad*, 'the most beautiful, and typical, English village.' [4]

Despite these eulogies and his obvious affection for the place, Merton, unlike his father, was not born in Tettenhall. He hailed from industrial Wolverhampton, a fact he was happy to acknowledge until relatively late in life. He also claimed descent from the Cotes family of Shropshire, whose seat was at Woodcote Hall, near Newport, and who were important enough to be included in Burke's *Dictionary of the Landed Gentry*. With a lineage stretching back to Norman times, the Shropshire Coteses were stalwarts of parliament, the Church, the law and the armed services. Merton adopted their coat of arms with its distinctive cockerel crest, but any connection between the two families is buried deep in the past. A dubious link to the gentry is, however, typical of an autobiography that often takes a fanciful view of personal and

1 An early 20th-century view of Tettenhall church from the Lower Green. The scene is little changed today. Merton believed that the houses either side of the church belonged to his grandfather and great-uncle, but they lived in a row of cottages, now demolished, behind the house on the right of the picture. (Author's collection)

family history.

Merton says that his great-grandfather bought an estate in Tettenhall in the early 1700s, but the truth is that the family settled there much later in the century and brought little with them by way of wealth. They were shoemakers and tailors, an integral part of village life but not among its most affluent residents. The more literate among them spelt their surname in several different ways, while the rest made do with making their mark with a cross. Later generations benefitted from a charity school in the village, an establishment where sand-filled trays stood in for slate and chalk. Blessed with the gifts of reading and writing, the family refined its name with a variety of results. Merton's father, born in 1796, settled on styling himself Samuel Coates. Samuel's much older cousin, Benjamin, preferred the Shropshire variety and so dropped the 'a'. Divided by one letter and a twenty-year age gap, confusing family ties brought the two cousins closer together. The avuncular Benjamin married the sister of Samuel's mother, thereby becoming his uncle in fact.[5] These two men, Merton's father and great-uncle, went on to start the business that formed the backdrop to his earliest years.

By the 1820s, young men were leaving the Staffordshire villages in their droves to look for work in Wolverhampton. Long renowned for its locksmiths, the town stood at the forefront of a manufacturing revolution. From hinges to hatchets and vices to vermin traps, if it was made in iron then Wolverhampton supplied it. The place was booming, and budding entrepreneurs could make a good living there. Samuel Coates was young enough to see the possibilities, while his uncle's standing in the community helped him to exploit them. Benjamin, who was a shoemaker by trade and had no children of his own, served as a churchwarden and as a trustee of the local union society – a sort of do-it-yourself welfare club.[6] He may have been inexperienced in the iron trade, but his reputation more than made up for it when it came to starting a business with his nephew.

Samuel Coates and Benjamin Cotes set themselves up as 'factors and wholesale ironmongers' in this age of opportunity. Merton refers to them as 'ironmasters and manufacturers', but factors stood lower down the supply chain and made their money by selling ironware, not making it.[7] The iron trade in those days consisted of a host of small factories making products destined for shops that were often more than a day's travel away. These firms relied on factors to sell their goods, a job that meant getting out on the road for many weeks at a time. Established factoring businesses hired men to carry out this work, but Samuel, as the younger partner in the firm, is likely to have done the job himself at the outset. A traveller – or bagman, as they were also called – followed regular routes that took in towns as much as a hundred miles away from home. He made the journeys in the saddle or by horse and cart, collecting payments and closing sales wherever he went.[8]

Soon after the firm opened for business, Samuel Coates married Elizabeth Law, a metalworker's daughter, at St Peter's Church in Wolverhampton. It was the spring of 1822. Heavily pregnant at the time of their marriage, Elizabeth gave birth to a daughter three days later. The girl, called Ann, survived only long enough for a baptism, and the couple returned to the church for a third time soon afterwards to bury her. A son was born the following year, named Samuel after his father. This marked the start of a procession of children over the next ten years – Emily, who died in infancy, then Mary, Clara, Georgina, Alfred and Charlotte. The family firm moved twice in this period, eventually settling at King Street in the heart of Wolverhampton. Samuel and Benjamin bought the freehold here, a big step up for men of their station. They were doing as well as could be expected in the competitive world of factoring and ironmongery.

Not long after the move to King Street, Elizabeth fell pregnant for the ninth time in thirteen years and delivered the couple's third son on Friday 8th May 1835. Having sided with convention for their other children, this time they settled upon a name that was something out of the ordinary. They called him Merton Russell Coates, which – as *Home and Abroad* cryptically explains – was after a link to Merton College, Oxford, with Russell adopted from an unspecified branch of the family. Whatever its source, the boy's first name was written as 'Morton' in the baptism register. His parents soon changed their minds if that was their first thought, as the name appears here and here alone. More likely, the parish clerk failed to decipher a note scribbled by a clergyman – an easy mistake to make with such an unusual name. Indeed,

2 The grave of Merton's father in Tettenhall churchyard, as restored in 1915. Samuel styled himself 'Coates' throughout his adulthood, and all ten of his children started out in life with that spelling. (Author's collection)

come the next census, he was the only Merton in the whole of Staffordshire. As for his middle name, Merton himself was in two minds about that. Having mentioned its family origins, he later claims to have been named after Lord John Russell (1792–1878), the architect of the Great Reform Act of 1832. The idea has merit, as this law granted the vote to middling men like Samuel Coates. Wolverhampton was a hotbed of the reform movement, and the town attracted thousands to public rallies in support of Russell's plans. Ousted from parliament in a sensational by-election two days before Merton's birth, the great man's name was much in the news at the time.

As Merton tells it, his baptism warranted the presence of one of the district's most notable figures. His godfather, he says, was Colonel Thomas Thorneycroft (1822–1903), the son of the ironmaster who served as Wolverhampton's first mayor. The colonel owned Tettenhall Towers, a gothic manor house in the village, and was a noted inventor and eccentric. His inventions included a glass umbrella, a portable dance floor and a mirror-fronted wardrobe. While trying out a pair of wings, his butler is said to have plummeted from one of the towers into a rhododendron bush, luckily with no lasting effects. For Merton to claim such a celebrated resident as his godfather evokes a certain image of his father's status in the business community. Thorneycroft, though, was only twelve at the time of the baptism – an unlikely age for a godparent.[9]

Merton's early life revolved around King Street. This was a harsh place to grow up, with smoke and soot from nearby factories choking the air and clogging the lungs. A short walk led to a maze of squalid, stinking alleys rife with disease. His youngest sister, Charlotte, died before Merton reached his first birthday and so became the third of the Coates children to suffer an early death. Elizabeth was expecting again within months, and it was to be another girl, Henrietta, who died in infancy. Merton's earliest childhood memories date from this period, but there is no talk of sickness and death. Tettenhall lies at the heart of his tales, an idyllic place untroubled by its neighbouring industrial giant. He recalls picking cowslips on the village green, strolling through bluebell groves and, more doubtfully, scrumping pears from the family's orchards. He tells of being saved by his nurse from a runaway carriage, of rescue by his sister after falling into a frozen pond, and of burnt legs caused by an ill-judged leap into a lime pit. Of his siblings, he mentions only Alfred and Georgina by name, while Samuel makes just two brief appearances as 'my eldest brother'.

By 1841 the family had moved to Newbridge, a hamlet clustered around the canal crossing on the road out to Tettenhall. The younger Samuel was involved in his father's business trips by then. That year's census captures the two of them in Bolton, a typical stop on a bagman's daily grind of customer calls, wayside inns and countless miles of atrocious roads. This was a punishing regime, enough to tax even the strongest constitution. For Merton's father, this journey was to be one of his last. The signs of illness would have been upon him on census night as one of the oldest diseases known to man took its toll. Called by many names – the white plague, phthisis, consumption, tuberculosis – it was killing someone in Britain, on average, every ten minutes.[10]

Samuel Coates died, aged forty-five, in January 1842. Merton, who was six at the time, blames his father's demise on a night in a damp bed while visiting a friend. He may not have known the real cause, but the reputation of tuberculosis as a disease of the urban poor did not encourage candour. 'My father's death came as a great and unexpected blow to all who knew him,' he wrote, one of just a few lines hinting at the devastating consequences of the loss.[11] The family laid Samuel to rest in Tettenhall, the place of his birth, and Merton twice arranged for the grave to be restored many years later. The second occasion resulted in the imposing, pink-granite monument seen in the churchyard today. *Home and Abroad* continues in the same vein, reproducing a portrait of Samuel from an unknown date. Possibly painted from life, more likely not, it depicts a man of around forty in a black suit and cravat, with a flush of youth belying his receding hair. Captioned 'Samuel Cotes, J.P., of Tettenhall', Merton takes away one letter from his surname, and adds two after it, to give another retrospective boost to his father's standing.

While it created no vacancy on the magistrate's bench, Samuel's death left an unfillable void in the family. 'He unfortunately died intestate,' wrote

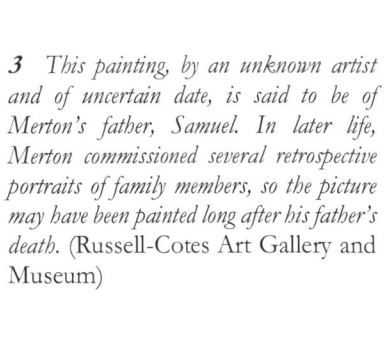

3 This painting, by an unknown artist and of uncertain date, is said to be of Merton's father, Samuel. In later life, Merton commissioned several retrospective portraits of family members, so the picture may have been painted long after his father's death. (Russell-Cotes Art Gallery and Museum)

Merton, 'and all the real property in Wolverhampton, Tettenhall and elsewhere, and the agricultural lands, were taken possession of by my eldest brother.' [12] This is the last reference to the younger Samuel in *Home and Abroad*, leaving his fate, and that of his inheritance, to the imagination. Merton hurries things along in this part of the story and gives no details about the seismic shock felt by the whole family. A period of hardship inevitably followed, as they struggled to adapt to the loss of their main breadwinner. Intestacy rules decreed that the younger Samuel inherited his father's landholdings, but there is no record of any property other than the business premises at King Street. These passed into the hands of Benjamin Cotes after his partner's death. The rest of the estate amounted to less than £300, a long way short of sustaining a widow and six children. Samuel, with youth and inexperience against him, faced the difficult task of taking his father's place in the family business. To complicate matters further, he had formed an attachment to a young woman in Cheshire – the sort of long-distance relationship that was an occupational hazard for an unattached bagman. Too young to marry without their parents' consent, the couple lied about their ages and tied the knot in Birkenhead in the summer of 1842. Samuel moved there for good a year later.[13] The family factoring firm, bereft of its driving force, ceased trading after more than two decades in business.

Merton's mother responded to this latest crisis with pragmatism. The year after her eldest son moved north, she married Henry Edwards (b. 1812), a Liverpudlian tailor about a dozen years her junior, and took the children to Merseyside. Eldest daughter Mary stayed behind in Wolverhampton and entered domestic service in a telltale sign of the family's plight. None of this is apparent from *Home and Abroad*. Merton skips over this distressing period by explaining how his sister Clara married a Glaswegian gentleman by the name of James MacEwan, who became his guardian and took care of his education. He says they took him to Glasgow, where he supposedly attended university with a view to entering the medical profession. The connection to Merseyside is only touched upon in his narrative, and there is no mention at all of his mother's remarriage. As it turns out, Clara's wedding did not take place until ten years after their father's death, leaving a large unexplained gap in the family's timeline.

There may be good reasons for Merton's silence on these events – and resentment of his stepfather might be one of them – but this mysterious period must have done much to shape his outlook on life. If he had the aptitude to learn about money and business at such a young age, then the travails of his eldest brother gave him some sort of lesson. Samuel, having left the iron trade in Wolverhampton, opened a beer house in Birkenhead, a town built around its shipyards. While serving ale to dockworkers might have seemed like a lucrative occupation, this new venture was soon hit by severe turbulence in the local economy. Rising costs of a new dockyard brought its construction to a halt, while the town bore the brunt of the Admiralty's reluctance to use iron ships. Hundreds of laid-off men left the area, a disaster for the businesses reliant upon them. Life was no better across the river, where Liverpool was the first port of call for the desperate thousands fleeing the potato famine in Ireland. In 1847, after a spell of unemployment, Samuel petitioned for bankruptcy at the height of the suffering.[14]

Merton's few hints about this period steer well clear of family trauma and, instead, refer to his boyhood love of art. This artistic bent was genetic, he believed, due to an improbable kinship with the artist Francis Cotes (1726–1770), a founding member of the Royal Academy.[15] He recalls poring over art journals and spending his pocket money on trinkets bought from doorstep sellers. He cut pictures from books and used them in a miniature theatre, charging his friends a penny to watch the show. While giving no details of his schooling, he lists music, botany, science and geography as his favourite subjects. Aged ten, he liked to draw the world on a blackboard and point to any country or city called out to him. He was fascinated by insects and brought them home to inspect at close quarters, much to the dismay of his mother, the cook and the rest of the household domestics. These servants were hardworking and devoted, thus rounding off an idealised view of hearth and home quite at odds with straitened reality.

While there is no evidence of servants, the signs are that Merton received a sound education in the face of difficult circumstances. His siblings, schooled in the more prosperous times before their father's death, no doubt passed on their knowledge as they did their best to fill the family coffers. Alfred, the middle brother, found a job in Liverpool as a junior clerk with the London and North Western Railway. It paid a pittance at first, but he spent the rest of his life working his way up the company ladder. His sister Clara, meanwhile, ran a tobacconist's in Birkenhead and later worked in Manchester as a barmaid. More ambitious than the steady and reliable Alfred, Clara soon cast off this modest beginning to play an important part in the life of her youngest brother. Merton's own movements in the lead-up to his sister's marriage are unclear, a situation compounded by a perplexing appearance on the 1851 census. A few weeks short of his sixteenth birthday, he is listed as a visitor in the house of a wine merchant's clerk in Bethnal Green.[16] Whatever took him there – and an early foray into the world of work is most likely – this was not a part of London where the streets were paved with gold. He must have been in the capital for some time, because he recalls a visit to the Great Exhibition in May of that year. In the first sign of an independent spirit, he tells of defying the police by clambering up a tree to watch the royal procession on the exhibition's opening day. As the Queen and Prince Albert passed by in their carriage, the Queen caught his eye, smiled, then drew the Prince's attention to the young man perched high above. Merton, like six million others who flocked to Hyde Park that summer, was awestruck by the spectacle of industry and culture. The impressionable youngster discovered the wonders of the age in the cavernous halls of the Crystal Palace and saw Britain's supremacy expressed in technology and innovation. Desperate for a souvenir, he stretched his pocket money to buy a 'Piping Bullfinch' – a mechanical bird he treasured for the rest of his life.[17]

The fog surrounding Merton's progress lifts only a little after Clara's marriage in the summer of 1852. Her husband, James MacEwan, worked as a salesman in various strands of the cotton trade, a line of business that took him between its strongholds in Lanarkshire and Lancashire. Whereas Merton barely mentions his eldest brother, and completely ignores his stepfather, he enshrines MacEwan in his memory. 'To him I owe a great debt of gratitude,' he wrote. 'He did all for me that my dear father would have done.'[18] This show of affection is *Home and Abroad*'s prelude to the move to Glasgow with his sister and brother-in-law. Merton claims to have studied to be a doctor there, met the girl he would later marry, then tried his luck in South America when illness thwarted his medical ambitions. While his account of these events is sketchy, the suspicion is that he uses Glasgow as a diversion to avoid raking over the family's struggles on Merseyside.

According to Merton, he studied medicine at Glasgow University and spent 'some years' at the old college in the High Street.[19] Towards the end of his time there, he says he met Annie Clark – a young lady who took his fancy from the start. Annie, so the story goes, had recently returned home to Glasgow after receiving a private education in London with the daughter of a family called Lloyd. The fact is, however, that Annie and the Lloyds were living in Liverpool in the early 1850s. They had a house in upmarket Falkner Street, less than a mile away from Merton's mother and stepfather in

THE ART OF A SALESMAN

4 James MacEwan, Merton's brother-in-law (1824–1857). He married Clara Coates in July 1852 at the Scottish National Church in Covent Garden, London – a long way from their home towns. Clara gave her address as a girls' school in Clapham Park, which suggests she may have found work in the capital. (From *Home and Abroad*)

working-class Toxteth Park. Only later did the Lloyds move to London, raising doubts about when and where Merton first met Annie. It also begs the question as to how much time, if any, he spent in Glasgow after Clara's marriage.

Merton reveals nothing of his university days other than a tale about a roommate called Syme. According to the story, Syme's father was an Edinburgh surgeon who worked with Joseph Lister (1827–1912), the pioneer of antiseptic surgery. While this can be dismissed as the innocent dropping of a famous name, the plot thickens when glancing through the university's admission records. A student called Syme enrolled at the right time, but he was the son of a provincial doctor, not an eminent surgeon. To add to the confusion, Merton is not listed among the names of the students. They do, however, include one of Annie Clark's cousins, who enrolled into the same class as Syme and went on to study medicine the following year.

If all this points to a university career borrowed from his wife's cousin, then it underlines Merton's reluctance to acknowledge his links to Merseyside.[20] University was out of reach for ordinary folk in those days, and the family purse, with or without MacEwan, was unlikely to have stretched that far. Merton was seventeen at the time of Clara's marriage, by which age his brother had already spent a year working as a clerk at the railway. He describes Alfred as the company's chief cashier, but it took nearly three decades of patience and hard work to reach that level and, even then, it was only in the goods department. To have shown Alfred's small beginnings would have revealed too much about the family's hardships in Birkenhead and Liverpool. By transporting himself to university in Glasgow, Merton manages to evade them altogether.

Based on the evidence of what happened next, it is more than likely that Merton went out to work as soon as he was able. Like Alfred, this meant starting at the bottom, albeit in a different line of business. MacEwan's connections opened doors in the cotton industry, but the evidence points to opportunities in Liverpool, not Glasgow. By Merton's account, he abandoned his university studies due to a 'slight congestion of the right lung'.[21] Doctors prescribed a long sea voyage by way of relief, prompting MacEwan to send the ailing 18-year-old across the Atlantic to Buenos Aires. There, Merton was to combine cure with career by embarking on what *Home and Abroad* describes as 'commercial pursuits'.[22] Regardless of what triggered it, a trip to that part of South America made perfect sense for an adventurous young man living in Liverpool.

Britain's trading links with Argentina went back several decades and offered good prospects for men of ambition. Argentine wool, beef, hides and tallow went one way, British cotton goods the other, in a cycle of trade that saw many a fortune won and lost. There were around 2,000 Britons in Buenos Aires by the early 1850s, most of them linked to one of the city's many mercantile houses. Like factors on a grand scale, these firms brought together buyers and sellers on opposite sides of the ocean. Liverpool, the largest port close to the Lancashire cotton mills, was well placed to service the trade. The town acted as a recruiting ground for British firms in Buenos Aires, with family and friends at the head of the queue for positions as clerks or bookkeepers. In this respect, MacEwan's contacts would have done much to help Merton's cause.

The trip to Argentina offered a chance for Merton to better himself, but it came with the risks of a long voyage to a country plagued with strife. It was a period of high tension in the region, caused by resentment in the provinces at the trade dominance enjoyed by Buenos Aires. Civil war had broken out in 1852, leading to a siege of the city lifted only a few months before Merton left England. British merchants, long used to a country where instability turned to violence, carried on as best they could. While things had calmed down by the time of Merton's departure, Argentina was not the ideal refuge for someone seeking respite from illness. Buenos Aires was a hotspot for a range of diseases, and the death rate was higher than most British cities.

Merton sailed from Liverpool into this uncertain future on New Year's Eve 1853.[23] His relationship with Annie Clark, whatever stage it had reached by then, was now tested by separation. 'The boat was very small,' he wrote of the voyage, 'and in rough weather we suffered considerable inconvenience.'[24] This, and some remarks about rock-hard biscuits and a broth cooked up by the captain's wife, are as much as he says about the nine-week journey. It sets the tone for a lightweight account of his time in Argentina that leaves many questions unanswered. *Home and Abroad* continues to move along in a headlong rush, as it races through more than two decades in the blink of an eye. Merton's trip to South America, coming at a key stage in his youthful development, deserves more space than the few lines he devotes to it.

Notes:

1. Merton's letter to Sala is held by Leeds University Library (BC MSC 19c).
2. The *Hastings and St Leonards Observer* of 12 March 1892 reported Furniss as saying: 'I hate the place [Bournemouth], if you have read my articles about it. We had a house in Dean Park three seasons ago on account of my wife's health. Had we stayed more than six months, we would have had to take permanent "diggings" in the cemetery close by; both the place and the people depressed us so much.'
3. The lines come from a poem published in 1814 by Rev. William Fernyhough.
4. *Home and Abroad*, p. 1. Tettenhall became part of Wolverhampton in 1966.
5. Benjamin Cotes married Appolina Thrustance, the sister of Charlotte, Merton's grandmother.
6. The Tettenhall Union Society met at the Rose and Crown, where Merton's second cousin, Edward Cotes, was the landlord.
7. *Home and Abroad*, p. 69, quoting a potted biography of Merton published in the *Midland Weekly News* in 1891.
8. The information about factors' working methods is taken from *Entrepreneurial Families* by Professor Andrew Popp, which draws on the archives of John Shaw, a Wolverhampton factor who was a contemporary of Merton's father.
9. In an odd twist to the godparent mystery, on p. 871 of *Home and Abroad* Merton quotes a letter from Florence Thorneycroft written in 1919. Miss Thorneycroft, who was the colonel's daughter, is said to have written: 'I am so thrilled to find that my grandfather, Col. Thorneycroft, was your godfather.'
10. The Russell-Cotes Art Gallery and Museum has a snuffbox labelled by Merton as follows: 'My father's snuffbox. Given to him by one of his travellers who collected a large sum of money and absconded. It represents therefore several thousand pounds.' While this suggests that Samuel employed a bagman, he was evidently doing the job himself in 1841. Thefts by bagmen were not uncommon, but Merton is likely to have been exaggerating the size of the loss.
11. *Home and Abroad*, p. 17.
12. ibid.
13. Samuel's first child was born in Birkenhead in the summer of 1843. He was baptised Frederick Merton – an apparent gesture of affection to his two brothers.
14. Samuel was working as an account collector for a coal merchant at the time of his bankruptcy. The 1851 census records him as a 'ferry collector', presumably meaning a toll collector on the Mersey ferry.
15. Merton describes Francis Cotes as his great-grandfather's first cousin on p. 704 of *Home and Abroad*, although no evidence has been found to support this. There is nothing to suggest that the artist was related to the Shropshire Coteses.
16. The clerk was Joseph Saunders of Queen Street – an area long since redeveloped.
17. John Maskelyne, a popular Victorian magician mentioned in *Home and Abroad*,

credits the Piping Bullfinch with inspiring his career.
18. *Home and Abroad*, p. 20.
19. ibid.
20. Annie's cousin was William Watkins, the son of her father's sister.
21. *Home and Abroad*, p. 21.
22. ibid., p. 69. Merton claims to have consulted 'three of the most eminent physicians in Glasgow' before making the voyage, but the family finances are unlikely to have permitted that, either there or in Liverpool.
23. Merton says that he left Liverpool on 10 November 1853 on a brig called the *Rita*, but shipping movements show it arriving in port on that date. A contemporary advertisement describes the vessel as a 192-ton clipper brig, registered at Lloyds for thirteen years, and a 'most superior conveyance for goods and passengers.'
24. *Home and Abroad*, p. 21.

2

TRAVELLER

Merton arrived in Buenos Aires in early March 1854, two months short of his nineteenth birthday. This was a vibrant, cosmopolitan city, where foreigners accounted for half the population. Italians, French, Germans and Spaniards were among those vying for a slice of the lucrative transatlantic trade. The British, while not the most numerous, dominated commercial life. As one contemporary guidebook observed: 'They usually make handsome fortunes, live in good style and get along pleasantly with their fellow foreigners and townsmen.' [1] With a British library, a British hospital, an English church and a Scots school among a host of expatriate institutions, a Briton arriving in Buenos Aires could feel a little at home in this far-distant land.

Merton had secured a position with Gifford Brothers, a well-established mercantile house in the heart of the city. He most likely began as a junior clerk, the usual point of entry for new starters. It was the ideal training ground for someone taking their first steps in the world of commerce. Merton says nothing about his work there, being more concerned with his later successes than recalling the events that laid the groundwork. Nevertheless, this must have been an important period in the life of a man who spent the rest of his career wheeling and dealing his way upwards. As well as their clerical and bookkeeping duties, clerks gained a thorough grounding in the firm's operations. This involved far more than importing and exporting goods. It meant mixing with the merchants, brokers, bankers and shippers who made up the busy commercial scene. Buenos Aires was an economic microcosm, where a clerk became immersed in the world of exchange rates, credit terms, bills of exchange, commissions and everything else that stood between a profit and a loss. In other words, a clerk in a mercantile house soon learned how to make money.

Merton spent around eighteen months in Buenos Aires before leaving abruptly in the autumn of 1855. The only real light he sheds on his experiences there concerns a curious change of employment in the last few weeks of the trip. Although not apparent from *Home and Abroad*, the roots of this diversion probably lay in a web of connections formed by his brother-in-law back on Merseyside. What may have begun in Liverpool's United Presbyterian Church ended with Merton taking brief charge of the only British school in Buenos Aires. Implausible at first glance, this appointment says much about the realities of life in a community cut off from home by 7,000 miles of ocean. It also shows that, despite the problems faced by his family, Merton had acquired enough education to be trusted with a class of fifty children.[2]

The British school was attached to St Andrew's Presbyterian Church – the Scottish community being a major force in the business life of Buenos Aires. Merton's appointment arose from the illness of the headmaster, described in *Home and Abroad* simply as 'Mr Holder'. This refers to William Holder (1828–1856), a man in his mid-twenties who left Liverpool at around the same time as Merton. They may even have sailed on the same ship. Although he gives no hint of knowing Holder beforehand, the evidence suggests that the two men had met on Merseyside. The circumstances also offer at least one explanation of how Merton came to meet Annie Clark. Holder's father owned a large drapery store in Liverpool's Mount Pleasant district, not far from where Annie lived with the Lloyd family. It may only be a coincidence that Merton's stepfather, Henry Edwards, was employed as a draper's assistant at the time. Be that as it may, the Holders were staunch Presbyterians and leading figures in their local congregation. William Holder served as the church's treasurer and taught music at the Sunday school. James MacEwan, a Presbyterian Scot with in-laws living nearby, is likely to have known the Holders through the church, the textile trade, or via Henry Edwards. Annie Clark, a devoutly religious young woman, may well have met Merton through this same labyrinth of connections.

William Holder chose not to follow his father into curtains and cloth. A bookkeeper by trade, he decided to start a new life in Buenos Aires after his marriage in the summer of 1853. There is, however, nothing to suggest that he left England for any other reason than to join a mercantile house. Indeed, he only took up the post at St Andrew's school about a year after arriving in the city. The headmaster had resigned, and the governors wanted to avoid the long delay of sending home for a replacement. Despite his limited experience, Holder emerged as the only candidate and got the job by saying he could teach bookkeeping, the three Rs, and a little astronomy and geology. As it transpired, he held the post for only nine months before falling ill. The governors asked him to arrange for Merton to take over while they sought another replacement – a sure sign that the two men already knew each other.

Whereas the switch from bookkeeper to schoolmaster may have been a career choice for Holder, Merton's appointment smacks of a favour called in,

5 Calle Piedad, the street in Buenos Aires where the firm of Gifford Brothers kept its office. The business evolved from that of McCrackan & Jamieson, which had been operating in the city since the 1830s. The ten Gifford brothers also had interests in China and India. (Public domain image)

or of the business community coming to the church's aid in its time of need. Regardless of what led to it, his tenure at the school lasted just one month, October 1855, before he relinquished the post in favour of the new incumbent. Merton, however, embellishes his account with a typical flourish. He puts the number of pupils at 140 – the school's records say it was less than half that – and he boasts of doing so well that the governors kept him on until Holder returned from his sickbed. In truth, Holder resigned under pressure from the governors and never taught at the school again. He died from tuberculosis a year later, leaving his wife and infant son to return to England without him.[3]

Merton completes his account of Argentina with a yarn straight out of a penny dreadful. It concerns a visit to the Holders' home in Barracas, a southern suburb where modest houses and grand villas lay at the fringes of a vast al fresco abattoir. Hundreds of cattle were slaughtered there daily, the source of the animal products so vital to the country's prosperity. As Merton rode out of the city to keep his appointment, a band of brigands appeared from nowhere and ordered him to stop. One of them struck him on the chest with the butt of a gun, almost knocking him off his horse. With the situation looking grim, a well-armed Scots settler arrived in the nick of time to scatter his assailants. 'Good God!' the man exclaimed. 'Cotes, what are you doing here? Don't you know the place is in a state of siege?' When Merton replied in the negative, his rescuer told him: 'If I had not come up, that man would have shot you just for the sake of getting what you had on your person.'[4]

With the siege of Buenos Aires more than two years in the past, this story of deliverance from banditry can be taken as an attempt to add a splash of colour. Merton had been in the country for eighteen months by this point so would have been aware of the risks of travelling alone. He says that he fell ill after the attack and that a doctor advised him to return home. Whatever the reason, Merton left Argentina two weeks after finishing at the school. He boarded the *Rhondda*, a ship sailing to England westwards via the Pacific – a route that took three times longer than the more usual Atlantic crossing. It suggests either that Merton arranged to work for his passage home by the best available means, or that his doctor prescribed an extended seagoing remedy. Poor health is a recurring theme of *Home and Abroad*, with nerve problems and bronchitis the most frequently mentioned disorders. Tuberculosis, the disease that killed both his father and William Holder, is never discussed, but it is possible Merton fell victim to it at some point. A long voyage was a common prescription at the time.

Merton's account of the journey home takes up two pages of *Home and Abroad*, more than he devotes to the whole of his stay in Buenos Aires. The ship's cargo of horses and mules suffered badly on the voyage and were thrown overboard to drown when they could no longer stand up. As for Merton's own health, it must have improved en route because he managed to cheat death again by evading a shark while swimming near the boat. This is a rare personal story in an account that sometimes sounds like a geography textbook. 'The island is small,' he wrote of Mauritius, 'being about nine miles across and about double the distance in length. The principal product is sugar.' [5] His narrative is at its most chaotic in these pages. He describes how a storm nearly sank the ship off the Cape of Good Hope – heroic work at the bilge pumps saved them – before jumping ahead four years to his marriage in the next paragraph. Buenos Aires is not given another thought, and yet the life experience he gained there rivalled any university study, medical or otherwise. It taught those willing to learn that success demands hard work, investment and tenacity. From business to friendships, and from civic projects to art collecting, the signs are that he took these lessons into all aspects of his life.

After sailing three oceans, the *Rhondda* docked in Liverpool on 15th May 1856. It was a week after Merton's twenty-first birthday, six months on from the ship leaving Buenos Aires, and two and a half years since he had last seen his native land. Britain had declared war in the Crimea, fought the fight and made peace in his absence. Benjamin Cotes, his father's old business partner, had died the previous autumn. What Merton did next is blurred by his jumbled version of events, as he skips through two decades in a couple of pages. These include *Home and Abroad*'s most troublesome sentence: 'On my return home, I was appointed by the late Mr William Spens, the founder of the Scottish Amicable Society, to the position of Resident Secretary and Superintendent of agencies for that Society in Ireland.' [6] The problem here is the extent to which this statement is, or is not, true. The puzzle is compounded by Merton's failure to provide any information about his time with the firm. Instead, he launches an attack on 'Popish priests and Jesuits' and the vagaries of the Irish tax system. This may have seemed apt to a man writing soon after the Easter Rising but does nothing to shed light on his personal progress.

The Scottish Amicable features in most potted biographies published after Merton's death but in just a few written in his lifetime.[7] It is the only employment he mentions in *Home and Abroad* over a twenty-year period. He outlines the Society's formation, a tale of the impoverished widow of a man who died of consumption. This gentleman had a life policy with another firm, which refused to pay out because he failed to disclose a family history of the disease. William Spens (1807–1868), one of the firm's managers, resigned in protest and went on to form the Scottish Amicable. This, at least, is Merton's account of its origins. In fact, Spens joined the Society more than a decade after its foundation, and there is nothing to suggest that he, or anyone else there, employed Merton in any capacity.

Rather than moving to Ireland, Merton spent a year or so in Manchester after returning from Buenos Aires. He contradicts himself by mentioning this but without saying what line of work took him there.[8] He talks only of visits to the Art Treasures Exhibition at Old Trafford, a mammoth event held during the summer of 1857.[9] It rivalled the Great Exhibition in scale, even down to the giant glass pavilion built to house it. By this time, Merton says that his childhood hobby had developed into a mania for acquiring art, an obsession helped by his eye for a good deal. He lists works by John Crome of the Norwich School (1768–1821) and J. M. W. Turner (1775–1851) among his growing collection, plus 'a small Corot' that cost him ten pounds.[10] This was over a month's wages for his brother at the railway, so he would have done well to afford it at this stage of his life. His chronology may be awry here, because he identified a later starting point for his art-buying habits when he catalogued his collection in old age. Besides, some of these paintings were not such great bargains after all. The so-called Turner, a view of St Michael's Mount, is not genuine, something he may have suspected based on his spirited defence of the work in *Home and Abroad*.

If his subsequent career is anything to go by, then Merton's stint in Manchester is likely to have involved working on the sales side of the textiles industry. His brothers remained on Merseyside, where Alfred was still working his way up the ranks of the railway company, and Samuel had gone back into the licensed trade. James MacEwan was now employed as a salesman for a firm of cotton printers in Liverpool but was labouring under the effects of tuberculosis. He moved back to Glasgow in 1857 and died there, aged thirty-three, that autumn – yet another of those close to Merton to succumb to the disease. While having few assets to his name, life assurance swelled MacEwan's estate to the tune of £1,000. He took out the policy with the Scottish Amicable two years before his marriage, an astute move at a time when few people bothered with such things. For Clara, the money cushioned the blow of her husband's loss, although one wonders if the firm questioned his family's medical history before paying out.[11] The fact that the policy provider was the same as Merton's supposed employer may or may not be a coincidence.

MacEwan's death is, with more certainty, the point that Merton moved to Glasgow. Although Clara's situation must have been a factor, Annie Clark may have been the most compelling reason for heading north. A mismatched pair when he left for Argentina, their circumstances had changed much in the intervening years. Merton was now a man of the world with great expectations, but the cultured and well-educated Annie had fallen on hard times. While not a universal truth, a single man in want of a fortune does well to find a good wife. Annie was the ideal choice for the aspirational Merton, a young woman capable of moving in higher social circles than either of them occupied in the late 1850s.

Although *Home and Abroad* says little about Annie's background, some reports link her to the illustrious Clark cotton barons of Glasgow and Paisley. Another branch of her family is said to have owned significant property on the south side of the Clyde.[12] While such claims should be treated with caution, cotton certainly played a big part in Annie's upbringing. Her grandfather did well enough in the trade to send his son to Glasgow University, but he was a middling player in a crowded field. Annie's father, John King Clark (1793–1874), also went into the industry, although an early attempt to set up his own business ended in the courts. He stood accused of plotting the bankruptcy of his partner, who was in turn blamed by Clark for an assault on their mill by an armed mob. By the late 1820s, Clark had established a weaving works on the banks of the River Kelvin and was soon employing more than a hundred people.[13] It allowed him to enjoy the finer things in life. An art connoisseur, he bought works attributed to Holbein, Hogarth and Turner, and indulged his passion for music by joining the Glasgow Musical Association and collecting antique violins.

Clark was forty-two when Annie, his only child, was born in Glasgow on 15th July 1835. Her mother, Ann Nelson, was a weaver's daughter from Girvan, seventeen years Clark's junior. She may have moved to the city to find factory work, which paid rather better than the jobs on offer in Ayrshire's declining cottage industries. No record of a marriage survives, so a liaison between mill owner and factory girl cannot be ruled out. Ann may have died in childbirth or shortly afterwards, as she disappears without trace after her daughter's arrival. Annie went to live with her grandmother in Girvan, a well-grounded childhood among people who knew the meaning of thrift, humility and hard graft. Back in Glasgow, her father weathered the ups and downs of the cotton trade, enjoyed a cultured social life and commanded the respect of his peers.

The highpoint of Clark's fortunes came in the 1840s. It was the era of the railway boom, when iron roads were sweeping across the country. A frenzy of public enthusiasm saw all manner of schemes springing up. Their prospectuses filled the press, grand ideas backed by the titled and the eminent, most of them based on pie-in-the-sky optimism or downright lies. These projects needed investors, people willing to exchange hard cash for bountiful promises. Clark yielded to the temptation and invested more than £8,000 – easily enough to pay his factory's wage bill for an entire year. So entangled did he become in the railway mania that he was described as a 'merchant and dealer in shares' when bankruptcy caught up with him in 1847.[14] Yet this was no ordinary insolvency. When his cotton business failed, proceedings against the firm went ahead at once, but Clark's personal assets, either by luck or forbearance, were left untouched for seven years. There was little impact on his other business dealings in the interim, and he kept his collection of paintings and violins. Nor was there anything, in theory, to stop him from setting assets aside for his daughter during this long period of limbo.

When she reached the age of fourteen, Clark was still affluent enough to send Annie to Liverpool to be educated with the Lloyd family. She found herself among the social superiors of her Girvan relatives. Harriet Lloyd, the head of the household, was the widow of a surgeon who came from a landed Welsh family. Annie acted as a companion for Mrs Lloyd's daughter, Charlotte, and joined in with her lessons. Why Clark chose to place her there is not clear, but he was a man of many connections. Even his musical interests may have played a part, as Charlotte's previous companion was the sister of a child piano prodigy. Sometime before Merton left England for Buenos

6 Annie Clark pictured with her father at around the time she moved to Falkner Street, Liverpool, to be educated with the Lloyd family. Elizabeth and Henry Edwards – Merton's mother and stepfather – were then living at Bedford (now Beaufort) Street in Toxteth Park. Within easy walking distance, the two streets were miles apart in terms of social standing. (Russell-Cotes Art Gallery and Museum)

Aires, the Lloyd family moved to Westbourne Park in London. Annie took singing lessons from Joseph de Pinna (c. 1799–1885), a musician and composer of some repute in the capital. Using his 'progressive system of vocalising and solfa-ing', she developed a fine contralto voice. 'For purity, richness and emotional qualities,' wrote Merton, 'I have heard no amateur's at all comparable to it.' So good was it, some reports say, that Signor de Pinna wrote several songs for her.[15]

The next stage of John King Clark's money woes took place soon after Merton's arrival in Argentina. In the spring of 1854, his creditors took decisive action after years of patience. Things were in a parlous state by then. Clark could offer only a penny in the pound on what he owed, despite selling his paintings and violins. Now in his sixties, he entered a period of unstable employment and frequent changes of address. Despite this, he kept himself involved in the city's cultural life and invested in two fledgling newspapers, the *Daily Bulletin* and *The Workman*. The latter, a radical weekly published under the strapline 'We uphold the dignity of labour', was an odd choice for a former cotton master.

Merton's brief account of Annie's childhood overlooks Clark's rise and fall. It touches on her Girvan schooling, then whisks her straight to London without going via Liverpool. He says they met when she returned to Scotland from the capital – a consequence, perhaps, of her father's money troubles. Annie's down-to-earth upbringing and genteel schooling made her an enticing prospect for the young Merton. 'She was so unlike the other young ladies I knew in Glasgow,' he wrote, 'that I was immensely struck with the difference.'[16] Her charms may have won him over in Scotland, but there is a good chance he first encountered them in Liverpool. Either way, he is adamant they met before he sailed to Buenos Aires. What is clear is that her father's problems left Merton in a far stronger position to win Annie's hand when he returned to England. Even so, the time spent in Manchester suggests he was in no rush to rekindle an old flame.

The first record of Merton in Glasgow is in an 1859 street directory published eighteen months after James MacEwan's death. He was now styling himself 'Merton R. Cotes', a defining moment in his personal branding. His siblings took some while to copy the spelling – and Samuel never did – but it was a bold statement. He was aligning himself not only with his great-uncle Benjamin but also with the Cotes family of Woodcote Hall. With the new name came a new home in St Vincent Crescent, an imposing terrace of three-storey houses on the western side of the city. These were fine middle-class dwellings facing two acres of grounds and a bowling green. He rented a suite of rooms here, an address to impress a refined young woman like Annie Clark.

Merton set about getting himself known in the city. This was the heyday of earnest clubs and societies, who filled newspaper columns with reports of

7 St Vincent Crescent, Glasgow, c. 1860. Merton's first known address in the city was at no. 50. He may have responded to an advertisement in the Glasgow Herald *of 22 November 1858 that read: 'A handsomely furnished drawing room and one or two bedrooms to be let in a widow lady's house, admirably adapted for merchants, or a lady and gentleman who desire every comfort and attention.'* (Mitchell Library, Glasgow)

their meetings. They provided a wealth of opportunities for a man to put his name down for whatever appealed to him. The Art Manufacture Association was typical, with its lofty aim to bring 'the application of high art to the manufacture of works of utility and ornament.' [17] As assistant secretary of its Glasgow branch, John King Clark was well placed to take Merton to its gatherings. 'I had the "Open Sesame" to all the art circles, sketching clubs and other artistic resorts,' he recalls. 'There was scarcely a popular or budding artist but whom I knew intimately, and from whom I purchased pictures as far as my income would allow.' [18] He bought his first painting in this period, or at least the one he described as such in later life. It is a small canvas called *Girl Combing Her Hair* by the Scottish artist James Giles (1801–1870). Spotted in a shop window in Aberdeen in October 1859, he paid four pounds for it. While the timing is at odds with *Home and Abroad*'s depictions of much earlier art collecting, the place of purchase and the price paid fit with his line of work at the time.

Merton had found a job as a salesman for Peter Scott & Co., a firm of textile manufacturers based in Buchanan Street. They specialised in sewn muslin, a cheap alternative to lace for adorning clothes and soft furnishings. While centred on Glasgow, production relied on a cottage industry in the surrounding towns and villages. Agents farmed out parcels of cloth to women and girls, who embroidered them according to a printed design. Ayrshire women were especially admired for their handiwork, but the job was low paid and tedious. Annie's grandmother was one of many who sewed for a few shillings a week between cooking and cleaning. Merton, as a salesman for the finished product, would have trailed around shops and wholesalers with samples of the ladies' work. In that context, a trip to Aberdeen makes perfect sense.

Back in his cotton-weaving days, John King Clark might have wished for a man with better prospects as a suitor for his daughter, but much had changed since then. As Annie descended from the heights, Merton met her on his way up. The couple married on 1st February 1860 at Hamilton, near Glasgow. They were both twenty-four. With the groom still to heed the Presbyterian call, they opted for a Church of England service in the home of a local jeweller – a friend of the bride's father.[19] To celebrate the happy day, but with the glum faces of early studio portraits, the newlyweds posed for a photograph in their finery. Annie, carrying a bonnet and parasol, gazed wistfully to one side. Merton, top hat in left hand, right thumb in waistcoat pocket, stared straight down the lens.

The couple made their first home in a tenement block on the Paisley road. It was on the outskirts of Govan, where the great Glasgow shipbuilding firms were churning out iron vessels by the dozen. Their neighbours included a clothier, a salesman and an ironmonger, each occupying a suite of four rooms. These were up-and-coming folk, all affluent enough to afford a servant. Merton gives nothing away about his early married life but does mention one event that dates from this period. A few months after the wedding, he attended an exhibition boxing match between John Heenan (1834–1873) and Tom Sayers (1826–1865) at Glasgow City Hall. The two

8 Annie and Merton on their wedding day, 1st February 1860. Queen Victoria may have started the trend for white weddings, but most women got married in a dress they could wear again. Even if they were prepared to wear white around town, the cost and practicalities of keeping the fabric clean would have been prohibitive for a salesman's wife like Annie. (From Home and Abroad)

men were enjoying a short burst of celebrity after an infamous clash in a Hampshire field some weeks before. There, thirty-six bare-knuckle rounds had featured a near strangling, a disputed draw and a visit from the local constabulary. The City Hall bout, while tame in comparison, was not the stuff of refined Glaswegian art circles.

The couple's first child, a daughter named Ella, was born in Glasgow in December 1860, six months after Heenan and Sayers stepped into the ring. Merton left the sewn muslin trade soon afterwards to join John Blair & Co., a well-established firm of hat and cap makers. They employed 500 people, most of them based at their flagship premises in the centre of Glasgow. The firm's top seller was the self-adjusting dress hat, an elasticated variety designed to prevent headaches. Merton joined the firm as a commercial traveller. These were the bagmen of the railway age but with a far more

9 The premises of John Blair & Co., on the corner of Howard Street and St Enoch Square, Glasgow. The building, designed in the early 1850s by Alexander 'Greek' Thomson (1817–1875), was demolished in 1966. (University of Strathclyde)

colourful reputation than their forefathers. Popular sentiment branded them as sots and womanisers who would do anything to close a sale. If they featured in the press, it was often in reports of bigamy and fraud. Many travellers saw themselves as a brotherhood, bound by the ties of lonely journeys and frequent separation from their families. They came together in the commercial rooms of hotels, where their sometimes noisy and inebriated after-work gatherings did little to enhance their image. Other travellers were nothing like this and took pride in a job that offered independence and decent pay. As their firms' ambassadors, they were respectable, educated and trusted with the large sums of money passing through their hands. They were renowned as dapper dressers too, an ingrained habit Merton seldom allowed himself to break.

This steady progress in Glasgow stood in stark contrast to that of his eldest brother, who was again experiencing a torrid time in Birkenhead. During another spell of unemployment, Samuel made the fateful mistake of visiting a jeweller's shop while under the influence of drink. Finding the place empty, he leaned across the counter and pocketed a gold chain hanging from a gas bracket on the wall. A girl entered the shop at the critical moment and alerted the jeweller. Samuel fled, was arrested in a pub, escaped on the way to the police station, then was arrested again after a chase. When hauled before the courts, he said he took the chain for a lark to teach the jeweller a lesson. The magistrate failed to see the joke and sentenced him to three months in prison with hard labour. A sobering end to a drunken prank, it goes a long way to explaining his anonymity in *Home and Abroad*.

As Samuel Coates found himself in the dock at Chester assizes, Merton R. Cotes was preparing to cross the Irish Sea. John Blair & Co. appointed him as their representative in Dublin in the summer of 1861. This, and not the Scottish Amicable, is what took him to Ireland. The move was a big step forward for a man of twenty-six, even if he failed to acknowledge it later on. Where future generations might have embraced it, Merton felt compelled to hide his steady climb up the social pecking order. There is not so much as a glimpse in *Home and Abroad* of Peter Scott, John Blair or the hardships of commercial travelling. The Scottish Amicable obscures them all, revealing a lot about how Merton expected to be judged by those around him. The higher he rose, the harder it became to let others – and himself – look back down.

Merton and Annie spent around two years in Dublin. They rented a terraced house in the suburb of Grangegorman, close to Phoenix Park and the zoo, and backing on to fields of grazing sheep and lowing cattle. It was a haven of peace compared to Govan. The couple's second daughter, Clarie, was born here in July 1862, giving Merton a chance to promote John Blair & Co. by slipping the firm's name into the birth announcement. This aside, he left little trace of himself in Ireland. He was an ordinary man going about his ordinary business, forming strong views about the locals as he went. The north of the country was a hive of honest endeavour, or so he believed, where industry thrived off the back of hard work. 'In the south and west, these qualities and traits are conspicuous by their absence,' he wrote.[20] To Merton, there could be only one cause of this difference: popish priestcraft. Not reserved for Ireland, he shows a commonplace disdain for the Catholic church throughout *Home and Abroad*.

Merton left Dublin towards the end of 1863. Why he did so is not clear, although a new cattle market being built next to their house may have helped to make up his mind. The work turned an expanse of farmland, meadows and trees into a wasteland of drainage ditches and construction materials. If he was already disenchanted with the country, then living next door to a building site was no inducement to stay. The family moved to Altrincham in

Cheshire, a short railway journey from Manchester and not far from Merton's old stamping grounds in Liverpool. They took a mid-size house near the town centre, although Merton preferred to say they lived in Bowdon – a nearby village of fine villas and mansions.

The family spent more than six years in Altrincham. *Home and Abroad* makes only vague references to this period, none of which say how Merton was earning a living. This again highlights how hard it was for him to admit that he had once been run-of-the-mill. Most contemporary sources say he was still working as a commercial traveller, although he is listed as an 'agent' elsewhere. While the latter raises the possibility of a role with the Scottish Amicable, his sister Clara later stated under oath that he was working for a Yorkshire firm at the time. This tallies with some accounts that link him to 'Brierley and Cotes', a firm of woollen manufacturers in Batley. This appears to be a misnomer and misspelling of Robert Brearley & Sons of that town, although there is no evidence to suggest that Merton was one of the principals. Brearley's son-in-law went by the surname of Coates, and became a partner in the 1860s, but he was not related to Merton and never featured in the firm's name. It seems, then, that 'Brierley and Cotes' may have been Merton's first attempt to plug the career gap he later chose to fill with the Scottish Amicable. Most likely, he worked for Robert Brearley as the firm's representative on the western side of the Pennines.

Annie delivered two more girls during their time in Cheshire – Anita in 1866 and Lottie a year later. Merton says he named his third daughter in honour of the late wife of Giuseppe Garibaldi (1807–1882), a man he hails as 'one of the greatest patriots the world has ever known.' [21] This is the precursor to one of Merton's most baffling stories, in which he claims to have met the Italian statesman in Glasgow during his much-publicised visit to Britain in 1864. 'I recall with delight the kindly grasp of that great man's hand,' he wrote, 'and his cheery smile when I said how proud I was to meet him.' Feted wherever he went, Garibaldi's fervent patriotism and staunch anti-Catholicism resonated with a large section of the British public. Town councils all over the country pleaded with him to visit, but annoyance in Westminster about his rapturous reception brought an early end to the tour. He went home without venturing further north than Bedford, so a meeting in Glasgow is, at best, a case of mistaken location.[22]

The great Italian is not the only eminent figure Merton mentions meeting in this period. He also talks of socialising in London with Henry Irving (1838–1905), Charles Wyndham (1837–1919) and other budding actors who became big stars of the late-Victorian stage. Commercial travellers roamed far and wide but, aside from the splash of showmanship required for a successful sale, were not kindred spirits of the theatrical profession. If social gatherings with the likes of Irving and Wyndham are hard to fathom, then Merton's recollection of the who, where and when of his personal history was not always reliable. He claims to have seen Ellen Terry (1847–1928) as Ariel in *The Tempest,* and as Puck [sic] in the same play, five years before the acclaimed actress made her stage debut, aged nine, in 1856.

While prone to exaggerating his connections, there are signs of Merton's status moving up a notch in Altrincham. Personal qualities aside, the misfortunes of his family and father-in-law provided the motivation to better himself. Good commercial travellers enjoyed a healthy income, while shrewd ones looked for other opportunities to make money. Merton was already doing that. His name appears in a long list of people – many of them butchers, drapers, grocers and the like – who bought shares in a start-up bank in Liverpool called the Adelphi. It hints at a man with at least some spare capital and the desire to make it work for him. The first firm evidence of his art collection emerges in the Altrincham period, too. In 1869, he lent several works to an exhibition at a church bazaar to raise funds for a new parsonage. A committed Christian as well as an art lover, Merton took on the role of exhibition secretary. This may explain how the *Manchester Times* came to describe it as 'one of the most unique and valuable collections exhibited for some time.' [23] His loan pieces, all works by established English and Scottish artists, included *Children*, a picture attributed to Sir Thomas Lawrence (1769–1830). One of Britain's greatest portrait painters, the chances of it being a genuine work by Lawrence are on a par with the so-called 'Turner'.

The church bazaar allowed all those involved to show themselves off as people of culture and charity. Merton made a useful contact – Charles Scotter (1835–1910), a local railway manager who would become a key ally many years down the line. Annie was his main supporter at the event, helping to run a stall during the day and playing the piano at a concert in the evening. They formed a strong team, with the practical and refined Annie complementing the strong-minded and ambitious Merton. His was a restless personality that demanded more than commercial travelling to satisfy his aspirations. A decade in the job was too much for some of his peers, who grew tired of the endless rush to display their wares in the commercial rooms of hotels. Infamous for their rowdy carousing after long days on the road, the lifestyle had its attractions for the younger traveller, less so for a man in his thirties. One seasoned campaigner, worn down by taproom rituals and drunken quarrels, bemoaned the 'melancholy condition of commercial travellers generally, many of them without God in the world.' [24]

If such thoughts gave Merton good reason to call time on his travelling career, then his daughter's health provided another. Anita had been suffering from a life-threatening liver abscess for the best part of two years at the time of the church bazaar. In March 1870, with Annie expecting their fifth child, Anita died at home in Altrincham.[25] Merton quit the town a few weeks later, intent on making a fresh start in a familiar city. There, he would put his commercial travelling experiences to the best possible use.

Notes:

1. *Handbook of the River Plate*, p. 14.
2. Merton says he was appointed at the school thanks to a letter of introduction from Dr Norman Macleod, a prominent Presbyterian minister in Glasgow. This may be dramatic licence. Even if Merton was in Scotland before he left for Buenos Aires, the evidence suggests he was a member of the Church of England until well into his forties.
3. William Holder's brother, Thomas, made a fortune in cotton broking and became the mayor of Liverpool in 1883.
4. *Home and Abroad*, p. 23.
5. ibid., p. 24. The island is more than twice as big as Merton describes.
6. ibid., p. 29.
7. The earliest known reference to Merton's employment with the Scottish Amicable is in a potted biography published in the *Bournemouth Guardian* on 11 February 1904.
8. The *Bournemouth Guardian*'s obituary of Merton, published in January 1921, says he 'entered into business at Manchester' after his return from Buenos Aires.
9. Merton mistakenly gives the year of the exhibition as 1856 in *Home and Abroad*.
10. *Home and Abroad*, p. 686.
11. MacEwan declared himself free of tuberculosis when he took out the policy in 1850. He was working in Liverpool for Godfrey Pattison & Co., calico printers, in the months before he died. Based in Glasgow, the firm spectacularly collapsed a few days before his death due to a commercial crisis triggered by the failure of the Western Bank of Scotland.
12. While there is some evidence to suggest that Annie was distantly related to the well-known Clark cotton families, her maternal grandmother, Isabella King, was a butcher's daughter.
13. The average workforce of a cotton mill at that time was about 250, so Clark's firm was smaller than most.
14. Clark put most of his money into three schemes: the British and Irish Union Railway, the Cornwall and Devon Railway, and the Enniskillen and Sligo Railway.
15. *Home and Abroad*, p. 21. The description of Joseph de Pinna's technique is taken from an 1857 advertisement in the *Morning Post*. He was based in Westbourne Park at the time – the area of London where the Lloyds were living.
16. ibid.
17. *Glasgow Herald*, 20 October 1856.
18. *Home and Abroad*, p. 699.
19. Scottish law allowed marriages to be conducted in private homes if a church minister performed the service. The family friend was James Muirhead, whose grandson, John Muirhead, subscribed to Merton and Annie's diamond wedding gift in 1920.
20. *Home and Abroad*, p. 818.
21. ibid., p. 661.
22. In one of his few other references to this period, Merton says he attended the

coming-of-age celebrations of Charles Cecil Cotes – the son and heir of the Shropshire Coteses – at Newport in April 1867. While the circumstances are not clear, the event took place on the day before Lottie's birth.
23. *Manchester Times*, 18 December 1869.
24. Malchow, *Gentlemen Capitalists*, p. 87, quoting a traveller's diary entry.
25. Merton's eldest sister, Mary, registered Anita's death, giving the surname as 'Coates'.

3

HOTELIER

As Merton steadily worked his way up the social ladder in Altrincham, his sister was sowing the seeds of the career move that would eventually define him. Clara ran a lodging house in Glasgow after her husband's death but moved to Manchester around the time Merton left Dublin. With her brother's help, she took over a 'Berlin Wool and Fancy Warehouse' in Deansgate, not far from where she had once worked as a barmaid. A grand title for a shop, it sold the threads and patterns used in Berlin wool work, a fashionable hobby much like needlepoint. It was a respectable business for a widow and, if Merton was indeed employed by Robert Brearley of Batley, dovetailed well with a job in the wool trade. Berlin yarn, while imported mainly from Germany, was also spun in Yorkshire.

Things went well for Clara in the first year or so. She extended the shop and brought in new stock advertised as 'most novel and *recherché*', a marketing turn of phrase Merton would have been proud of.[1] No sooner had she done so than a serious fire broke out in the premises next door. Although Clara's shop survived, smoke damage obliged her to sell off the entire stock at knockdown prices. The business never recovered. In the summer of 1865, she was forced to make a deal with her creditors, who agreed to write off two-thirds of what she owed. It allowed her to carry on trading but came with the proviso that Merton underwrote the arrangement. This was not only a matter of fraternal love. He had ploughed more than £500 into the shop – money he would lose if the business failed.

The size of this investment shows that Merton was operating in a league above his commercial travelling peers. A traveller could expect to earn about £200 per year, perhaps twice that for a good salesman with an established firm. Merton's business acumen would have helped to increase his earnings, but there may have been other reasons for his financial strength. James MacEwan's life insurance, assets squirrelled away by his father-in-law, or even a South American windfall could have boosted his position. No matter how he acquired it, Merton's money mingled with his sister's businesses in ever more mysterious ways over the next few years.

In the summer of 1868, Clara shut up shop in Manchester and returned to Glasgow. Still in debt to her brother, she took over the management of a hotel lying within easy reach of the city centre and a railway station. Although the business appeared in trade directories under her name, it was Merton who provided the real driving force behind the enterprise. He took out the lease himself and paid his sister a commission to run things on his behalf. This first step into the hotel trade was marked by a matter-of-fact announcement in the *Glasgow Herald*: 'Hanover Hotel, 45 Hanover Street, George Square. First-class. Charges moderate. Splendid Commercial, Coffee, Billiard and Smoking Rooms.' [2] This low-key pitch, with its eye towards the commercial travelling market, appeared eighteen months before the Altrincham art exhibition.

Although Merton's work in England kept him away from the hotel, he had good reason to keep tabs on its progress. Put simply, he was better with money than Clara. Whether they both accepted this at the time of her husband's insurance payout is a moot point, but Merton held all the purse strings now. The hotel, previously almost invisible outside Scotland, benefitted from his investment in promotion. A wave of advertising targeted cities in the north of England to tempt those considering a break across the border. The commercial rooms and billiard table still ranked among the attractions, but there was now talk of a piano and a coffee room for ladies. While these were undoubted selling points, describing the hotel as 'quiet' stretched the marketing brief in a way that became a Merton trademark. The hotel formed part of the perimeter of Queen Street station, putting it well within earshot of whistling steam engines and slamming train doors.

Clara ran the hotel for two years before Merton took over. A complete novice on the face of it, he was entering a business in which he had plenty of experience as a customer. That fact alone encouraged many former commercial travellers to enter the hospitality trade. In Merton's case, his sister's stint in charge of the hotel smoothed the transition from one to the other. He applied to transfer the alcohol licence into his own name in March 1870, but Anita's death at the end of that month meant it was late spring before he arrived in Glasgow to embark on his new career. Such an important milestone ought to have warranted at least a few lines in *Home and Abroad*. As it is, the Hanover Hotel is not mentioned at all.

As Merton moved in at Hanover Street, Glasgow, Clara moved out and went to Hanover Street, Edinburgh. A coincidence perhaps, but this was not the only curious alignment of names in a year punctuated with business and family expansion. Within weeks, Clara had set up a new Hanover Hotel in the capital a few yards off Princes Street. She engaged Mary and Georgina, her two unmarried sisters, as employees. That September, the family's Scottish contingent was given a further boost by the birth of Merton and

Annie's only son. Herbert Victor Merton Cotes – known as Bert or Bertie – entered the world shortly after the author Victor Hugo (1802–1885) returned to Paris after a long exile. If intended, this further coincidence of names would in time prove ironic. Hugo's triumphant homecoming marked the overthrow of Napoleon III (1808–1873), the French Emperor, during the Franco-Prussian War. The desperate flight to England of the Empress Eugénie (1826–1920), Napoleon's much-talked-about wife, sent the British press into a frenzy in the days before Bert's arrival. Already subject to a host of colourful stories, Merton would create one of his own about the ill-starred Empress a decade or so later.

For now, Merton sat at the head of his own small empire. More than a loose family alliance, the two hotels hired staff on each other's behalf and featured the same logo in their advertising – a coronet placed between the words 'Hanover' and 'Hotel'. Still, the Glasgow establishment had more to shout about. Boasting 'superior arrangements' and 'the comforts of home', it assured continentals that *On Parle Francais* and *Man Spricht Deutsche*. Merton

10 Advertisements for the Hanover Hotels in Glasgow and Edinburgh taken from the 1872 edition of The Tourists' Handy Guide to Scotland. *Despite the impressive endorsements quoted by Merton, the former did not feature in the* Glasgow Herald*'s review of the city's foremost hotels in 1876.* (Author's collection)

was gaining experience that would serve him well in the future, but he was not the only man in Glasgow learning lessons about promoting a business. A young grocer called Thomas Lipton (1848–1931) had also discovered the power of marketing. The two men became friends in later life and may have known each other in this period. While not as brash as Lipton, who hid gold coins in giant cheeses and paraded pigs through the streets in fancy dress,

Merton sought to attract a more select clientele. So keen was he to spread the word that a bogus salesman duped him into buying space in a fictitious American travel guide. Such setbacks were to be expected when competing in a crowded hospitality market.

Merton worked hard to forge an identity for the hotel, even though it was not among Glasgow's elite. An early coup saw him host a breakfast for the Chief Rabbi of the British Empire, who was in the city to officiate at the Glasgow synagogue.[3] The hotel served up a kosher meal for the occasion, making a change from the usual fare dished out at regimental suppers and pigeon fanciers' dinners. Merton built on this success when Prince Henry of Bourbon-Parma (1851–1905) stayed at the hotel during a spring tour of Scotland in 1873. The Prince was a great-grandson of Charles X of France (1757–1836), whose abdication led to the uprising described by Victor Hugo in *Les Misérables*. Although the Prince's visit to Scotland attracted little attention elsewhere, the *Glasgow Herald* managed to get wind of his stay at the Hanover Hotel. Drawing attention to eminent patronage was another useful marketing trick.

Merton used the hotel's success as a platform to diversify his business interests. He ran an agency for the Scottish Fire Insurance Company – the only sign of a role in that industry – and imported wine and brandy. The latter meant competing against local branches of well-known names like Gilbey, Hennessy and Martell, but Merton most likely bought in low volume to sell through his trade contacts. All the same, these firms offered more examples of clever branding. There were no such sidelines for Clara in Edinburgh, who was able to concentrate her efforts on the hotel alone. The business here, although entirely in her name, relied on her brother's cash injections to stay afloat. Despite this, Merton kept the Edinburgh hotel at arm's length and wanted the outside world to believe it was unconnected to the one in Glasgow. He failed to convince everyone, and the illusion almost shattered when he became embroiled in a public spat with an accountant named James Paterson.

Paterson was the collector of poor rates for the Edinburgh parish of St Cuthbert's and operated from the same building as Clara's hotel. For a few days each year, ratepayers arrived en masse to contribute to the cost of the parish workhouse. To do so, they were obliged to climb a narrow, winding staircase past the Hanover Hotel on the way up to Paterson's office. According to one local councillor, the fairer sex fared badly in the resulting crush. He claimed to have witnessed a pitiful horde of swooning, insensible women on the staircase, desperate to part with their money. A cry went up for the rates office to move elsewhere. Paterson, in an indignant letter to the press, dismissed the councillor's vision of stairwell Armageddon as sensationalised nonsense. He admitted to problems in the past but believed he had resolved them by taking personal charge of crowd control on payment days. This, he said, worked to the satisfaction of all the other occupants of the building. All of them, that is, bar one.

Although Paterson chose not to name the objecting party, Merton wrote to the same newspaper to rebut his claims. Portraying himself as a regular hotel guest, he bemoaned the hindrance to his business affairs caused by the pandemonium on the stairs. 'I have seen women and children very much crushed,' he wrote, 'and have repeatedly seen them faint away and carried into Mrs MacEwan's hotel.' [4] Paterson, in response, identified Merton as the owner of the Hanover Hotel in Glasgow and accused him of 'utter untrustworthiness' for failing to point out his links to its Edinburgh namesake. Faced with such a personal attack, Merton refused to let the matter lie:

> *The truth of the statements made in my former letter are, I think, fully proved, by Mr Paterson carefully avoiding in his reply the subject at issue and indulging in a series of unkind personalities. In stating that I am the proprietor of the Hanover Hotel, Glasgow, Mr Paterson is simply informing the public what they are already fully aware of; but his statement to the effect that I have "intimate business relations" with Mrs MacEwan's hotel is false and incorrect. Mrs MacEwan's business and mine are of a totally different nature, and I have less "business communication" with her hotel than any other in Edinburgh. I further beg emphatically to deny Mr Paterson's insinuation contained in the latter portion of his letter. Mrs MacEwan knew nothing of the letter I addressed to you, nor its substance.*[5]

This letter, which appeared in *The Scotsman* in February 1874, shows how Merton was willing to stand his ground when under fire. His measured, assertive and well-argued prose would fill many a newspaper column in the years to come. In this case, Paterson backed down and moved away from Hanover Street a few months later.

Merton's use of a poker face to call an opponent's bluff was matched by his determination to make the best of an ordinary hand. He added a 'Royal' prefix to the name of the Glasgow hotel in 1875, bringing a touch of class to catch the eye of potential visitors. Why he did so is uncertain, but the visit of Prince Henry of Bourbon-Parma is the most plausible explanation. The strategy paid off in any event. Although silent on his Glasgow hotel career, many of the theatrical acquaintances listed in *Home and Abroad* are likely to have stayed at the Royal Hanover while performing in the city. German opera singer Karl Formes (1815–1889), Italian actress Adelaide Ristori (1822–1906) and the French soprano Marie Rôze (1846–1926) all visited Glasgow in the early 1870s.

Formes, Ristori and Rôze are among a host of names featured in a chapter of *Home and Abroad* called *Friends I Have Made*. It includes around seventy distinguished figures and runs to more than a hundred pages of biographical detail.[6] Merton, while rarely saying how he knew these luminaries, sometimes gives the impression of intimacy with people who could only have been passing acquaintances. He met Charles Dickens (1812–1870) twice during one of the author's lecture tours, describing him as morose on first meeting but 'a very cordial and staunch friend' when he warmed up.[7] Sir Arthur Sullivan (1842–1900) is introduced in the same chapter as 'one of my most intimate friends'. Merton claims to have been present while the musician composed *The Light of the World* but gives no details about the circumstances. Indeed, it is by no means certain the two men had even met at the time of the oratorio's premiere in 1873. There is, however, no doubt that the composer stayed at the Royal Hanover two years later.

Fresh from the triumph of *Trial by Jury*, Sullivan arrived in the city at the end of 1875 to conduct a series of concerts for the Glasgow Choral Union. He found himself billeted in a filthy lodging house, where his valet was forced to sleep on a grubby sofa and share his master's meagre breakfast. Disgusted, Sullivan paid a fortnight's rent to escape and made his way to the Royal Hanover. This is likely to have been his first meeting with Merton, who surely would not have allowed a close friend to stay somewhere so unbefitting. Sullivan, for his part, gave no sign of having previously met his host when he wrote a letter to his mother from the hotel. On the contrary, he complained of a 'wretched creature' playing his hymn tunes on the floor above. 'I hope they don't do it out of compliment to me,' he wrote, 'for they put in their own harmony, which to say the least isn't as good as mine.'[8]

Sullivan returned to Glasgow a year later for another season of concerts, although it is not clear if he stayed at the Royal Hanover on that occasion. Even so, *Home and Abroad* refers to other events that, taken at face value, could only have occurred between his two visits to the city. According to Merton, the composer asked him to lend paintings to an exhibition at the Royal Aquarium – a palatial building in Westminster opened to great fanfare in January 1876. Conceived as a fusion of fish, art and music, many visitors were left disgruntled by the venue's dearth of marine life, second-rate art and poor acoustics. Merton, while saying nothing of that, tells an anecdote about a painting called *The Watchers Asleep*, which he claims to have lent to the exhibition.[9] The picture turned out to be a fake, so he instructed his lawyers to serve a writ on the dealer who sold it to him. When they failed to track down the guilty party, Merton took on the role of sleuth and traced the culprit to a house in Bloomsbury. There, he discovered a stack of paintings propped against a wall, each of which was an exact copy of *The Watchers Asleep*. The dealer agreed to pawn the forgeries to cover part of the debt, a creative solution that needed the threat of arrest to recoup the full amount.

This tale shows Merton indulging in one of his frequent time warps. The link to the Royal Aquarium places the story in the 1870s, but close inspection of the detail, such as the address of the pawnbroker mentioned in *Home and Abroad*, dates the events to the early 1880s.[10] Sullivan had cut his ties with the Aquarium by then, casting further doubt on Merton's account. The story serves to portray him as a man of artistic benevolence from his earliest days as a collector, but the Altrincham bazaar is the only real sign of it at this stage of his career.[11] He never used art to promote the Royal Hanover, suggesting that his collection was not yet big enough to cause a stir. Besides, a hotel next to a busy railway station is not a typical place for a cultural hotspot.

As a man of ambition, Merton would have felt the limitations of his situation in Glasgow and must already have been looking to the future when Sullivan took umbrage at the mystery pianist. Bouts of bronchitis, made worse by harsh Scottish winters, convinced him of the need to move on. Reluctant at first to leave Glasgow on Annie's account, he changed his mind after a warning from his doctor. 'What's all the world to a man,' asked the medic, 'if his wife's a widow?'[12] Health aside, there were other reasons to move away. John King Clark died in September 1874, having spent more than a decade as the registrar of births, marriages and deaths for the Anderston district of Glasgow. A staid line of work for the erstwhile entrepreneur, it did little to improve his finances. His will named Annie as executor, but his death came just weeks after another loss in the family. In July of that year, Lottie – Merton and Annie's 7-year-old daughter – died from hydrocephalus at her great-uncle's house in Girvan.[13] Perhaps too distraught to deal with her father's paltry estate, Annie entrusted its administration to one of her cousins. Its value came in at a shade over twenty pounds.

11 Merton captioned these photographs of his daughters in Home and Abroad *with 'Our darling little Anita' and 'Our darling little Lottie'. Their deaths, at the ages of four and seven respectively, may account for his and Annie's fondness for children's charities in later life. (From* Home and Abroad*)*

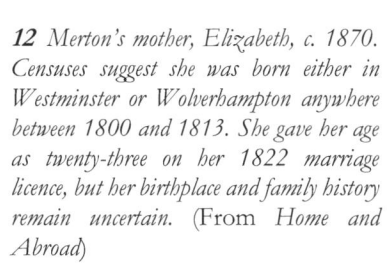

12 Merton's mother, Elizabeth, c. 1870. Censuses suggest she was born either in Westminster or Wolverhampton anywhere between 1800 and 1813. She gave her age as twenty-three on her 1822 marriage licence, but her birthplace and family history remain uncertain. (From *Home and Abroad*)

The family suffered another bereavement a few months later. Merton's mother died at the Royal Hanover at the beginning of 1875, having lived out her twilight years under her son's roof. He delegated the task of registering the death to Ella, his 14-year-old daughter, who no doubt went armed with the information supplied by her father. The registrar recorded the deceased as 'Elizabeth Cotes, widow of Samuel Cotes, iron merchant', thus ignoring her second marriage to Henry Edwards.[14] Merton's stepfather, who spent much of the 1850s running a tobacco shop in Birkenhead, seems to have lost everything, including his wife's companionship, in the 1860s. As well as being expunged from the family history, he may have ended his life in poverty. A tailor of the same name, and of precisely the right age, died in Tranmere's workhouse hospital a year after Merton's mother.

In addition to the loss of his three close relatives, developments at the hotel gave Merton another reason to leave Glasgow. He was a tenant of the North British Railway Company, which owned the adjacent Queen Street station and much of the property nearby. The station was built in the 1840s, when few could have anticipated the upsurge in traffic. By the 1870s, it was common for passengers to step out of their train onto a wooden plank instead of a platform. After negotiating that hazard, they had to pick their way across several lines of rails in order to reach safety. In the spring of 1875, the company's directors came up with a radical plan to resolve the problem: the station was to be extended to the north, south and east, with the land on all sides acquired by compulsory purchase. The Royal Hanover, together with several other buildings, would be knocked down to make way.

Whether triggered by poor health, family bereavements or threats of demolition, Merton set his sights on pastures new. He embarked on a tour of the resorts of southern England, beginning in Margate and working his way westwards. After a stopover on the Isle of Wight, he crossed the Solent to Lymington and then moved on to Bournemouth – a small town on the Hampshire coast.[15] One part of *Home and Abroad* paints this stop on the itinerary as a piece of good fortune at the end of an otherwise fruitless quest. Later, Merton reveals that he was carrying a letter of introduction to Dr J. Roberts Thomson (1844–1917), a prominent Bournemouth physician. In other words, his visit to the town was no accident. Merton remembers meeting Thomson in April 1875, contradicting many later accounts that say he first came to Bournemouth in 1876. As *Home and Abroad* twice mentions the earlier date, it is unlikely to be a mistake. It also fits with a story told by William Pickford (1861–1938), a local journalist who was a friend of Merton's in later life. Pickford recalls him saying that he first stayed in Bournemouth in 1875, when he took a room over a shop in Old Christchurch Road.[16] Merton thought it a fine town to live in but had no thoughts about its business potential when he first arrived. Until, that is, he struck up a friendship with Arthur Briant (1830–1912), the owner of the Bath Hotel.

Merton gives the hand of fate a leading role when describing his dealings with Briant. There is no sense that he might only have been a hotelier in search of a new opportunity on the south coast. The two men enjoyed each other's company, which prompted Briant to show his new friend around the hotel. Merton, who was more used to seeing passengers running for trains at the Royal Hanover, admired the Bath's clifftop position and stunning views across the bay. It was, he says, a 'unique and idealistic spot', but the response to this praise took him aback.[17] Briant announced that he wanted to sell up and leave Bournemouth so that his daughters could live in London. He claimed to be ignorant of the hotel business and reliant on his manageress to do everything for him. All Briant had to do was sit back, count the cash and enjoy the fruits of her labours. The hotel, he said, was like a home with benefits, not the least of which was the rising value of land in the town.

By telling this story, Merton comes across as a hotel trade virgin tempted by the patter of a man desperate to sell. The pitch worked regardless, because he seriously considered buying the place right there and then. According to William Pickford, all was going well until Briant brought the hotel's parrot and a carriage and horses into the bargain. Merton had no use for a parrot – not at five pounds, anyway – and so the deal broke down.[18] Aside from the animals, this account is consistent with *Home and Abroad* in saying that Merton abandoned the negotiations and returned to Glasgow. Where they differ is in what happened next.

As Pickford tells it, Merton later changed his mind and contacted Briant to see if the hotel was still up for sale. In *Home and Abroad*, it was Briant who rekindled the deal after another buyer dropped out. In the latter version, Merton was taking a holiday to relieve his bronchitis when he received a message from Charles Mathews (1803–1878), a well-known comic actor. Mathews had arrived in Glasgow for a series of performances and begged Merton to cut his break short as he felt uncomfortable 'without his host and hostess'.[19] This, incidentally, is as close as *Home and Abroad* comes to mentioning the Royal Hanover. When Merton returned to Glasgow, a letter arrived from Briant offering him first refusal of the Bath Hotel. While the exact timing of these events is hazy, the discussions had reached an advanced stage by the autumn of 1876. By then, the railway company had prepared a parliamentary bill to pave the way for the enlargement of Queen Street station.

To add complication to the negotiations with Briant, simmering problems at Clara's hotel boiled over at this crucial moment. As Merton tried to reach a deal in Bournemouth, his sister was on the verge of bankruptcy in Edinburgh. Her difficulties harked back more than a year, when she closed the hotel for improvements. To provide income during the six-month hiatus, she borrowed heavily to open a second hotel a few doors down the road. By December 1876, her many creditors had lost hope of ever being repaid. The gravity of the situation became clear at the bankruptcy hearing the following month, which showed Clara to be hopelessly insolvent and revealed debts totalling £5,000. Worse, she had failed to keep proper accounts in her early years in business and had lost all her records prior to 1874. These included details of the loans she had received from Merton. Portrayed in court as naïve and reckless, Clara became so distressed during the hearing that she struggled

13 Clara MacEwan (née Coates), c. 1870. Merton says nothing of his sister's business ventures in Home and Abroad *and only mentions her first name in the caption to this photograph. When her Edinburgh hotels went bankrupt, the debts included a hefty £800 to an upholsterer in Glasgow.* (From Home and Abroad)

to sign her statement.

Merton submitted claims against his sister for well over £2,000 – more than five times the combined annual rent of her two hotels.[20] A mixture of IOUs, bills and promissory notes, the trustee in bankruptcy greeted the claims with scepticism, believing that at least one of them had been made up. Another, he concluded, related to loan guarantees that were subject to separate claims by the lenders concerned. In effect, he was accusing Merton of trying to recover a non-existent debt. The trustee's concerns are given added significance by the timing: Merton completed the purchase of the Bath Hotel less than two weeks after the first meeting of Clara's creditors. The trustee, suspecting collusion between brother and sister, dismissed the claims in their entirety. In doing so, he left an air of suspicion hanging over the proceedings.

The bankruptcy ended the family's involvement in the Edinburgh hotel trade. Clara and her sisters faded into the background of their brother's affairs and eventually settled into a quiet life in Rothesay on the Isle of Bute. *Home and Abroad* gives the impression that Merton made a clean break with Glasgow after completing the deal with Briant, a seamless move that saw him divert his energies to Bournemouth. In truth, he kept the Royal Hanover for two more years, providing welcome extra income as he established himself on the south coast. Work on Queen Street station began in January 1878, but the hotel continued to welcome guests, advertise in guidebooks and hire staff. A notice appeared in *The Scotsman* in the summer of that year stating that the hotel was 'to be disposed of, with connection, licence and possession.' [21] Whether the railway company compensated Merton for his loss is an open question, but he is unlikely to have gone down without a fight. As he tried to squeeze the last drops from the business – the lease was surely worthless – the last rites came in November 1878 when he sold off the furniture. After that, the Royal Hanover Hotel was no more.

Notes:

1. *Manchester Times*, 26 November 1864.
2. *Glasgow Herald*, 20 July 1868. The hotel had previously been known as Whyte's.
3. The Chief Rabbi was a native of Hanover in Germany, so no doubt appreciated the choice of venue.
4. *The Scotsman*, 24 February 1874.
5. ibid., 26 February 1874.
6. *Home and Abroad* names more than 700 individuals in total.
7. *Home and Abroad*, p. 873. *Home and Abroad* includes a facsimile of a letter from Dickens thanking an unnamed person for a book of poetry. It is dated 3 May 1855, when Merton was in Buenos Aires, so he may have bought the letter at a later date.

8. Jacobs, *Arthur Sullivan: A Victorian Musician*, p. 97.
9. Merton does not name the artist but describes the painting as a girl sitting beside a cradle. It contains a child, a dog and a canary, all of whom are asleep.
10. The hotel Merton used during his detective work was owned by the father of the actor Charles Wyndham, who is mentioned several times in *Home and Abroad*. Wyndham's father died in 1882, whereas the pawnbroker moved to the address used in the story in 1880. Merton must, then, have pawned the paintings between these dates.
11. Merton served as an agent for the Art Union of London while he was in Glasgow. A members' club, it gave out artworks by lottery with the aim of widening art ownership.
12. *Home and Abroad*, p. 31.
13. Annie's uncle was master joiner James Nelson, her mother's brother. He died in Girvan in 1876.
14. Merton may not have realised that Scottish death records require the names of both of the deceased's parents. Ella only provided the father's name, which she incorrectly gave as Thomas Law. His first name was, in fact, Richard.
15. Bournemouth became part of Dorset following local government reorganisation in 1974.
16. In the *Bournemouth Guardian* of 5 February 1921, Pickford mentioned that Merton took 'a room over a shop that is now the Capital and Counties Bank.' This suggests it was where Lloyds Bank is now, on the corner of Albert Road and Old Christchurch Road.
17. *Home and Abroad*, p. 31.
18. By coincidence, Merton reported the loss of a grey parrot in the small ads of the *Glasgow Herald* in 1871.
19. *Home and Abroad*, pp. 32–33. Merton says he holidayed in Bridge of Allan (near Stirling) in the autumn after his first visit to Bournemouth – implying the latter part of 1875. This is consistent with p. 444 of *Home and Abroad*, which says he last saw Mathews in November of that year. The actor performed in Glasgow in October 1876, but there is no evidence of a visit to the city a year earlier. This suggests a muddle over dates and that Merton received his letter from Briant in the autumn of 1876.
20. The Edinburgh valuation rolls for 1875 show that Clara's annual rent was £281 for the main hotel and £170 for the other one. Merton was paying £300 a year for the Glasgow hotel.
21. *The Scotsman*, 22 June 1878.

4

NEWCOMER

The Bath Hotel in Bournemouth was a remnant of a plan devised in the 1830s by Sir George Gervis (1795–1842) to develop the heathland and pine woods around the Bourne stream. With its sandy beaches and mild climate, Gervis saw the area's potential as a fashionable watering hole. Bournemouth was then no more than a hamlet. Its origins went back to 1810, when Lewis Tregonwell (1758–1832), the town's acknowledged founder, started a modest spate of building. Gervis, a man with much bigger ideas, instructed his architect, Benjamin Ferrey (1810–1880), to design 'The New Marine Village of Bourne'. Ferrey had in mind an exclusive resort of wide, curvaceous streets lined with elegant Georgian houses. What emerged was a row of Italianate villas overlooking the stream, along what is now Westover Road. At the eastern end stood the Bath Hotel, which opened, according to many accounts, on Queen Victoria's coronation day in 1838.[1] Plain from the front, but more pleasing from the sea-facing rear, it featured two floors for guests plus a cramped top storey for servants and staff. To one side lay the taproom, stabling and an office, stretching the frontage to well over fifty yards. A clifftop garden offered fine sea views from the Isle of Wight to Old Harry Rocks.

As Bournemouth flourished and grew around it, the hotel changed little before Merton's arrival. A peaceful sanctuary in a genteel resort, it was a place where the rich, such as Lord John Russell, revived over the winter.[2] It welcomed Dr Augustus Granville (1783–1872) as a guest in its early days, a man whose opinions of his stay mattered a great deal. An Italian by birth, Granville had made his name in London in the 1820s by carrying out the first autopsy of an Egyptian mummy. As the author of the influential *Spas of England*, a few words from him could make or break a resort or hotel. His review called Bournemouth 'a winter residence for the most delicate constitutions requiring a warm and sheltered locality.'[3] These words defined the town for decades. Invalids' Walk, a pine-fringed path through the

14 *The Bath Hotel in 1860, sixteen years before Merton took over. Opened in 1838, James Lampard of Winchester paid a lump sum of £1,200 for the original 14-year lease. Merton was paying that same amount in rent every year by the late 1890s, but the price he paid to Arthur Briant in 1876 is not known.* (Bournemouth Library)

pleasure gardens, was an apt choice of name. As for the hotel, Granville found much to admire. He considered the exterior handsome and its position unrivalled but thought the views from the top floor were far too good for servants. 'This storey should be rebuilt,' he suggested, 'and applied to a series of lofty and well-furnished bedchambers, each of which would be a little belvedere.' [4]

Granville's advice went beyond the hotel. He urged the town to resist vulgarising influences, a warning that became a mantra for its landowners. Restrictive leases kept a tight control on development, establishing Bournemouth as a place of good taste and refinement. The Bath Hotel was no exception to this leasehold rule. The freeholder in 1876 was Sir George Meyrick (1827–1896), the son of the man who built it.[5] Acquiring the hotel meant not only buying Briant's lease but also obtaining Meyrick's seal of approval. Merton needed to confirm his financial status for the sale to go through – a tall order with Clara's bankruptcy muddying the waters. His track record suggests a man adept at working his way up in business, using gains from one venture as a platform for the next. The Bath Hotel was the biggest step of all, but he did enough to impress Meyrick. Merton's granddaughter, Phyllis Lee-Duncan (1904–1996), believed he borrowed most of the money to fund the purchase. If so, then the risk paid off in ways that neither he nor his lender could have imagined.

Merton celebrated the deal by taking a three-mile walk with Arthur Briant along the beach to Boscombe and back. It was Christmas Day 1876, with the weather warm enough for the new man to roll up his shirtsleeves. William Pickford could scarcely believe it when told the story years later. 'I doubt if he ever repeated it,' he said of a man whom he never saw looking anything less than pristine.[6] Bournemouth, the haunt of well-heeled convalescents in bath chairs, was already working its magic. At forty-one, Merton had plenty of years ahead of him to make an impact on this seductive place.

He began by announcing his arrival in the press. 'Mr & Mrs Cotes,' ran the notice, 'beg to intimate to the nobility and gentry that they have taken this old-established and first-class hotel.'[7] It added that the tariff would be forwarded 'on application to Mrs Cotes.' Always ready to credit Annie's unstinting support, here Merton recognises her role in his business affairs. Nowhere else is it made so plain. Pickford describes her as 'a pleasant, motherly woman, who made the guests feel at home.' Merton, he says, was 'top hole as a landlord.' They were the ideal combination – one a calm presence in the background, the other leading from the front. 'Under the Patronage of His Royal Highness the Prince of Wales,' Merton declared in his announcement – a marketing gift that Briant and his predecessors had somehow managed to miss. In 1856, the future Edward VII, then aged fourteen, had stayed at the hotel for one night during an incognito tour of the West Country.

Merton suffered an early setback when a young man hanged himself in the taproom closet, but this was no harbinger of doom. Undeterred, he was soon trumpeting Lord Beaconsfield, the Archbishop of Canterbury and the King of the Belgians as former guests. Beaconsfield, when known only as Benjamin Disraeli (1804–1881), had stayed at the hotel two years earlier to recover from an attack of gout. This connection was a godsend for Merton, who described the great Conservative as 'one of the most brilliant statesmen – if not the most brilliant – that Britain has ever possessed.'[8] While Disraeli's visit was a matter of fact, describing the hotel as 'Established Half a Century' stretched the truth by more than a decade.[9] If that invited challenge, the small print spelled out the new owner's no-nonsense approach to business: the advertisement was under his copyright, and he would take action against anyone infringing it.

Despite its reputation as Bournemouth's best, the Bath Hotel was a small establishment in a fast-growing resort. Numbered in the dozens back in 1838, the town's population stood at around 10,000 in 1876. Previous owners had failed to address the problems mentioned by Dr Granville, but Merton came in with fresh ideas. Having discharged Briant's manageress, the hotel's fate rested in his hands alone.[10] Yet, according to *Home and Abroad*, its small size occurred to him only when he fell into conversation with the Duke of Argyll a few weeks after arriving. 'If you are prepared to invest some capital in the improvement of this property,' said the Duke, 'I am quite sure that it will be a gold mine.' Merton recalls how the suggestion spurred him into action. 'I communicated these views to my friend Mr C. C. Creeke, who was then the leading light in Bournemouth, being the Town Surveyor and in fact the all-in-all. He at once jumped at the idea and said he would rejoice to enlarge the hotel and make his mark and leave it a distinguished building in the town.'[11]

This story of a chance remark by a Duke inspiring the engagement of a leading light is dramatic licence. A canny operator like Merton would not have bought the hotel without first discussing its potential. A contemporary press report confirms as much, which revealed his plans for 'considerable improvements' at the same time as announcing his arrival.[12] Even so, he did well to secure the services of such a well-known architect. Christopher Creeke (1820–1886) played a big part in Bournemouth's rise and was responsible for many of its landmarks. As town surveyor, he had laid out the road, drainage and sewerage systems. Nevertheless, with the weight of private work distracting him from his civic duties, Creeke's official position was under threat at the time Merton engaged him. This heavy workload may account for the late submission of the plans for the hotel to the local building committee. In June 1877, with the work already under way, the committee threatened Merton with penalties if he failed to rectify the omission. Although the plans materialised two months later, it was not the best of starts to his relationship with Bournemouth's grandees.[13]

The hotel stayed open for business throughout the alterations. Those guests willing to put up with the disruption saw an imposing building start to emerge from behind the scaffolding. Unrecognisable from its former self, the hotel was undergoing more of a rebirth than a renovation. It boasted a much-improved top floor and new wings on each side, but such drastic changes to one of the town's best-known buildings was bound to attract its share of doubters. 'There seemed to be no one in Bournemouth except myself who believed in its future success and prosperity,' Merton complained.[14] True, there were some – he dubbed them the 'do-nothing party' – who saw almost any change in the town as an attack on its character. Others pressed ahead regardless. The Winter Gardens, a concert venue opened with private money earlier that year, attracted similar criticism. While not a success, its mere existence proves that Merton was not the only one taking risks in Bournemouth at the time.

A hotel of such grandeur needed an air of distinction to set it apart from the competition. And so, with the construction work still in progress, Merton added a 'Royal' prefix to its name in the autumn of 1877. This time, the boyhood visit of the Prince of Wales served to justify the elevation.[15] What with the pressure and worry of a major building project, plus his ongoing

THE ART OF A SALESMAN

15 Albert Edward, the Prince of Wales (1841–1910), pictured around the time of his visit to the Bath Hotel in 1856. He became King Edward VII in 1901. A year after his accession, his office demanded that Merton remove the royal feathers from his advertising for the hotel. (National Library of Wales)

involvement with the hotel in Glasgow, Merton had more than enough to keep him occupied. The future success of the Royal Bath was, however, bound up with the fortunes of Bournemouth itself. Rapid growth brought its own stresses and strains, with many of the town's newcomers wary of it being ruined by its own popularity. Merton, for his part, believed that resorts needed visitor attractions if their businesses were to prosper, and he expected those in power to do their best to provide them.

Bournemouth, despite its remarkable expansion, was not yet big enough to warrant a council and a mayor. As in some other small towns, a board of elected improvement commissioners served as the local authority. The board was established by the 1856 Bournemouth Improvement Act, which allowed for thirteen commissioners. This had grown to seventeen by 1876.[16] Much of the board's work concerned mundane matters, but the commissioners played an important role in developing the town's amenities. They took on the task of building the first pier, completed in 1861, and made the fateful decision to use wood instead of iron. Efforts to shore it up had met with limited success, and it was near to collapse when Merton moved to Bournemouth. In one of his earliest contributions to civic affairs, he spoke up at a public meeting in favour of building a new one out of concrete. Even so, replacing the ramshackle structure was not the most pressing issue for the commissioners at the time. Sewage disposal stood at the top of their to-do list. A common problem for urban areas with a growing population, no one could have foreseen how the debate would develop in Bournemouth. What began as a row about effluent evolved into an epic, thirty-year struggle for the future of the seafront. For Merton, it became a cause célèbre.

His interest in the debate began, like everyone else's, with the arguments about sewage. He got involved as early as August 1877, when Sir Joseph

Bazalgette (1819–1891) came to town to advise Christopher Creeke and the board of commissioners about what to do. Bazalgette, the man responsible for ridding London of its Big Stink, had been trying to solve the problem in Bournemouth since well before Merton's arrival. The town discharged its effluent into the sea through an outfall beyond the pier, an arrangement branded as a risk to public health by local medical professionals. They wanted sewage and promenaders kept as far away from each other as possible. Besides that, a wave of new development on the eastern side of the district had created the need for a new outfall further along the coast. Bazalgette came up with a novel solution to this dilemma. Rather than discharging sewage near the pier, he suggested sending it down a pipe running for more than a mile along the beach to a single outfall at Boscombe.[17] There, east would meet west in a mighty confluence of effluent before floating out to sea in one giant slick. As a bonus, the design incorporated an esplanade at the base of the cliffs to hide the pipework on the beach.

Many in the town praised Bazalgette's idea for solving a problem and creating a visitor attraction at the same time. As they saw it, the esplanade – or 'undercliff drive' as it came to be known – would allow promenaders and carriage riders to enjoy the shoreline without the annoying inconvenience of sand. Others condemned the plan as a shameful waste of money. The residents of Boscombe, aghast at the prospect of a torrent of sewage flowing in their direction, objected to the entire concept. They were happy to have an outfall for their own waste but expected the rest of the town to make its own arrangements. Merton sided firmly with the undercliff drive plan and, as Bazalgette was staying at the hotel in the summer of 1877, he had the perfect opportunity to make his views known. *Home and Abroad* goes further, placing Merton in the thick of the debate at the outset. It talks of his 'intimate relations' with Bazalgette and Creeke, and how the three men spent hours poring over the plans for the undercliff drive. Merton was entitled to express his views but, as a strong critic of what he called 'amateur experts and would-be engineers', fails to explain why two qualified men would take a newly arrived hotelier into their confidence.[18]

Merton made his first attempt to gain a seat on the board of improvement commissioners against the backdrop of the sewage debate. It was something of a longshot for a man still new to Bournemouth and with no practical experience of local government elsewhere. Elections to the board took place every April, allowing those members retiring by rotation to be re-elected or voted off. Six vacancies came up in 1878, with Merton one of fourteen men vying to fill them. With a new iron pier approved by the commissioners the previous autumn, the sewage problem was the main point of contention. The candidates divided themselves along effluent disposal lines. 'One Outfall' and 'Two Outfall' parties sprang up to press their views, with most candidates signing joint statements in support of their preferred option. Merton chose to plough his own furrow, but his nomination – by one of the doctors in favour of Bazalgette's scheme – made his views clear. He also wrote to the press asking why anyone would think it a good idea, with a new pier in the offing, to have an outfall under the nose of every promenader using it. As far as he was concerned, one outfall at Boscombe was the only answer. Removing the outfall at the pier also had the advantage of keeping offensive smells well away from the Royal Bath.

Merton says nothing about this first election effort in *Home and Abroad* but was in no doubt about how people perceived him back then. 'The native-born people of the place always look upon newcomers with suspicion and jealousy, and as interlopers,' he wrote. 'Such was the case with myself for many years.'[19] This may be how Merton came to terms with his failure to win the trust of the electorate, but being an outsider was not an issue in itself. After all, natives were a rarity in a town as new as Bournemouth. More likely, Merton's way of working was already raising doubts about his motives, just as it had done with his sister's trustee in bankruptcy and James Paterson of the poor rates office. While many shared his views about a new pier and better sewerage, others may have seen the line between common good and personal benefit beginning to blur. Needing around 800 votes to win a seat on the board, Merton mustered less than half that. Only one candidate polled fewer. Worse followed when Westminster, in the guise of the all-powerful Local Government Board, ruled in favour of two outfalls a few months later.[20] The outcome seemed to crush the hopes of those, like Merton, who dreamed of an undercliff drive. Nevertheless, the scheme would return at regular intervals to haunt its detractors in the years to come. In doing so, it would inflict the most acute of the town's many growing pains.

With a seat on the board out of reach for the time being, Merton could concentrate on the Royal Bath. Alfred Cotes visited the hotel that same spring – probably the last time the two brothers were reunited. Either in poor health when he arrived or taken ill after his departure, Alfred died of pneumonia a few weeks after returning to Liverpool. His death, at the age of forty-six, robbed Merton of the only sibling given more than a passing mention in *Home and Abroad*. That summer, he invited Alfred's widow to stay at the hotel. The railway cashier's wife checked in on the same day as Prince Louis Lucien Bonaparte (1813–1891), a nephew of the great Napoleon. The contrast could hardly be more stark, yet the Prince was exactly the sort of guest Merton needed if he wanted to see a return on his capital. Where the titled and the famous brought glitz, wealthy businessmen and annuitants were bound to follow with their cash.

By the time of the Prince's visit, the builders had finished the structural work at the Royal Bath. A chateau-style roof now crowned the enlarged building, bringing a hint of the Loire Valley to the Hampshire coast. For Merton, it marked the start of a period of consolidation. The Royal Hanover

16 Merton's brother, Alfred, c. 1875. He married Elizabeth Griffiths, his former landlady, in 1871, by which time he had adopted Merton's way of spelling the surname. Like his brother, Alfred lent money to his sister Clara, but he was not a rich man. His estate was valued at £450 when he died in 1878. (From *Home and Abroad*)

closed its doors for the last time in November 1878, the same month that work started in Bournemouth on the new pier. More disruption near to the Royal Bath was not ideal, but he could take comfort in a visitor attraction taking shape within walking distance of his guests. Having invested so much in the hotel's exterior, Merton made sure the internal fittings matched the same high standards. The work took many months, resulting in what he called 'every improvement modern science can suggest' and sanitary fittings 'of the very highest order.' [21] Things did not always go to plan, however. One evening, after a gasfitter failed to seal some new pipework, Annie carried a candle into the room where he had been working. The resulting explosion blew out the windows and sent glass flying across the road into the pleasure gardens. Lucky not to be killed, she escaped without so much as a scratch.

As the hotel started to gain a reputation for the highest standards of service, Merton took care to nurture his other business interests. The Royal Bath, he says, was only one of the properties he bought when moving to Bournemouth, although he gives no details of the others. There are hints elsewhere of landholdings in the rising suburbs of Boscombe and Springbourne, and he owned a number of houses in the growing conurbation down the years.[22] Income from these properties helped to finance his various activities, as did his continued involvement in the wine and spirit trade. An early advertisement for the hotel names him as the sole proprietor of 'Abbotsford Blend', a whisky using the home of Sir Walter Scott (1771–1832) as a brand name. This gives some idea of the breadth of his interests, even if the Royal Bath is alone in receiving attention in *Home and Abroad*. As these other ventures raked in the cash to plough back into the hotel, Merton chose art as the vehicle to take it to the next level. Part promotion, part investment, part obsession, he applied the same verve to the Royal Bath's décor as he did to the rebuilding. He talks of arriving in Bournemouth with an established art collection, but there is no doubt that he bought far more in the years afterwards. *The Watchers Asleep* illustrates the point, a painting acquired much later than he was willing to admit. As well as adding to the aesthetics and sophistication of the hotel, buying and selling art offered a release from business pressures. 'A hobby of some sort,' he wrote, 'is as necessary to the human brain as food is to the body.' [23]

Unswayed by the whims of fashion, Merton preferred what he called 'the modern British School of Art' to the work of foreign artists and the old masters. The Pre-Raphaelites lay at the fringes of his tastes and later art movements largely passed him by. For him, exhibition at the Royal Academy guaranteed a painting's quality, but reliance on the art establishment led to a conservative approach. Besides, anything too controversial might have offended his high-end clientele. Merton took pride in buying everything himself, which set him apart from the wealthier collectors who used agents. Provenance was vital – experience had taught him that. He labelled the artist Sidney Cooper (1803–1902) 'a covetous elf' for charging five guineas to authenticate his own work.[24] Merton could also be creative in his dealings with the art world. He commissioned a bust of Disraeli for the newly named Beaconsfield Room at the Royal Bath, where the great man was said to have conducted cabinet business during his stay. As well as underlining the hotel's links to a prime minister, publicity from the unveiling helped the sculptor to sell copies to Conservative clubs up and down the country.

This tactic of inducing press coverage became Merton's favoured way of promoting the hotel. News stories came to the notice of far more people than an advertisement hidden away among a glut of others. The bigger the event, the more the column inches, and events seldom came much bigger in Bournemouth than the completion of its long-awaited new pier in the summer of 1880. The result of years of wrangling, it demanded the presence of a person of high rank to carry out the opening. With the Queen shunning public appearances in her widowhood, the improvement commissioners invited the Prince of Wales to do the honours. He would have been the perfect choice for Merton. When the Prince declined, the board then received a refusal from Prince Arthur, Duke of Connaught (1850–1942), the Queen's third son. With time running out, they persuaded the Lord Mayor of London, Sir Francis Truscott (1824–1895), to do the deed instead.

In most places, such an occasion would have meant receiving the guest of honour at the town hall. Bournemouth did have such a thing, but it was owned by a private company and was not geared up to large civic functions. The commissioners consulted a group of influential residents, known as the Town's Interest Committee, about suitable venues. The committee soon received an offer of a suite of rooms at the Highcliffe Mansions, an upmarket hotel on the West Cliff with a good view of the new pier. However, on the day the commissioners were due to ratify the arrangement, Merton turned up unannounced before the committee assembled for the meeting. Not only was he prepared to match the Highcliffe Mansions' offer of rooms, but he was also willing to supply, free of charge, the food, wine and everything else the Lord Mayor and his retinue might require. The commissioners, believing they understood the extent of his offer, voted to accept it. The committee, presented with this fait accompli when they arrived, walked away in disgust when the commissioners refused to change their minds. The committee's anger was more than just a reaction to the board's refusal to reconsider a deal made behind their backs. They had earlier rebuffed Merton's efforts to join their ranks, believing his generosity was nothing more than a ploy to advertise the Royal Bath. By taking over the arrangements, they felt it would appear as if he, and not the board, was playing host to the Lord Mayor.

Merton puts forward his own angle on these discussions in *Home and Abroad*. He mentions the offer from an unnamed hotel but says that his rival 'could not supply food or drink, not even bread and cheese.' [25] As for what followed, he saw himself first as the victim, then as the saviour, when the atmosphere turned sour: 'A jealous-minded member of the board of commissioners (whose name I refrain from mentioning) sent an anonymous letter stating that the invitation from myself was really for the purpose not so much of opening the pier as of reopening the Royal Bath Hotel.' [26] This letter, he says, threatened to derail the visit, as Truscott took fright at the prospect of a commercial hijacking. Merton claims to have smoothed things over by dictating a telegram on the board's behalf.

Having seized the chance to play host, Merton did his best to make the most of it. Board and committee members greeted their honoured guest at the railway station, but from there the Royal Bath took centre stage. Led by the town band, a procession of carriages made its way through a sea of decorations to the hotel, where four heralds trumpeted its arrival. Merton had set aside thirty rooms for the Lord Mayor's entourage. The party included Truscott's son, a sheriff, two under-sheriffs – all with their wives – the City Marshal, the Sword Bearer, the Mace Bearer and many others. Press coverage was equally bloated, with the Royal Bath as much the focus of attention as its guests. 'The decoration and furnishing are of a most costly and handsome character,' declared the *Bournemouth Observer*, a prelude to a gushing review of the hotel's delights.[27] It spared no words to describe the art – 'curiosities of every conceivable kind, with some of the finest oil and watercolour paintings and drawings, we should think, to be seen in the neighbourhood.' On and on it went, conducting a grand tour of the *salle à manger*, the coffee room, the Burroughes and Watts billiard table, the ladies' boudoir and a downstairs lavatory. Such adulation addled the grammar of the reporter caught up in it. 'Having said thus much of the interior arrangements,' he concluded, 'we do not know that we have not exceeded our original intentions.'

17 The Royal Bath Hotel in the 1880s after extension and renovation. Despite the hotel's prominent position and distinctive facade, Merton's advertising warned new arrivals 'to be careful that they are taken there, as mistakes have occurred, causing much disappointment.' [28] This may be one reason why, in his first year in the town, Merton joined the board of a new cab company and allowed it to use the hotel's stables as a base. (Bournemouth Library)

The next morning, a host of bands and dignitaries marched behind the Lord Mayor's carriage as it made its way to the pier. Truscott performed the official opening with a golden key. After enjoying a civic lunch and a regatta, he returned to the Royal Bath for a banquet arranged by Merton. The hotel, adorned with 3,000 coloured oil lamps, dazzled the crowds watching the comings and goings from outside. Inside, the guests sat down to a sumptuous feast. The menu, printed on white satin, included *quails farce en caisse, canard aux cressons* and *Royal Bath pouding glacé*. After seven courses and a surfeit of speeches and toasts, the diners decamped to the garden to watch a firework display on the new pier. As the party wound down and the guests started to drift away, a cry arose from the people gathered in the street for a speech from the Lord Mayor. Truscott claimed fatigue at first but was prevailed upon to appear on the hotel balcony. After a few words in tribute to Bournemouth and the warmth of his welcome, he reserved his best praise for the Royal Bath. 'I understand that the hotel has been partly rebuilt,' he remarked. 'I believe that, if it treats all its guests as it has done me, it will receive its well-merited success.' [29] These comments, Merton suggests, were Truscott's way of showing his disgust at the affair of the anonymous letter. Perhaps so, but Merton also chose to interpret the Lord Mayor's words as a formal reopening of the Royal Bath after its revamp. Despite finishing the work many months earlier, this was to become an established part of the hotel's story in the years to come.

Newspapers across Britain reported on the pier opening, with many of them making special mention of the Royal Bath. A key milestone in the town's progress, Merton's willingness to back the occasion with cash gave it attention-grabbing glamour. This, as events would prove, created its own problems. For some, Merton had stolen too much of the glory, giving rise to lingering tensions and a bitter aftertaste. 'I have been the object of so much personal animus and jealousy,' he complained. 'Every effort I have endeavoured to make for the prosperity and advancement of Bournemouth has been, not the outcome of selfishness and egoism, but of an earnest desire to serve the whole town.' [30] Those with the opposite view waited for a chance to take their revenge, and it would not be long in coming. Yet even the strongest of Merton's critics could not deny that Truscott's visit had confirmed the Royal Bath as *the* haven for the town's most discerning patrons. The point would be underlined a few months later when the hotel received its most illustrious visitor to date. Merton would seldom meet anyone more feted, or more colourful.

Notes:

1. The hotel was open for business several weeks before the coronation.
2. A brochure for the hotel from c. 1899 claimed Lord John Russell as its first ever guest.
3. Granville, *Spas of England*, p. 515.
4. ibid., p. 521.
5. Sir George Gervis (1795–1842), properly known as Sir George Tapps-Gervis, was the son of Sir George Tapps (1753–1835). Gervis's son, another George (1827–1896), took the additional surname of Meyrick in 1876 after an inheritance, thus becoming Sir George Tapps-Gervis-Meyrick. He was generally known as Sir George Meyrick.
6. *Bournemouth Guardian*, 5 February 1921.
7. *Bournemouth Observer*, 11 January 1877.
8. *Home and Abroad*, p. 918.
9. *Bournemouth Observer*, 12 September 1877.
10. A series of managers, and not the owners, ran the hotel from its earliest days. The first, Thomas Holloway, died in 1839 and was succeeded by his sister-in-law, Mary Toomer. Her niece, Emma Bailey, took over in 1868. Mary Martin, who became Arthur Briant's manager when he bought the hotel c. 1871, left when Merton arrived.
11. *Home and Abroad*, p. 34. Merton was referring to George Campbell (1823–1900), the 8th Duke of Argyll. William Pickford attributes the 'gold mine' phrase to Arthur Briant.
12. *Poole and Bournemouth Herald*, 18 January 1877.
13. Creeke's involvement in the hotel's alterations is not recorded in the minutes of the building committee, but obituaries list it as one of his achievements. Another firm of architects, Kemp Welch & Co., submitted proposals to extend the hotel stables towards the end of 1877. Either that work was too small for Creeke, or he had no capacity to carry it out.

14. *Home and Abroad*, p. 34.
15. Merton may have run into trouble with the use of the 'Royal' prefix, because the National Archives holds records under the heading 'Title royal: Royal Bath Hotel' (ref. HO 144/7016). The files are closed to the public until 2028.
16. Two seats on the board were reserved for the lord of the manor (Sir George Meyrick) and his nominee, but neither attended any meetings after 1870.
17. Bazalgette's outfall plan led to the first of Bournemouth's many boundary extensions. Boscombe was then outside the commissioners' district – defined by the Bournemouth Improvement Act as 'a circle of the radius of a mile, whereof the centre is the front door of the Belle Vue Hotel.' The Belle Vue, near the mouth of the Bourne stream, made more geographical sense than the Bath Hotel. As the proposed outfall lay beyond this boundary, the commissioners annexed Boscombe in 1876.
18. Merton's comments come from a letter to the *Bournemouth Daily Echo* in November 1903. It begins with the words 'Upwards of a quarter of a century ago', clearly referring to Bazalgette's 1877 visit.
19. *Home and Abroad*, pp. 53–54.
20. The commissioners extended the existing outfall further out to sea after the Local Government Board's decision.
21. *Bournemouth Observer*, 16 April 1881.
22. An 1882 court case, in which Merton lost a civil claim by a firm of auctioneers over a disputed bill, revealed that he owned property in Old Christchurch Road.
23. *Home and Abroad*, p. 701.
24. ibid., p. 698.
25. ibid., p. 261.
26. ibid., p. 263.
27. *Bournemouth Observer*, 11 August 1880.
28. ibid., 16 April 1881.
29. ibid., 14 August 1880.
30. *Home and Abroad*, p. 131.

5

CANDIDATE

In January 1881, Merton received a telegram from Osborne House, Queen Victoria's home on the Isle of Wight, asking him to send a carriage to the station. It was to collect Eugénie, the exiled Empress of France, who was arriving in Bournemouth to visit Sophia, the Queen consort of Sweden (1836–1913). The Swedish Queen, who preferred her own space to the delights of the Royal Bath, had rented a villa on the East Cliff to regain her health over the winter. Merton's role was to convey the Empress to the hotel, provide refreshments, then arrange for her to be taken to see the Queen. Choosing one of the town's hoteliers for this task was not a snub to the improvement commissioners. As a private visit, the Empress wanted to get away with as little fanfare as could be managed. Even so, the fact that the Royal Bath was selected to host such an important figure says everything about the hotel's standing. As yet, nowhere else in the town came close.

The erstwhile Empress was then in her mid-fifties. The days of grand palaces and lavish parties may have been behind her, but she retained an air of celebrity mystique. Often troubled in her youth, she attempted suicide as a love-struck teenager by drinking milk laced with ground up match heads. Later, she is said to have ridden bareback to bullfights and flirted with matadors. She settled in Kent after fleeing the Prussian advance on Paris, but her husband died soon afterwards. More anguish followed when her only son was killed fighting for the British in the Anglo-Zulu war of 1879. A reporter saw these troubles etched on her face as she stepped off the train at Bournemouth: 'The Empress, we are sorry to state, had by no means the appearance of being in the best of health.' [1]

Eugénie's visit to the town lasted three hours and fourteen minutes. So say the train times. She made two stops at the Royal Bath, one on arrival and one on departure. Brief as they must have been, they were long enough for a new legend to emerge about the tragic lady. 'On walking through the lounge,' recalls Merton, 'she noticed a cabinet, at which she seemed to be very much upset. She was almost in a fainting condition and sat down in a chair. I immediately ordered one of the waiters in attendance to bring Her Majesty a glass of water, which she drank and recovered herself.' [2] An aide asked Merton how the cabinet came to be there, as the Empress recognised it from her boudoir at Saint-Cloud, a palace destroyed by fire after her flight into exile. Merton explained that he bought it from a Glaswegian gentleman, who had acquired it in Paris in the early 1870s. Apparently satisfied, Eugénie made her way to a waiting carriage. 'On her departure,' wrote Merton, 'she expressed herself as being extremely pleased and delighted with everything and said she hoped to pay another visit to Bournemouth. She also expressed a hope that my wife and I would pay Her Majesty a visit at Farnborough Hill.' While it is no surprise that neither of these calls took place, Merton says he received a diamond ring to thank him for his services. Its current whereabouts are not known, but Eugénie's cabinet now stands opposite her portrait in the Russell-Cotes Art Gallery and Museum.

The local newspapers failed to sniff out this fine addition to Eugénie folklore. Merton was always discreet when it came to goings-on in the hotel – loose talk was bad for business – and he resists the temptation to gossip in *Home and Abroad*. Press coverage praising himself or the Royal Bath meant far more to him. He kept scrapbooks crammed with newspaper cuttings, to which he added notes, ticks and crosses by way of emphasis. Tea and grocery magnate Thomas Lipton kept similar scrapbooks but made little use of them in his autobiography. Merton, by contrast, sprinkles extracts from his own collection of cuttings throughout *Home and Abroad*. Sometimes he takes liberties with the original wording, fuelling the doubts of those unconvinced by his Empress Eugénie anecdote.

18 The Empress Eugénie, by the court painter Franz Winterhalter (1805–1873). She lived at Chislehurst, Kent, after fleeing to England but moved to Farnborough Hill in Hampshire in the early 1880s. Merton's colourful account of her visit to the Royal Bath was not echoed in the local newspapers, which talked only of her walking in the hotel grounds, signing the visitors' book, and receiving a bouquet of flowers from Ella Cotes. (Russell-Cotes Art Gallery and Museum)

One example of Merton's creativity with quotations concerns the King of Sweden, who joined his wife in Bournemouth a few weeks after Eugénie's visit. During his stay, the King laid the foundation stone of a potential rival to the Royal Bath called the Mont Dore, a hydropathic hotel being built overlooking the town's pleasure gardens. Merton, in quoting an article in *The Times* about the event, omits all references to the Mont Dore. He prefers to focus on the gift given to the King to celebrate the occasion – an album containing pictures of the local area. Among these, according to *Home and Abroad*, were 'the new pier, opened by the Lord Mayor of London, and the Royal Bath Hotel, reopened by his Lordship on the 11th August last.' [3] While these words seem to endorse his interpretation of Sir Francis Truscott's speech on the hotel balcony, the original article provided no detail about the pictures in the album. The point of embellishing it, one imagines, was not so much to edit out a rival but to emphasise a link, however small, between the Royal Bath and one of the town's distinguished visitors. Such unabashed promotion was, together with its art, décor and first-class service, one of the main ingredients in the hotel's success. Merton himself preferred to put it down to his 'special genius for the love of art' and a 'weakness for building and developing property.' [4] While indulgence in both had left him well placed to take on the likes of the Mont Dore, his most potent talent was for marketing. When asked the question 'Which is the best hotel in the United Kingdom?', readers of one London magazine voted the Royal Bath into thirteenth place. This was quite a publicity coup for a hotel outside the capital, even allowing for votes cast by owners and their friends.[5]

Merton's next investment in the Royal Bath turned the hotel itself into a work of art. In 1881, he employed the decorative artist John Thomas (c. 1826 – c. 1900) to paint scenes on the walls and ceilings. A former wallpaper designer, Thomas specialised in murals reflecting the fashion for Far Eastern art and design. Merton was not alone in following the trend in Bournemouth. That same year, John Elmes Beale (1847–1928) opened his Fancy Fair and Oriental House, the shop that went on to become the well-known department store bearing his name. At the Royal Bath, the *Bournemouth Observer* eulogised the hotel's new Japanese Drawing Room: 'The general tone of the walls is a soft Japanese yellow, on which are painted by Mr Thomas innumerable specimens of the feathered tribe, like peacocks, flamingos, herons, storks and owls, and small birds of a rare and brilliant hue. Among these are dispersed armorial bearings of Japanese nobility, from the Mikado downwards, the ceiling being treated in a similar manner.' [6] Even the gas brackets, fashioned out of bamboo, blended in with the theme.

The Royal Bath was now one of the main attractions in a town not noted for excitement. One guest remembers going out for a stroll with his friends after a sumptuous dinner at the hotel. They explored the pier, the pleasure gardens and the Invalids' Walk, then wandered around aimlessly trying to

19 Most of Merton's advertisements, like this one from the 1880s, played on the hotel's royal connections. In truth, its foundation stone was laid in June 1836 – two years before the coronation – at which time it was intended to be named 'The Gervis Arms'. (Author's collection)

work out what to do next. 'We inquired of a passer-by if there were any entertainments in the town,' the visitor recalled. 'He reflected carefully for several seconds, and then said he was afraid not, unless there might possibly be something of some kind or other going on at the theatre.' The friends gave up and went back to the hotel, only to encounter more of the same the next evening. It was a tale familiar to many who were visiting Bournemouth for the first time in the early 1880s. The town, with its reputation for dullness, lacked amenities for those who expected more than a pier, fine scenery and fair weather. Unlike the old guard of health seekers, a more demanding clientele wanted a variety of things to do. This presented Merton with a problem, despite the success of his first five years on the south coast. He knew the outlook was less rosy if Bournemouth failed to attract visitors, yet many in the town resented spending money on new facilities. To win the argument, he needed to persuade the improvement commissioners to invest for the future. His best chance of doing that was to try once more to become a commissioner himself.

After being nominated by an outgoing board member, Merton again stood for election in April 1881. This time, he fought a much more visible campaign than his low-key attempt to win a boardroom seat three years earlier. In a letter to the ratepayers, he spoke of 'the large sums I have expended in improvements and the pleasure it gave me to entertain the Lord Mayor as your guest.' [7] While supporting measures to enhance 'the comfort of residents and visitors', he also sought to appease the more conservative element of the electorate. He would curb waste, plant more pine trees – 'the primary cause of Bournemouth's rise'– and resist plans for civic offices in the pleasure gardens. This softened any alarm caused by his closing remarks: 'An accelerated train service is much needed to and from London. Deputations to the London and South Western Railway Company should be persisted in.' This was a delicate subject to introduce to his campaign, as Bournemouth and the railways had never been the best of friends. The main Southampton to Dorchester line ignored the town when it opened in 1847, passing instead through Ringwood and Wimborne on its way westwards. Passengers travelling from London alighted at Holmsley, a tiny station on the edge of the New Forest, and then completed their journey with a bone-shaking, twelve-mile ride in an omnibus. Things improved with the construction of a branch line to Christchurch in 1862, which reached Bournemouth eight years later. Visitors still had some way to go, however, as the station stood a mile east of the Bath Hotel.[8]

By 1881, nothing much had changed. The Empress Eugénie's opinion of her visit to Bournemouth that year is not recorded, but she trundled into town along the same tortuous branch line as lesser mortals. Merton often travelled the route himself so knew the difficulties. He recalls how clerks at Waterloo scratched their heads when asked for a ticket to Bournemouth, so far off the beaten track was it. With a journey time of four hours, little wonder that many Londoners preferred Brighton and Eastbourne. Their stations were better, too. One resident described Bournemouth's as a 'primeval edifice' after seeing a consumptive with a respirator struggle with their bags in a howling gale.[9] Some saw advantages in this situation, as it deterred day trippers and put the brakes on growth. The town mushroomed regardless, and 17,000 people were calling it their home by the early 1880s. Residents needed a good rail service as much as visitors, and demand for direct trains from London went back way before Merton's time. Pier and sewage pushed the subject down the list of priorities, but there was good reason for him to bring it to the fore during the 1881 campaign: Wyndham Portal (1822–1905), the deputy chairman of the London and South Western Railway, was staying at the Royal Bath in the run-up to the election.

Merton knew a thing or two about trains and stations from his time in Glasgow. In advance of the poll, he brought together a group of tradesmen to draw up a set of proposals. Portal agreed to take time out from his holiday to discuss them at a meeting of interested parties. It gave the aspiring commissioners a chance to show their mettle. Those who took up the opportunity included Joseph Cutler (1830–1910) and Enoch White (1830–1890), two men who would go on to have a big say in Merton's political career. Cutler, a maverick builder, took pride in his humble origins and claimed to have witnessed the laying of the Bath Hotel's foundation stone back in the 1830s. He was the most unsuccessful candidate in the history of the commissioners, having lost seven times in the space of eleven years. Enoch White, a nurseryman by trade, had failed six times, but the odds lay against men of their class. Commissioners were elected under a system where property values determined the number of votes cast by each ratepayer. It favoured candidates who appealed to wealthier voters.

In opening the meeting, Portal noted how Merton was 'very active and zealous in trying to promote the good of Bournemouth.' [10] This, one presumes, was a reference to being collared in the hotel lounge. As a past guest, he spoke of his admiration for the changes at the Royal Bath and its role in the Lord Mayor's visit. Merton replied to this welcome election boost by setting out the tradesmen's proposals. They demanded a fast service from Waterloo, leaving out all the stops between Eastleigh and Bournemouth.[11] They also wanted a new station to rid the town of its existing embarrassment. Much discussion followed, with opposition expressed to Sunday trains – including from Merton – and with a consensus that the town should be on the main line to London. In accepting that principle, Portal suggested that Holmsley, the starting point for the omnibus journey in bygone days, was the right place to begin a new line.

Press reports of the meeting appeared on the day of the count. They came too late to influence the ballot, as most people had cast their votes by then. That said, with only nine candidates vying for five seats, Merton's campaign gave him reason to be confident. Tension mounted as updates appeared throughout the day. A late surge saw him closing in on fifth place, but he was thirty votes short when the returning officer read out the final tally. As the nonplussed Merton tried to make sense of the result, the town clerk refused his request to inspect the ballot papers. Most galling of all, Joseph Cutler and Enoch White had at last won their coveted seats on the board.

That year's election saw Bournemouth on the cusp of change. The system

20 *Joseph Cutler crossed swords with Merton on several occasions. Born in Christchurch, he emigrated to Australia as a young man, where he worked as a fisherman and, unsuccessfully, as a gold prospector. On returning to England, he entered the building trade, survived bankruptcy and went on to become one of Bournemouth's most industrious and eccentric figures. 'Joseph's Steps', a footpath on the West Cliff, was named after him.* (Author's collection)

failed to disbar Cutler and White, while those relying on upper-class votes occupied the last three places in the poll. Most of Merton's support came from tradesmen and the middle classes, the groups with the most to gain from better rail links. A different outcome might have arisen if he could have capitalised on his intervention a few days earlier. Not to be put off, he met Portal again soon after the poll and shared the outcome with the press. The London and South Western, he announced, would 'consider the question of cutting a direct line, as the crow flies, from here to Brockenhurst or Holmsley Junction.' [12] In raising the prospect of the former, he may have been the first to publicise the eventual route.

After the election, an undercurrent of tension crept into Merton's dealings with the commissioners. The first signs had appeared before the pier opening, when he claimed damages for an accident caused by a badly maintained road. The nature of the incident is not known, but he twice rejected the board's offers of compensation before reaching a settlement.[13] Later, it transpired that some of those involved in the pier opening had misunderstood certain details about the arrangements. No one was sure, for instance, who ordered the 3,000 lights for the Royal Bath, let alone who had agreed to pay for them. With the debt outstanding more than nine months on, the commissioners paid the contractor's bill to avoid legal action. This situation prompted Thomas Hankinson (1831–1905), the treasurer of the Town's Interest Committee, to ask awkward questions. In a letter to the press, he drew attention to a bill sent to the commissioners by the Royal Bath for costs associated with the Lord Mayor's banquet. This, he said, went against Merton's pledge to cover the entire cost himself. Hankinson also took issue with an account sent to his committee for 'attendance' and 'showing the public over the hotel'.[14] When another correspondent turned the cause into a crusade, Merton went on the offensive in his reply: 'I undertook to entertain, at my own cost, the Lord Mayor and his personal suite, not the commissioners and their invited guests and friends. I carried out to the very letter – and far more – all I undertook at a cost out of my own pocket of about £270.' [15] His claim against the commissioners, he went on, related to their personal consumption at the banquet.

Other niggles came to light as the affair rumbled on. The commissioners greeted with suspicion Merton's request to widen a footpath in front of the hotel and to invoice him for the cost. He had, they recalled, deducted strange expenses when billed for similar work in the past. They then dismissed as 'a joke' his application to erect signposts to the Royal Bath in the pleasure gardens. Later, a board member named him as the author of an unsigned note calling a commissioner to account for using a board employee for private work. For Merton, who often complained of being the victim of anonymous letters, the tables had been turned.

The distrust created by these spats spilled over when Merton again stood for election in 1882. Things soon turned sour, despite his success in scraping together enough support from members of the Residents' Association for them to endorse him as a candidate.[16] An unsigned handbill began to circulate that raised doubts about his fitness to serve as a commissioner and queried his conduct over the Lord Mayor's banquet. He dismissed it as a 'dastardly, contemptible and cowardly attack', but the handbill's origin was an open secret.[17] At one election meeting, someone called out from the floor that the author was 'quite plain'. Another added, 'They say there's no colour more pure than white.' Although Merton glossed over the exchange by quoting *Othello* ('Who steals my purse…'), the reference to Enoch White would have been obvious to all.[18]

Against this backdrop, Merton secured his nomination from James McWilliam (c. 1824–1897), an experienced commissioner who managed to broker a settlement in the expenses row. Board members paid for what they ate at the banquet, leaving Merton to pick up the costs of the Lord Mayor's party. Yet still the issue refused to go away. Questions kept coming from the floor at meetings, despite his efforts to talk about policy matters. His cause suffered another blow when rumours surfaced of a deal to pledge himself to a faction on the board in exchange for campaign support. He refuted this claim in an otherwise tepid address to the ratepayers, in which he focused on cutting costs, planting pine trees and providing help to the town's outlying districts. 'I should be glad to further the development of the West Cliff,' he concluded, 'by assisting in the promotion of the Undercliff Walk, provided such can be constructed without undue demands on the pockets of the ratepayers.' [19] He said nothing at all about a drive beneath the East Cliff.

Merton saved his more radical views for public meetings. He joined the clamour for Bournemouth's incorporation as a municipal borough, which many saw as the best way for the town to control its own destiny. It had outgrown Christchurch, and yet it still relied on its neighbour for a range of local government services. Greeted with apathy by the commissioners when mooted by Joseph Cutler at the turn of the year, Merton was one of those who liked the idea at first. He also favoured the construction of tramways, except in the town centre, but had little to say about railway matters. With Wyndham Portal still some months away from revealing his plans, Merton found himself without a campaign issue to call his own. He presented himself as a centre-ground candidate committed to bringing unity to a divided board. His pitch failed to convince the electorate. With five seats available, he was beaten into sixth place by the man who nominated him the year before.

Another chance to gain a seat on the board arose a few months later. Although elected by the ratepayers, the rules allowed the commissioners to appoint a new member themselves if someone died or resigned between the annual polls. Such a vacancy arose in the summer of 1882. On the day of the meeting to agree a replacement, officials from the railway company presented

21 As deputy chairman of the London and South Western Railway, Wyndham Portal was instrumental in bringing the direct line from London to fruition. Although Merton claimed credit for proposing the Brockenhurst route, Jude James, in his book about the line's construction, singles out Herbert Nankivell (1843–1912), a Bournemouth doctor, as the instigator of the idea. Whatever the truth of the matter, the route had a complex genesis. (Library of Congress)

their plans to the board. Keen to press ahead with the direct line via Brockenhurst, they wanted support for a bill lined up for the next session of parliament. Their proposals would have come as a surprise to no one, as engineers had already surveyed the planned route. Still, Merton felt free to announce the company's intentions in the *Bournemouth Observer* the following day: 'I am authorised to state that Mr Wyndham Portal has obtained the approval of his board to a scheme he has long advocated to accelerate the train accommodation between London and Bournemouth, viz. a direct line, as the crow flies, from Christchurch to Brockenhurst.' [20]

Although this statement seems to give Portal the credit for the route, Merton would claim it for himself in the years to come. That should have earned him the board's gratitude, but his private dealings with the railway company raised many hackles. With three names in the ring for the vacant position, one commissioner felt Merton's near miss at the last election justified his appointment. Others refused to support him out of personal dislike. One said: 'I cannot vote for Captain Elwes, because I do not know him, and I cannot vote for Mr Cotes because I do.' [21] The board opted for the retired army captain, with Merton pushed into third place. He chose not to put his name forward when another vacancy arose a month later.

In the ensuing weeks, the London and South Western sought approval from the landowners affected by the new line. Reports claimed that Sir George Meyrick, whose Hinton Admiral estate lay in its path, had raised objections, but he soon denied it. Merton says the railway company asked him to mediate with Meyrick, using the promise of a station at Hinton Admiral as an inducement. A change to the route may also have won Meyrick

THE ART OF A SALESMAN

over, as the one finally agreed ran a little to the south of that first intended.

With the route settled, in 1883 Merton made a fourth attempt to gain election to the board. This time he could speak at hustings without fielding awkward questions about banquets. Largely absent from the press since the furore died down, his most recent appearance was upbeat. He donated a portrait of Sir Stafford Northcote (1818–1887), a former hotel guest and Chancellor of the Exchequer, to the local Conservative club. As well as benefitting the Royal Bath and underlining his political allegiances, the publicity painted Merton in a far better light than the expenses row. His election address steered well clear of reopening that old wound: 'My personal efforts to further the interests and prosperity of our lovely town are sufficiently known to you, and being a large owner and ratepayer myself, you may rely upon my opposing all extravagant and wasteful expenditure.' [22] He made no other pledges, not even for a single pine tree.

Of the fourteen candidates on offer, only four had served as commissioners before. Christopher Creeke, the board's former surveyor, finished at the head of the poll, gaining a seat at the first time of asking. Merton came in second – a comfortable place to be with seven seats available. A quarrel-free campaign helped his cause, but business success and progress on the railway seem to have been the main reasons for the upturn in his fortunes. As Bournemouth got ready to embrace the direct line, Merton could rightly claim to have played his part in bringing it to fruition. After five years and three unsuccessful campaigns, he was at last in a position to exert more influence over the town's affairs. And yet he was destined to spend less time occupying his seat on the board than he had spent trying to win it.

Notes:

1. *Bournemouth Visitors Directory*, 2 February 1881.
2. *Home and Abroad*, p. 39.
3. ibid., p. 40. The original article appeared in *The Times* on 26 May 1881.
4. ibid., p. 33.
5. The poll was run by *St Stephen's Review* magazine. The *Bournemouth Guardian* of 23 February 1884 reported: 'The Royal Bath Hotel, Bournemouth, stands thirteenth on a list of about a hundred, with 72 votes. Many of the hotels have only one vote, probably that of the proprietor himself.'
6. *Bournemouth Observer*, 2 April 1881.
7. ibid., 30 March 1881.
8. The original station was built to the east of Holdenhurst Road and became known as Bournemouth East in 1874. It closed when the current main station, to the west of Holdenhurst Road, opened in 1885.
9. *Morning Post*, 31 May 1878.

10. *Home and Abroad*, p. 59. In 1877, Merton brokered a meeting between the commissioners and representatives of three railway companies, including the London and South Western. The main concerns were the regulation of cab fares, timetables and the charges for goods traffic.
11. Eastleigh station was known as Bishopstoke at the time. The tradesmen's idea meant taking trains straight onto the branch line at Ringwood.
12. *Hampshire Advertiser*, 9 April 1881.
13. The incident took place in Norwich Road, Bournemouth. The *Poole and Bournemouth Herald* of 16 October 1879 reported that Merton had also claimed twenty guineas for 'injuries received by a horse and carriage in Suffolk Road.' The two roads are close by, but the claims do not appear to be related.
14. *Bournemouth Visitors Directory*, 28 May 1881.
15. *Bournemouth Observer*, 10 September 1881.
16. The Residents' Association gave its support to five candidates (out of eight nominees) via a ballot of members. Merton came fifth.
17. *Bournemouth Observer*, 29 March 1882.
18. *Poole and Bournemouth Herald*, 30 March 1882. Merton is alluding to Iago's lines: 'Who steals my purse steals trash, 'tis something, nothing; 'Twas mine, 'tis his, and has been slave to thousands; But he that filches from me my good name robs me of that which not enriches him and makes me poor indeed.'
19. *Bournemouth Observer*, 25 March 1882.
20. ibid., 16 August 1882.
21. *Poole and Bournemouth Herald*, 17 August 1882.
22. *Bournemouth Observer*, 15 March 1883.

6

COMMISSIONER

In one of the few reliable statements in *Home and Abroad* about his time as a commissioner, Merton recalls topping the poll alongside 'my dear old friend, the late Mr Creeke.'[1] He ignores his previous election losses and chooses not to reveal that success came in 1883 after many years of trying. Instead, by quoting his address to the ratepayers from two years earlier, he makes it seem as if he was elected at the first attempt in 1881. This time distortion allows him to present the direct line discussions as one of the highlights of his contributions to the board. In doing so, he portrays himself not just as a keen campaigner on the issue but as the scheme's sole instigator. Nonetheless, the board approved the Brockenhurst route, and a new main station, two weeks before he swore the commissioner's oath of office.

As well as the railway, Merton boasts of being the prime mover on one other big development during his spell as a commissioner. It concerns the building of a hospital for infectious diseases. His nomination that year came from a member of the local Medical Society, a body of men holding great sway in any self-respecting health resort. The doctors saw the hospital as vital to protecting Bournemouth's reputation and, according to Merton, were banking on him to deliver it. There was already a tuberculosis sanatorium in the town – it was next door to the emergent Mont Dore hotel – but the planned hospital had a broader remit. Described as a 'fever hospital' even by its supporters, some residents took fright at what they perceived would be little better than the plague and pest houses of old. Few wanted one of those within contagion's reach of their backyard.

Merton describes how he joined one of the board's committees, determined to keep his promise to the doctors. He talks of infighting from the start: 'The greatest opposition I received in my campaign on this matter was from two gentlemen who were too ignorant and obstinate to listen to any comments whatever on that subject. I spent days and nights in communicating with the medical officers of health of other seaside resorts,

22 Christopher Creeke's election as a commissioner in 1883 saw him make a triumphant return to public life after falling victim to boardroom squabbles in 1879. As the town's consulting surveyor at the time, a faction on the board forced him to resign after the main sewer at Boscombe was laid at the wrong gradient. (Bournemouth Library)

both at home and abroad, and in getting up every scrap of evidence that could be adduced to carry out my project.' [2] He tells of how his opponents played dirty, their anger stoked by his two committee colleagues. As irate residents confronted him in the street, anonymous letters poured through his letter box. 'In whatever direction my committee went for the purpose of obtaining a site,' he wrote, 'we were met with rancorous abuse.'

Merton refers to the 'insuperable obstacles' thrown in his way, of which the use of the word 'fever' in the same breath as the hospital proved the most formidable. He recalls: 'I was telling my wife about it, when she said, "But why use the word *fever* at all? Why not substitute *sanitary* and call it the sanitary hospital?"' [3] This revolutionary idea is said to have caused consternation when he suggested it at the next board meeting. 'San-nar-tarry? What do you mean by san-nar-tarry?' asked one commissioner, flummoxed by the exotic new word. 'If you will be good enough when you get home to consult your dictionary,' replied Merton, 'you will find all the information you require.' [4] He accuses his opponents of resorting to insults, with the word 'sanitary' acting as their rallying cry. 'They eventually burned myself and one or two others on the committee in effigy,' he wrote, adding further spice to the story.

This vivid retrospective is far removed from contemporary accounts of what happened. Despite talk of 'my committee' and 'my project', it was Christopher Creeke who played the leading role in bringing the hospital to fruition. Vast experience of major building projects, plus an insider's view of town politics, made him a good choice as the committee's chairman. Three other men served alongside him – Merton, Joseph Cutler and Enoch White. These last two, no doubt, are the 'ignorant and obstinate' gentlemen referred to in *Home and Abroad*. It is true that the committee inherited a few problems, but acquiring a site was not among them. Efforts to find one dated back several years, most of them thwarted by protests from the affected householders. Then, a year before Merton's election, the board used its compulsory purchase powers to buy five acres of land between Boscombe and Pokesdown. The plot lay in an area called Freemantle, just beyond the district's eastern boundary.[5] Nothing had happened at the site since, hence the doctors' desire for the building work to start.

One part of Merton's story does fit with the evidence. The change of name from 'fever' to 'sanitary' took place soon after he joined the board, but no commissioner would have needed a dictionary to understand it. He and his three colleagues were members of the Sanitary Committee, which had gone by that name for the past six years. Other towns applied the word to their own hospitals, and Torquay was in the process of building one. This aside, the project's progress bears little relation to the version given by Merton. The committee set to work on the plans straight after the election and, thanks to Creeke's firm guidance, went ahead without much ado. 'I had fought my fight and conquered' is how Merton describes it, although his efforts received no credit when the hospital opened in 1886.[6] Like the direct line from London, he later amplified his role in the project and made it a highlight of his civic contribution. In fact, he attended only a fraction of the committee's meetings and was not present for many of its key decisions. There is little sign of opposition once Creeke took charge, nor of Merton falling out with anyone – about the hospital, at least – as the work progressed. That said, he was absent from all boardroom duties for three months from June 1883 – just six weeks into his tenure. Illness may have been the reason, as the Royal Bath acquired the services of a manager at around this time.[7]

In *Home and Abroad*, Merton begins his stint as a commissioner with the direct line and ends it with the fuss over the hospital. His temporary absence is not mentioned, but he makes no bones about finding his time on the board a stressful experience. Health was a big factor. Lung problems were one thing, but his 'highly strung mental qualities', as one newspaper later put it, made him ill-equipped to deal with the after-effects of boardroom tensions.[8] A commissioner's job was demanding, with or without a hospital project. Sessions often ran all day and long into the evening, and members were obliged to sit on three or four committees.[9] The press portrayed the boardroom as a battleground, with petty sniping stifling debate and paralysing decision making. Rows could erupt over trivial matters or points of procedure. 'The place is getting a perfect bear garden,' complained one commissioner after a protracted squabble over a byelaw. 'Yes,' replied another, 'and you are one of the best performers in it.'[10] If Merton had found it hard to work with Messrs Cutler and White on the hospital committee, then the real bearbaiting began when he returned to his duties in the autumn.

The remaining commissioners ploughed through their long to-do list in his absence. They debated the pros and cons of the town's incorporation and mulled over extending the district to cover Westbourne and the site of the planned sanitary hospital. Sir George Meyrick gifted an area of common land to the board, the first step towards creating the public park – Bournemouth's first – that would bear his name. Progress on the hospital continued, allowing the plans to be sent to the Local Government Board for approval. Yet old tensions still simmered. Two commissioners, including the board's chairman, resigned in protest at a decision to build a pavilion on the pier. Spending money on visitor facilities always aroused excitement, and the idea was later scrapped. Merton returned to the boardroom in October 1883, but his sporadic contributions in the first few weeks hint at a man trying to ease himself back in. After a debate about a new sewer, he admitted to abstaining from the vote because the fine details of the discussion were beyond him. Enoch White's advice on that occasion was to 'keep your hair on', words many on the board would have been wise to heed in the days ahead.[11] After a period of relative calm, a minor mishap near the Royal Bath provided the unlikely trigger for a string of spats between Merton and his colleagues.

In January 1884, Thomas Beechey (1823–1894), a commissioner and wine merchant, was walking home after an evening out when he bumped into a lamp post outside the hotel. After checking his hat for damage and collecting his wounded pride, he turned his attention back to the offending object. The lamp post was, he noticed, dark brown instead of the regulation grey – an obvious hazard to unwary pedestrians. Determined to hold someone to account, he took his indignation to the next board meeting. It transpired that the new colour was the result of one of Merton's ideas to bring a touch of elegance to the street outside the Royal Bath. Keen to apply gold embellishments to the hotel's nearest lamp post, he had first persuaded the chairman of the Lighting Committee to paint it brown. Some commissioners questioned the chairman's authority to make such an agreement, while others wondered why they were wasting their time in discussing it.

An hour went by, during which Beechey denied being drunk at the time of the accident. Having inspected the lamp post on three evenings since, he assured his colleagues that it could only be seen when the moon was bright. Joseph Cutler agreed, contending that brown was, without doubt, the worst possible colour. In fact, a brown lamp post was one of the most dangerous things the town had ever seen. Henry Newlyn (1844–1912), a rival hotelier elected to the board at the same time as Merton, took a different view. Where would it end, he wondered, if the board allowed everyone to change the colour of the street furniture to suit themselves? The arguments went back and forth. Cutler raised a motion to repaint the lamp post grey, declaring that Merton was 'always parading his honour and honesty' and yet was prepared to use his position to get his own way.[12] Christopher Creeke could see both sides of the dispute but deplored the personal insults thrown into a debate about fourpence worth of paint. As most of the commissioners agreed with his opinion that the work should stand, the board voted to allow the gilding to proceed at Merton's expense.

The 'great battle of the lamp post', as the *Bournemouth Guardian* called it, is a sign of the lingering distrust surrounding Merton as he tried to make his mark as a commissioner.[13] The pier opening may have been more than three years in the past, but the main accusation in the lamp post row – that he served himself first and foremost – was common to both controversies. Something in his personality also created friction. Whereas Henry Newlyn was laying the foundations of a solid career in public service, Merton found it hard to make a positive impression. And yet the lamp post affair, and others like it, contributed to a much bigger debate within the town. Advocates of Bournemouth's elevation to municipal borough status used it to fight one of the main arguments against incorporation. Those in favour of retaining the improvement commissioners claimed that infighting and bickering would be an inevitable result of the party divisions found in the council chamber of a municipal corporation. An improvement board, on the other hand, was made up of sober, impartial gentlemen intent only on the common good. The lamp post battle proved otherwise, a fact not lost on the pragmatic Christopher Creeke. When Joseph Cutler proposed an increase in the number of commissioners at their next meeting, Creeke spoke against it. In his view, most ratepayers had already decided that the board's days were numbered. Merton now believed they should carry on as they were for a while longer but switched back to supporting incorporation a few months later.

Although an ardent Conservative, Merton saw himself as non-partisan when it came to local affairs. Political parties were not recognised within the board, but other divisions had the same effect. As well as rifts between progressives and small-c conservatives, issues of class also created conflict. Shopkeepers and publicans served alongside professionals and retired military men, all of whom had their own ideas about the town's future. Business rivalries also played a part. Henry Newlyn owned the Royal Exeter Hotel, which aspired to the same sort of clientele as the Royal Bath. Cutler and White added a degree of volatility to the mix, with one rival builder describing the former as having a 'crack in the head'.[14] These divisions mattered less outside the boardroom, where members could unite behind a common cause. Merton, Cutler and Newlyn, for example, were all big-C Conservatives when it came to national politics. They also served as directors of the Bournemouth, Swanage and Poole Steam Packet Company, which ran pleasure cruises from the pier. Merton was routinely re-elected to the company's board in February 1884 but attended a commissioners' meeting the next day that turned out to be anything but routine.

The proceedings began with mundane debates about pier shelters and a railway bridge, then moved on to plans submitted for his business premises by Edward Rebbeck (1842–1913), a commissioner and prominent estate agent. It was a trifling matter referred to the main board by the Buildings

23 The SS Bournemouth *was built in Leith for the Bournemouth, Swanage and Poole Steam Packet Company. Launched in 1884, it is shown here after running aground at Portland in August 1886. The vessel had been returning to Bournemouth from Torquay when it encountered thick fog.* (Portland Museum Trust)

Committee over a minor breach of the byelaws. Enoch White complained about the referral, insisting that the committee should have 'acted like men' and settled the matter themselves.[15] These murmurs of discontent became howls of protest when Merton entered the fray. He believed that the committee failed to agree the plans only because Rebbeck was a commissioner. They would not have been so picky for anyone else. Joseph Cutler, a member of the said committee, took exception to this accusation and demanded its withdrawal. Uproar followed, with commissioners pitching in on both sides. 'This is not the lamp post business today!' bellowed White, as the chairman called for order. Merton tried to apologise when the noise died down, but White joined forces with Cutler to share in his indignation. He branded Merton's criticisms of the committee 'a falsehood' – a serious charge to make against another commissioner. When others spoke up in Merton's support, the chairman tried to end the discussion. 'I think Mr Cotes ought to retract,' Cutler insisted. 'If he does not, I shall resign altogether.' With most of the board siding with Merton, the chairman closed the subject by referring it back to the committee.

They moved on to the next item on the agenda, a matter dear to the chairman's heart. To his dismay, a long line of continuous seating had recently been installed in the pleasure gardens. It made the place look like a tea garden, he complained, and served as a race track for unruly children. Merton suggested replacing it with individual benches, as the current arrangements were suitable only for 'chawbacons'. When asked to explain the remark, he replied: 'Persons who come from Bristol and elsewhere find it a most convenient spot to bring their baskets, to eat their luncheons and to open their bottled beer.' [16] Such people, he added, were driving away the town's elite.

Enoch White pooh-poohed the idea of ripping up the seating as a waste of ratepayers' money. He objected to the constant carping, especially from Merton, about everything the Pleasure Grounds Committee did. If they put in more trees, he said, some people would complain they were planted upside down. He accused Merton of damaging an area of the public gardens for the benefit of the Royal Bath, a charge that raised the boardroom temperature to boiling point. A bout of insults and name-calling broke out, with 'Knocker' dismissing 'Chawbacon' as an empty vessel making too much noise. 'I am not going to submit to the lah-di-dah of Mr Cotes,' declared White, adding that Merton would doubtless prefer 'iron chairs with ornamental backs filled in with little cupids.' The exasperated chairman, worn down by a marathon session and endless squabbling, sent the issue back to the committee and adjourned the meeting.

These new scenes of rowdiness drew derision in the local press. One wag, caricaturing the exchanges in the *Bournemouth Guardian*, homed in on Merton's supremacy in matters of style and vocabulary: 'There was one gent as is mostly got up not exactly like a new pin, as the saying is, but more as if he was French polished all over. He always looks so spick and span and new. Well, he got trampling on those new seats in the pleasure gardens, which he's so awfully afraid other people will do. He's very choice of his words – he is always trying to bring out one that's original.' [17] Of greater concern to the board's chairman was the embarrassment caused by reports of the word 'falsehood' emanating from the mouth of a commissioner. He confronted Enoch White at their next meeting, pointing out that, irrespective of personal enmities, he expected business in the boardroom to be conducted in a civil manner. 'Withdraw that word, sir – never!' White replied when asked to retract it.[18]

With no prospect of an apology, the chairman asked the other commissioners to make their own judgement about their colleague's conduct. If he hoped that would lead to a reckoning at the ballot box, then it failed to influence the outcome of the forthcoming election. White, who retired by rotation in April 1884, was re-elected with ease, while Joseph Cutler polled second from bottom and lost his seat. Merton was not obliged to seek re-election on that occasion, but he may not have stood anyway. The animosity with White ran deep, and the row over Bristolian beer drinkers highlighted their differing attitudes to class. White, the son of a farm labourer, wore his roots on his sleeve and could be a formidable adversary.

Merton attended only two more board meetings after the chawbacons episode and was not allocated to that year's Sanitary Committee. He took up other briefs instead, but distractions outside the boardroom meant that he rarely went to the sittings.[19] In the early months of 1884, he was in the process of buying the business of Gustavus Lane (1831–1914), an established wine and spirit merchant based in the centre of Bournemouth. He completed the purchase in June of that year, adding a lucrative sideline to his growing interests in the town. In the spring, he found himself in court defending a claim for damages arising from a crash at the station between a cab and a Royal Bath omnibus. He appeared before the judge several times over the next few months in a failed attempt to overturn the decision against him. In May 1884 he was again before the courts, this time charged with keeping the hotel's taproom open after hours. His bar manager received a fine, but the bench deemed Merton responsible and fined him, too. The accumulated stress proved too much. Citing poor health, he resigned as a commissioner in October 1884 after eighteen months on the board. When Christopher Creeke tabled a motion regretting his departure, all but one of his colleagues supported it. Enoch White abstained.

Merton lays the blame for his resignation on his efforts with the sanitary hospital and the impact of the alleged effigy burning. The two combined to cause what he called 'a serious nervous breakdown'.[20] While there were other reasons for his departure, the fact is that the rows about lamp posts and park

24 G. Lane & Co. was Merton's most visible venture in Bournemouth other than the Royal Bath Hotel. He paid £6,000 for the business, raising the money by mortgaging the premises back to Lane – in effect borrowing from the seller to buy him out. The interest provided income to the retiring Lane, while Merton acquired the business without laying out a penny. He kept the firm's name, which continued to trade until well after his death. (Author's collection)

benches dominated his lacklustre spell as a commissioner. Not only that, but his attendance rate at meetings – less than forty per cent – was the lowest of anyone elected to the board after 1876. This presented Merton with a problem in *Home and Abroad*, where only misguided opposition gets in the way of a string of achievements and triumphs. He solved it by leaving out the minor controversies and by using the direct line and the hospital to bolster his contribution. As fate would have it, the issue Merton went on to champion – the undercliff drive – began to stir from its slumbers in the months before he resigned. It awoke not as a cover for sewage pipes but as a way of protecting the town's fragile cliffs. Debated for more than a year, he played no noticeable part in this latest attempt to promote the idea.

With health now his overriding concern, Merton turned to a rival for advice in his time of need. He consulted Dr Horace Dobell (1828–1917), a Harley Street doctor hired by the Mont Dore to develop its hydropathic treatments. Dobell recommended a trip abroad to recuperate, but Merton had no intention of sipping tea on the manicured lawns of a European hotel. He had a more challenging journey in mind and needed to plan accordingly. The transfer of the Gustavus Lane premises into Annie's name just days before their departure may well have been part of those preparations, but she and the three children were also making the trip. Merton may, then, have simply decided to take belated advantage of a change in the law that made it possible for a wife to own property in her own right.[21] If that, in turn, was no more than astute financial planning, then it could also be a sign that Annie brought more to their marriage than her father's trifling estate might suggest. Regardless of the reason, it would not be the last time Merton transferred

25 Dr Horace Dobell conceived the idea of bringing the Mont Dore cure to Bournemouth. Named after the French spa town where it originated, the regime consisted of a system of thermal baths for the treatment of respiratory and rheumatic ailments. The author Robert Louis Stevenson (1850–1894), who wrote The Strange Case of Dr Jekyll and Mr Hyde *while living in Westbourne in the 1880s, was one of those to use it. Dobell retired to Poole in 1892, a move that led Merton to consider doing likewise a decade or so later.* (Public domain image)

assets into his wife's name.

With none of the family staying behind, Merton required good staff at the Royal Bath to cover what promised to be a lengthy absence. He needed people he could depend upon to look after a hotel that now boasted a national reputation. For front of house, he hired Charles Reingpach (c. 1844–1924), a Frenchman whose most recent engagement had been at the upmarket Athole hydropathic hotel in Pitlochry, Scotland. As the former chef de cuisine at London's prestigious Langham Hotel, where the guests included Napoleon III and Oscar Wilde, Reingpach was a good fit for the Royal Bath. For financial matters, Merton turned to Arthur Painter (1849–1924), a man he knew and trusted from the wine and spirit trade. Five years younger than the 40-year-old Reingpach, Painter was to become a key figure in Merton's business affairs in the years ahead.[22]

Before leaving England, Merton hosted a banquet at the Royal Bath to bid farewell to commissioners, friends and associates. Enoch White was conspicuously absent. Christopher Creeke generously praised Merton's contribution to the town and hoped he would 'return with renewed vigour to cooperate with his fellow townsmen to ensure the future prosperity of Bournemouth.'[23] The Cotes family travelled to Plymouth two weeks later to begin what, for Merton, turned out to be more than a journey of recovery. The perfect tonic after his boardroom struggles, the time spent abroad would transform the way people perceived him. Although Creeke would not live to see it, his words proved to be prophetic.

Notes:

1. *Home and Abroad*, p. 65.
2. ibid., pp. 65–66.
3. ibid., p. 996.
4. ibid., p. 66.
5. The name 'Freemantle' is no longer used, but it lay at the edge of what is now King's Park.
6. *Home and Abroad*, p. 67.
7. The manager, Henry Grover, had previously worked at a restaurant in The Strand where the clientele included Gladstone and Disraeli. Grover's tenure at the Royal Bath appears to have been brief, but his CV illustrates the sort of experience the hotel now needed.
8. *Bournemouth Guardian*, 26 June 1909.
9. Merton sat on the Horse, Pier, Railway and Pleasure Grounds Committees, as well as the Sanitary Committee, during his first year on the board. He won first prize for his mare 'Beauty' in the 'park hacks and ladies horses' class at the 1882 Andover Horse Show, so the first of those committees played to one of his strengths.
10. *Hampshire Advertiser*, 24 February 1883.

THE ART OF A SALESMAN

11. *Bournemouth Guardian*, 22 December 1883.
12. *Bournemouth Guardian*, 19 January 1884.
13. ibid.
14. Barker, *Bournemouth, 1810–2010*, p. 37.
15. *Bournemouth Guardian*, 9 February 1884.
16. *Bournemouth Observer*, 9 February 1884.
17. *Bournemouth Guardian*, 23 February 1884.
18. ibid.
19. Merton was appointed to the Lighting & Water, Pier, Pleasure Grounds and General Purpose Committees at the start of his second year on the board. It was standard practice to reallocate the committees after the April elections. He had served alongside Enoch White on the Pleasure Grounds Committee during his first year, hence White's annoyance over the continuous seating.
20. *Home and Abroad*, p. 687.
21. The Married Women's Property Act of 1882 made it possible for a wife to own property in her own right. When they married in 1860, anything Annie owned would have passed to Merton.
22. In 1897, the *Bournemouth Observer* stated that 'for fifteen years he [Painter] had been treasurer and secretary of the hotel affairs and was the managing partner of Mr Cotes.'
23. The *Bournemouth Guardian* listed 'Mr W. Spens of Glasgow' among those unable to attend the banquet. His father was the man said to have hired Merton at the Scottish Amicable. The younger Spens, who was the Society's secretary at the time, appears in the list alongside a London solicitor and two of Sir George Meyrick's agents. Taken together, it suggests a commercial connection to the Scottish Amicable via the hotel.

7

GLOBETROTTER

'I have an inordinate love of timetables and maps,' wrote Merton, as he mused upon his travels in *Home and Abroad*.[1] On boarding the clipper *Torrens* in November 1884, he began to indulge his passion in a journey that would stretch to five continents and 50,000 miles. The original plan was less ambitious – a few weeks in Australia to regain his health, then back home again via New Zealand. Some of his fellow passengers had the same idea. Fred Hargreaves (1858–1897), a footballer for Blackburn Rovers and England, hoped to be back in time for the next cricket season.[2]

In his preface to the trip, Merton vows to avoid 'all descriptive matter of a guidebook character.'[3] Although failing to meet this promise, his intentions hint at the nature of the journey. The places the family visited would be untouched by mass tourism for decades, but they were by no means the first to pass through them. Nor was Merton alone in recording his experiences of the emerging travel industry. Anthony Trollope (1815–1882) had written an account of his tour of Australasia ten years earlier, and Richard Tangye (1833–1906), a Cornish engineer, published his experiences of a similar itinerary. While lacking Trollope's skill and Tangye's wit, Merton reveals himself to be an intrepid tourist. The trip required stamina for a man with health problems in his fiftieth year, even allowing for comfortable cabins and cosy beds. Annie, who took almost everything in her stride, belied the stereotype of Victorian female fragility. Her book, *Westward from the Golden Gate*, records her thoughts on the second half of the trip. Based on a journal that no longer survives, its value lies in providing an alternative perspective of their travels. Annie's style is much easier to read than *Home and Abroad*, and she sometimes differs from Merton about where they went.

The *Torrens*, commanded by Captain Henry Angel (1829–1923), sailed from Plymouth to Adelaide, a taxing voyage via the Cape of Good Hope. Angel had steered that course for the past ten years and could run 300 miles on a good day. He was carrying around seventy passengers, most of whom,

26 The clipper Torrens *at Port Adelaide. A passenger on the 1883 run recalled how the crew, by tradition, made a mock-up of a horse a fortnight into the voyage. After a tour of the deck and a comic speech from a sailor, they threw the beast overboard.* (State Library of South Australia, PRG 1373/2/22)

like the Cotes party, were in the first-class saloon. It threw together health seekers from all walks of the affluent side of life. Merton, a veteran of months at sea in the 1850s, found the voyage uneventful and tedious. In stories to her grandchildren, Annie told of being becalmed for a week, learning shorthand to pass the time, and of her disgust at seeing the crew dry cutlery with bedsheets. A traveller on the previous year's run recalled how passengers staved off boredom with music and games. Some took to spotting marine life or taking potshots with rifles at passing seabirds. At Christmas, Angel decked the ship with evergreens and mistletoe – he encouraged kissing – and left greeting cards at the festive table. His efforts failed to convince Merton to go under sail again. In one of his many travel tips, he advises the use of steamships, as they laid on better entertainment and broke the journey by stopping for coal. He took his own advice for the rest of the trip.

They arrived in Adelaide at the end of January 1885 after a voyage of eighty-four days. Merton found the heat unbearable and was in low spirits after being cooped up for so long. 'I consulted a doctor,' he wrote, 'who earnestly advised me on no consideration to contemplate returning home at once but to extend my travels in search of health to at least twelve or eighteen months.'[4] Their itinerary swelled to occupy the full extent of that time – a remarkable journey that only a privileged few could undertake. After a tour of Australia's south-east, they planned to go on to New Zealand, the Hawaiian Islands and San Francisco, then cross the United States by train to catch a steamer home from New York.

The family lingered in Adelaide for a few days before moving on to Melbourne, where Merton sent a cable home. To his annoyance, the telegraph office charged him more for the word 'Bournemouth' because it was too long. The clerk refused to leave out the 'e' to save him half a crown. From there, they travelled to a sheep station owned by one of Annie's childhood friends who had emigrated to Australia in the 1860s.[5] To have remained in touch for so long says much about her diligence as a correspondent. The family did as tourists do during a relaxing two-month stay. They fished for sharks, gazed at scenery, observed the wildlife, and posed in mining gear for a snapshot outside a goldmine. Bert, as was expected of a 14-year-old boy back then, killed a snake and skinned it for a souvenir. When they moved on to Sydney, Merton wrote to the stationmaster for tickets to the Blue Mountains and received a reply from an old London and South Western Railway acquaintance. Their friend took care of everything, the first of many favours curried during the trip. They returned to Melbourne a month later to board an eastbound steamer. *Home and Abroad* switches to guidebook mode to describe their brief stopover in Hobart, as Merton summarises the parts of Tasmania they had no time to see. In a potted history of New Zealand, he reveals that its first seat of government – Russell, on the tip of the North Island – was named, like himself, after the eminent British statesman.

Ella, Clarie and Bert returned to England when they reached

27 *Merton (centre), Annie and Bert pictured with their guides in March 1885 before visiting the Last Chance Mine in Ballarat, Australia. Gold was discovered in the area in 1851, a matter of days after the state of Victoria came into being. The subsequent gold rush contributed to a sevenfold increase in its population over the next ten years.* (From *Home and Abroad*)

Christchurch, and it would be more than a year before they saw their parents again. In their absence, Merton and Annie set about adding to the growing collection of art and artefacts sent back to Bournemouth. They bought several stuffed birds during their week in the city, including a kea – a species of parrot noted for gorging on the fat of live sheep. As well as making striking ornaments, these specimens attracted much attention from naturalists when they were exhibited back home. From Christchurch, they travelled to what Annie dubbed 'wet, windy, wooden Wellington'.[6] Here, in unexplained circumstances, Merton met Sir Julius Vogel (1835–1899), the colony's former Prime Minister. The two men shared a joke when Merton added 'wretched' to Annie's list of adjectives.

Auckland served as the starting point for the tourist trail to the Maori heartlands and the geothermal area around Rotorua. This part of the trip brought them into close contact with indigenous culture for the first time. 'They all sleep packed like herrings, head to feet,' Annie wrote of the Maoris, 'and they drink as much whisky as they can get.'[7] Merton found some of what they saw distasteful. 'It is very open to question whether the haka, even in its ordinary form, is a thing to be encouraged among the natives.'[8] This, and a lack of interest in sport, makes it unlikely that he saw its first performance on an English rugby field three years later. Still, he acknowledged that the women dancers 'were delicately formed, some even fragile and approaching the European standard of beauty.' Such casual comparisons were common at the time, although these opinions, as it turns out, were not his own.

As Merton begins to describe the area and its traditions, the style of his writing shows a marked change. They secured the services of a guide called Kate for this part of the tour – 'an exceedingly robust specimen of the Maori women, shrill-tongued and well able to protect any party to whom she acted as cicerone.'[9] His narrative becomes even more showy when eulogising the scenery and reaches its peak when describing the Pink and White Terraces – a spectacular geological feature on the shores of Lake Rotomahana. He tells of walking over a 'glistening surface of rippling silica' to reach warm pools of an exquisite colour. 'It is blue,' he wrote, 'but such a blue as is seen nowhere else in Nature – more delicate than the shade of the sky – a milky, pellucid blue, with a gem-like iridescence like the shifting light of an opal.'[10] This is a better word picture than managed by Richard Tangye, who conceded that it was 'useless to try and describe it' and so gave up.[11] *Home and Abroad* even outdoes Trollope, who devotes more time to the effects of tourism than he does to the landscape. There is, however, a reason for this change in Merton's prose. His descriptions of Kate, the haka, the women dancers and the terraces were copied from a guidebook published by the local shipping company a year earlier. More than a dozen pages are transplanted into *Home and Abroad* with only minor changes.[12]

Trollope's concern for the area's future was in one way fulfilled, save that Mother Nature, not man, wreaked the greatest havoc. A year on from Merton and Annie's visit, nearby Mount Tarawera burst into life with devastating effect. The eruption killed scores of people and laid waste to the terraces.[13] As one of the last to set eyes on this lost wonder, Merton may have overstepped the mark in his eagerness to record the fact. In a touch of irony, he recalls a conversation with the journalist George Augustus Sala later in the trip. 'He wrote most graphic descriptions of the Hot Lakes and the Pink and White Terraces and other scenery throughout New Zealand, although he had never visited them! I chaffed him on this, and he said, "That was the true art of writing descriptive matter."' [14]

Merton and Annie left Auckland in June 1885 for the Hawaiian Islands, sailing via Fiji and Samoa. They checked into the Royal Hawaiian in Honolulu, a government-owned hotel formed of pretty cottages set in lush tropical grounds. The press somehow discovered that the owner of another regally named hotel was staying there but got into a muddle when reporting the fact. 'Mr Cotes is proprietor of Claridge's Hotel, London,' the *Daily Bulletin* assured its readers, 'and the Royal Hotel [sic], Bournemouth.' [15] From then on, Merton popped up in the newspapers more often than might be expected of an ordinary visitor. After joining a tour of a luxury Japanese liner, their group was said to consist of 'Mr and Mrs Merton R. Cotes, of London, England, and a party of ladies and gentlemen.' [16]

Merton enjoyed himself immensely in the islands and revelled in his encounters with local dignitaries. He describes how he was given membership of the Royal Club in Honolulu by the Right Honourable Archibald Cleghorn (1835–1910), a Scots émigré who was the Hawaiian King's brother-in-law. This led to introductions to other luminaries, including Mormon ex-communicant and former gunrunner Walter M. Gibson (1822–1888), the Hawaiian interior minister. They fell into a discussion about leprosy – a disease so common in those parts that the government exiled sufferers to a nearby island and declared them dead. Merton, a keen student of medical conditions, said he had visited every country where leprosy prevailed and blamed it on a diet of raw fish. Much

28 The White Terraces at Lake Rotomahana, captured by the artist Charles Blomfield (1848–1926). Despite Merton's teasing, George Augustus Sala had seen the terraces first-hand towards the end of 1885. Indeed, his celebrity was such that he was invited to open a geothermal bath in Rotorua during his tour of the area. (Museum of New Zealand)

THE ART OF A SALESMAN

impressed, Gibson presented him with a copy of his book, *Sanitary Instructions for Hawaiians*.

From Honolulu, on the island of Oahu, Merton and Annie embarked on a trip to Kilauea, an active volcano on the island of Hawaii. Too remote and arduous for some tourists – Tangye chose not to bother – it was a must-see highlight for many others. The boat called in at Maui, where they toured the giant Spreckelsville sugar plantation on Annie's fiftieth birthday. They landed on Hawaii the following day, not far from the spot where Captain James Cook (1728–1779) met his grisly end. According to Merton, the King of Hawaii later told him that his ancestors killed the celebrated sailor upon realising he was not the deity they had been led to believe. As the monarch said to the hotelier, a true god never yelps with pain when struck on the foot by a lump of wood.

Among the adventurous souls in the Kilauea party was Jules Tavernier (1844–1889), a French artist living in Honolulu for health reasons.[17] He earned his keep by painting night scenes of the volcano and joined the group at Merton's request. Their first challenge was an uphill trek on horseback towards the Volcano House – a small hotel within walking distance of the crater. Rudimentary when it first opened in the 1840s, it now boasted six comfortable bedrooms and fine dining. They made their first foray to the volcano the next day, setting off in the late afternoon and trekking for three miles across the lava field as the sun went down. 'Cat-like,' wrote Merton, 'we had to pick our way after the two guides with lanterns, in Indian file, in case of the layer of lava giving way and engulfing us all in the molten sea below.'[18]

They made it safely to the lava lake within the crater of Halemaumau – the home of Pele, the fire goddess. The spectacle intensified as the sun sank below the horizon and reached its full glory under the moon and stars. Tavernier went to work, completing his commission as the others marvelled at the scene around them. Although after midnight when they returned to the hotel, Merton found time to dash off an excited letter to the Honolulu press before going to bed. 'Halemaumau was one mass of rolling molten fire,' he wrote, 'running in huge waves from six to ten feet high, just like the surf after a severe storm. In many places, jets of the most brilliant fire played, throwing up thousands of sparkling diamonds in the air fifteen and twenty feet high.'[19]

They spent five nights at the Volcano House and visited Halemaumau twice. Merton ignored the guides' instructions on one occasion and ventured to the edge of the lake to break off a few strands of 'Pele's hair' – fine filaments of lava spun by volatile gases. As the guides yelled a warning, he regained the path just as a fountain of molten rock plummeted to earth on the exact spot where he had been standing. Merton, although unharmed, had aroused the wrath of the fire goddess: Annie lost her footing as they made their way across the lava field and badly injured her ankle.[20] The guides helped her back to the hotel, but Merton wrote an entry in the visitors' book warning ladies to stay at the crater all night rather than risk the return journey in the dark.[21]

In great pain and unable to walk, Annie endured a twenty-mile mule ride to the town of Hilo to seek help from a doctor. During a three-week stay there, Merton killed time by making friends and writing about their travels for a church magazine. They returned to Honolulu in early August but were too late to catch the intended boat to San Francisco. Merton used the enforced wait to good effect by arranging with Archibald Cleghorn for an

29 Engineer Richard Tangye may never have met Merton, but he visited many of the same places and shared a disdain for New World manners. When a seasick American on the boat from Honolulu to San Francisco asked him where he could throw up, Tangye answered: 'We don't "throw up" at all. We "go up" and lean over the lee side.' [22] (Author's collection)

audience with the King and a tour of the royal palace and mausoleum. During their conversation, he says the King sought his advice on a stock market flotation for a mooted volcano railway and talked of sending a band of native performers to England.[23]

Annie had recovered enough by mid-August to make the voyage to California. They travelled with Claus Spreckels (1828–1908), the owner of both the sugar plantation on Maui and the ship on which they were sailing. A royal insider, Spreckels' departure merited the King's presence among a crowd of well-wishers at the dockside. On reaching San Francisco, Annie sought advice about her ankle from another doctor, who prescribed a few weeks in the city to recover followed by another change to their itinerary. Rather than catching a train to New York as intended, he recommended taking the westward route via Japan and India. This, he believed, would be less taxing than a railway journey across the United States. Merton, perhaps mindful of the Japanese Drawing Room at the Royal Bath, required little

THE ART OF A SALESMAN

persuasion to change the route. A guest at the Volcano House had also recommended the detour, so the couple submitted to doctor's orders and altered their plans.[24] Already nine months away from home, they were now only halfway through the trip.

Thanks to an introduction from Spreckels, Merton and Annie checked into a suite at San Francisco's 700-room Palace Hotel. Its art treasures rivalled the Royal Bath's, but it was built on a vastly different scale. Lifts, messaging tubes and a fire brigade left Bournemouth's idea of modern conveniences far behind. Merton found it overpowering, more machine than hotel, and lacking homespun charms. 'I may mention that if you put your boots outside your door to be cleaned,' he wrote, 'the probability is that you would never see them anymore, as no boots are cleaned by the hotel people. You have to put on your dirty boots and go down before you have breakfast and have them polished by one of the numerous shoeblacks.'[25] Nor was he impressed with American manners. Waiters and cab drivers were 'intensely familiar and cheeky' unless he tipped them, while labourers lacked respect and were full of their own importance.[26]

With Annie ordered to rest, Merton went solo for much of their time in the city. He was introduced at the elite Bohemian Club, which counted businessmen, authors and artists among its members. This, presumably, is where he became 'very intimate friends' with Josh Billings (1818–1885), a well-known writer in the Mark Twain mould who died later that year. While vague about Billings, Merton is more specific about how he met Karl Formes, one of the greatest opera stars of his generation: he stopped him in the street while out for a walk. With a little prompting, the singer professed to remembering Merton from Glasgow and took him home to meet his wife.

The couple left San Francisco in mid-September and sailed to Yokohama. Annie's *Westward from the Golden Gate* begins at this point.[27] She opens by observing that their ship carried fifty first-class passengers, more than a thousand people in steerage and only twelve lifeboats. A Thomas Cook 'Round the World' party were among those on board. 'We did not care for them,' wrote Merton, 'because they were always quarrelling.'[28] A typhoon raged for thirty-six hours as they crossed the Pacific, doing little for Annie's recovery and ending the lives of seven of the people in steerage. The ship's surgeon embalmed their bodies and placed them in one of the precious lifeboats for later burial.

They spent seven weeks in Japan, touring widely and soaking up the culture of the Mikados and Shoguns. Merton describes it as 'a wonderful country, the Britain of the East' and lauds the Japanese working classes over their British counterparts.[29] Buddhism was the only drawback, which he thought a little too close to Catholicism. 'It only requires time and perseverance,' he wrote, 'to accomplish the conversion of an intelligent and progressive people, like the Japanese, to the truths of the Gospel.'[30] The

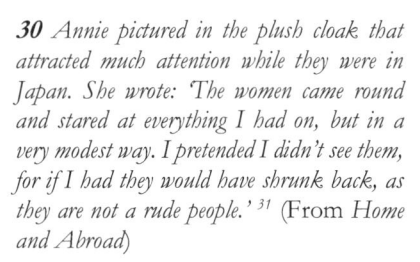

30 Annie pictured in the plush cloak that attracted much attention while they were in Japan. She wrote: 'The women came round and stared at everything I had on, but in a very modest way. I pretended I didn't see them, for if I had they would have shrunk back, as they are not a rude people.' [31] (From Home and Abroad)

couple attracted attention everywhere – Annie's plush cloak intrigued the locals – and curio dealers pestered them with their wares. Merton set his sights on filling the Japanese Drawing Room with anything he could lay his hands on. With little cash and no prearranged credit, he pleaded for help from the Hong Kong and Shanghai Bank in Yokohama. The manager, who claimed to be able to judge a man from the cut of his jib, lent the money with minimal fuss. Upon returning for more, the banker confessed to having checked Merton's credentials with the British mission in Tokyo.

The couple relied on their guide to sort the artistic wheat from the touristic chaff and gave him plenty of leeway to haggle. By Merton's reckoning, they filled a hundred packing cases with art and artefacts. Some of their cash went on items of national importance, such as a kakemono belonging to the Mikado, a Buddhist shrine and a decorative platter. On a visit to Bournemouth many years later, the Japanese ambassador was astounded to find such treasures in the hands of a private collector. Indeed, Merton only succeeded in exporting his purchases by appealing for help from the British mission.[32] Through this intervention, an astute guide and a little luck, he acquired one of the most important collections of Japanese art in Britain.

Merton and Annie's accounts of their itinerary diverge after Japan. Annie talks of catching a boat from Nagasaki in early December, then arriving in Singapore after a stopover in Hong Kong. Merton includes a visit to Shanghai and Peking after Hong Kong – a round trip of over 3,000 miles in the wrong direction. His description of the two cities bears a striking resemblance to *China: Its Marvel and Mystery*, a book published a few years before he began *Home and Abroad*. Annie's version of their route is, then, more likely to be correct.

They saw in the new year in Ceylon, spending most of their time at the colonial hill retreat of Nuwara Eliya. While this was gentle sightseeing compared to Kilauea, they still managed an ascent on horseback of the island's highest peak. Merton devotes most attention to the Temple of the Sacred Tooth Relic at Kandy, home to a giant incisor said to have come from the Buddha's funeral pyre. Visitors view it through a glass screen upon payment to a priest. 'A more completely fraudulent imposture could not be conceived,' he protested. 'The human being to whom it belonged would have been a man at least from 40 or 50 feet high! It is this sort of thing in all religions that reduces them to an absurdity and disgusts the mind of any independent thinker.'[33] He dismisses the relic as a piece of ivory or the tooth of a wild beast, but the priests refused all inducements to let him touch it.

India, an exhausting two-month tour, was the last big stop on their travels. They took in Madras, Calcutta – where they met George Augustus Sala – Delhi, Bombay and some of the bloodiest scenes of the Indian Mutiny. Merton, following established norms, shows no qualms about colonial rule. He writes at length about British heroism at the Siege of Lucknow and of native atrocities at Cawnpore.[34] There is talk, too, of the dangers and discomforts of exotic travel, as he recalls dinners shared with giant moths, and – to the wonder of the hotel staff – an epic battle with a snake discovered in his bathwater at Jaipur. He tells of how he and Annie tried to intervene when they saw an English army officer thrashing a cart driver for failing to let him pass. The officer rejected their charge of cruelty by explaining that the driver had subjected him to the most loathsome curses. 'We both apologised to him for having interfered,' wrote Merton, 'and heartily endorsed what he had done.'[35] On an excursion from Delhi, they asked a local man to fetch a replacement for a skittish horse but were left stranded when he failed to return. They found him in the next village without a care in the world. 'This is an admirable example of the average native – lazy and irresponsible,' wrote Merton. 'We rated him soundly, got two fresh horses and drove back to Delhi.'[36]

In all these things, Merton portrays himself as a proud colonialist, unshakeable in his belief in the British right to rule. His tales of the heat and the flies in the sacred outposts of Empire would have been greeted with admiration back home. Disdain for the local religions is part of the same narrative. 'This Krishna of the Hindus is nothing more than a very low and crude counterfeit of our Saviour,' he wrote. 'Many of the incidents said to have occurred during the life of this Hindu deity correspond with what actually occurred during the life of Christ.'[37] In her own book, Annie brands the Hindus as 'untruthful, deceitful, and most ungrateful' and seems surprised that the British could not win them over. 'The Indians are peculiarly jealous of our interference in their religion,' she observed.[38]

For all the talk of empire and religion, Merton and Annie spent most of their time in India on well-worn tourist trails. They travelled around 3,000 miles, most of it by rail, and may even have visited Burma. Merton says they made a detour to 'unutterably wretched' Rangoon, but its omission from Annie's account raises doubts about his own.[39] Both agree they left India via Bombay. There were re-coaling stops at Aden, Port Said, Valletta and Gibraltar, but there was little time to go ashore. They arrived in London in May 1886, a shade over eighteen months after leaving Plymouth. Weary from the voyage, they decamped to Claridge's – as guests not owners – before returning to Bournemouth a few days later. Although they travelled by the same old rickety branch line, the train pulled into the magnificent new station opened in their absence.

Dozens of packing cases sent back from far-flung places awaited them at the Royal Bath. As well as a host of treasures and artefacts, Merton brought back something just as important from their jaunt around the globe. Journeys to exotic places attracted a huge amount of curiosity and kudos, while tales of distant lands stood any number of retellings. This gave Merton a prestigious new label – 'traveller' – to add to his CV. With his confidence restored, he was almost a new man as he resumed his place in the life of Bournemouth.

Notes:

1. *Home and Abroad*, p. 701.
2. Hargreaves won three England caps and played in a record 13–0 win over Ireland in 1882.
3. *Home and Abroad*, p. 375.
4. ibid., p. 376.
5. Annie's friend was Robert Anderson, whose father, a Girvan farmer, co-wrote a book called *The Birds of Ayrshire and Wigtownshire*. Annie also took an interest in ornithology, which may have stemmed from that source.
6. *Home and Abroad*, p. 391.
7. ibid., p. 394. Merton was quoting Annie's journal.
8. ibid., pp. 399–400.
9. ibid., p. 402.
10. ibid., pp. 403–4.
11. Tangye, *Notes of My Fourth Voyage to the Australian Colonies*, p. 110.
12. The guidebook referred to is *Maoriland: An Illustrated Handbook to New Zealand*.
13. Merton says the eruption occurred during the latter part of the tour, but it took place a month after their return to England.
14. *Home and Abroad*, p. 499.
15. *Daily Bulletin* (Honolulu), 10 July 1885.
16. *Pacific Commercial Advertiser*, 11 July 1885.
17. Merton spells the name 'Taverniers', but other sources omit the 's'.

18. *Home and Abroad*, p. 418.
19. *Pacific Commercial Advertiser*, 21 July 1885.
20. Merton does not mention an ankle, but he quotes a letter from a Hawaiian friend who refers to Annie's 'limb'. The friend adds: 'You know, of course, I must not mention the other name for it.'
21. Merton's entry in the hotel's visitors' book is dated 21 July – apparently their last day – and refers to two visits to Halemaumau. *Home and Abroad* refers to three visits, on 21, 23 and 27 July.
22. Tangye, *Reminiscences of Travel in Australia, America and Egypt*, p. 28.
23. Merton recalls attending a birthday party given in the King's honour, but this is unlikely as the celebrations took place in November. In a postscript to these events, some newspapers reported the King's intended visit to Bournemouth in October 1890. However, the *St James's Gazette* of 28 June that year said he planned to stay at the Boscombe Chine Hotel, not the Royal Bath. The visit never took place, and the King died the following January.
24. The Volcano House guest was Eugenio-Martin Lanciarez, the Italian chargé d'affaires in Tokyo.
25. *Home and Abroad*, p. 445.
26. ibid., p. 570.
27. Although undated, *Westward from the Golden Gate* must have been published more than a decade after the trip, as it contains a reference to 1896. Annie presented a copy to the Glasgow Corporation in 1899, so it may have been published that year.
28. *Home and Abroad*, p. 454.
29. ibid., p. 466.
30. ibid., pp. 459–60.
31. *Westward from the Golden Gate*, p. 41.
32. Merton names Sir Julian Pauncefote as the British ambassador who helped him, but Pauncefote never served in Japan. He was, however, the head of the British legation in Washington when Merton and Annie were there in 1890.
33. *Home and Abroad*, p. 490.
34. Parts of Merton's description of the Indian Mutiny come from *The Guide to Lucknow*, published in 1911.
35. *Home and Abroad*, p. 511.
36. ibid., p. 527.
37. ibid., p. 522.
38. *Westward from the Golden Gate*, p. 147.
39. *Home and Abroad*, p. 505.

8

FELLOW

Merton toyed with writing a full account of his adventures in the months after returning to England. He dismissed the idea in the end and, instead, set to work on a paper describing their experiences on Kilauea. His brush with death in pursuit of Pele's hair spiced the tale with a dash of derring-do. He sent his work to the Royal Geographical Society and asked the local MP, Charles Baring Young (1850–1928), to nominate him for a fellowship.[1] The Society conferred the distinction in November 1886, taking Merton's social network in a new direction. He was one of 200 fellows appointed that year – all of them men – who were joining a club some 3,000 strong. Many were explorers and scientists, but others, such as Richard Tangye, were simply tourists willing to share their knowledge of faraway places. Merton embraced the honour with a passion. From the ashes of Merton R. Cotes, improvement commissioner, rose Merton Russell Cotes, F.R.G.S. It would be some years yet before he added the hyphen between his middle and last names. The honour marked him out as a man of the establishment, while the post-nominal letters gave him an air of gravitas whenever he needed to make himself heard. So proud was he of his geographical appendage that it appears more than fifty times in *Home and Abroad*.

By the time of his fellowship nomination, the family had moved to Branksome Park, a suburb to the west of Bournemouth. This meant they were now living in Dorset, although Merton evoked thoughts of Staffordshire by calling the house 'Tettenhall'.[2] With a major extension to the Royal Bath in the offing, this new home provided some respite from the hotel when the work started. The move may also have been a factor in Merton taking a break from civic affairs at a time when Bournemouth's development showed no signs of letting up. Construction of the direct line from London was well advanced, and there was talk of the town launching a bid for incorporation. The sanitary hospital opened at the beginning of 1886, but Christopher Creeke, who did so much to deliver it, died soon after Merton's return to England. The town hailed him as 'The Father of Bournemouth' as it mourned his loss. On the seafront, a novel solution to an old problem led to a familiar outcome. Amid floundering talk of new piers at Boscombe and Alum Chine, the latest attempt to build an undercliff drive had ended in chaos. After voting to press ahead with it in the summer of 1885, the commissioners set up a competition for the best design. It came with a generous cash prize and no less a figure than Sir Joseph Bazalgette as the main judge. A farce ensued nonetheless. The winning entry, although sent in by a third party, turned out to be the work of the board's own surveyor. As heated arguments broke out about the prize money, the townsfolk, many of whom were not sold on the idea in the first place, rose up in anger. Once again, the scheme came to nothing.

Merton may have cast jealous glances along the coast as he pondered this lack of progress. Southbourne-on-Sea, a new resort to the east of Bournemouth, managed to build 500 yards of promenade while he was away. The vision of an enterprising local doctor, Southbourne proved what could be done along the same stretch of coastline. It was not enough at this stage to encourage Merton to agitate for a more progressive outlook by the authorities in Bournemouth. That only started to change when he moved the family back to the Royal Bath around two years after setting up home in Branksome Park. Wary, perhaps, of history repeating itself, he never again stood for election as a commissioner. The nearest thing to controversy in this period came when daughter Ella knocked down a boy in the town centre after losing control of a pony and trap. The child suffered only minor injuries, and the courts cleared Ella of furious driving.

While attracting people to Bournemouth remained a big issue, Merton came home to growing competition at the upper end of the hotel market. The Mont Dore was now open to the better class of health seeker, and a large new hotel – The Imperial – was taking shape less than half a mile from the Royal Bath.[3] The emergence of these newcomers forced the old guard to improve to survive. Henry Newlyn embarked on a major extension of the Royal Exeter within weeks of Merton's return, copying the Royal Bath's lead almost a decade on. Like his rival, Newlyn played heavily on the patronage of foreign royalty and on the hotel's significance in Bournemouth's rise. While the Royal Bath could boast of being the town's first hotel, the Royal Exeter occupied its own unique place in local history: Lewis Tregonwell's original mansion, often cited as the town's first house, lay at the heart of the premises. Newlyn, a steady and reliable commissioner, was now serving a second term as the board's chairman. His progress, and the rise of the Mont Dore and The Imperial, demanded a response from Merton. In 1887, he submitted proposals to double the size of the Royal Bath by adding a new south-facing wing. When the commissioners refused to endorse the plans due to an encroachment on the public highway, he started the work anyway

31 The Mont Dore (top) and the Royal Exeter were among the Royal Bath's main rivals. The Mont Dore became a military hospital during the First World War and has been the town hall since 1921. The Royal Exeter – also known as Newlyn's Hotel, the Exeter Park and various combinations of the same – was named after the Marchioness of Exeter, who rented what was then a private residence prior to her death in 1837. (Author's collection)

while arguing his case. The board turned down the plans for a second time the following month, but the main part of the scheme later went ahead without further hindrance.

In tandem with the building work, Merton again turned to the decorative artist John Thomas to apply his talents to the hotel. This time it was on a breathtaking scale. Thomas and his son spent around two years adorning the walls and ceilings with classical and bucolic scenes. In a typical piece of Merton media manipulation, *Plumber and Decorator* magazine ran a feature on the work. Opening with a description of the hotel's 'distinctive natural advantages', the article lavished praise on Thomas's 'graceful entwinings', 'blooming peonies' and 'Pompeian corridors'.[4] Some of the designs noted by the magazine resurfaced in Merton's later commissions by the same artists – friezes of rooks and peacocks, faux-leather wallpaper and the patron saints of Britain and Ireland depicted in stained glass. In a flight of literary fancy, Thomas painted the phrase 'Welcome the coming, speed the parting guest' on the balcony above the lobby. Bram Stoker (1847–1912), a future visitor to the hotel, later placed these words – a quotation from Homer's *Odyssey* – on Count Dracula's lips.

Thomas's original Japanese Drawing Room, crammed with the contents of a hundred packing cases, became the hotel's artistic hub. It gave Merton another unique selling point to stay ahead of the competition, while invitations designed by Thomas added an air of exclusivity to the exhibition.[5] For the right guest, the new Fellow of the Royal Geographical Society would give a guided tour to add even more colour to the dazzling display. Visitors could hear first-hand stories of the costume, cuisine and customs of a land

THE ART OF A SALESMAN

32 The Japanese Drawing Room at the Royal Bath, crammed with the souvenirs collected by Merton and Annie. Most Westerners had little understanding of Japan, which only began to open up to the outside world as a result of American gunboat diplomacy in the 1850s. (From *Home and Abroad*)

all but closed to foreigners until the 1860s. Merton claims to have shown the collection to the Prime Minister, Lord Salisbury (1830–1903), although reports at the time say it was his Lordship's wife and daughter who took the tour. They received a small item of Japanese ware as a memento.

With the Royal Bath's new wing nearing completion, The Imperial opened for business in early 1888. What it lacked in Japanese curios and a globetrotting proprietor, it made up for with luxurious rooms, fine art and electric bells. A telephone hotline to a local doctor helped to sell it to health seekers. That said, Merton held a commercial trump card over this latest newcomer. The Imperial's landlord was Sir George Meyrick, who refused the hotel permission to apply for an alcohol licence. This, in turn, arose from an agreement between Meyrick and Merton, probably dating back to 1876, that the former would permit no new licensed hotels on his land.[6] The restriction failed to stop The Imperial from poaching Charles Reingpach from its established rival. In his place, the Royal Bath hired German-born Franz Kuntze (c. 1849–1916), a former waiter with the London and North Western Railway. Merton's late brother had, of course, worked for the same company. If that smacks of sentiment, then perhaps it was: Kuntze had most recently worked as the steward of the Wolverhampton Conservative club.

To add salt to the wound of the loss of Reingpach, The Imperial used the advent of the direct line from London in its first wave of advertising. The line opened in March 1888 after four years of work to build the ten miles of track from Brockenhurst. Several lives had been lost and a contractor bankrupted in the process. Merton kept a low profile during the celebrations and was neither heard nor mentioned at the civic luncheon to mark the occasion.[7] The speeches dwelt less on individual contributions to the scheme's completion and more on the line's importance to the town's development. Some speakers threw in words of caution and warned that the railway risked turning the resort into another Margate. The Kentish town offered the fine folk of Bournemouth a glimpse of something close to the Apocalypse. First-class ticket holders arriving on fast trains from the capital counted for little if a flock of five-shilling day trippers travelled with them.

With both of Bournemouth's 'Royal' hotels boasting new facilities, the battle for patronage intensified. Merton struck the first blow two weeks after the opening of the direct line when the marriage of Prince Oscar (1859–1953) – a son of the King of Sweden – took place in the town. The Prince was marrying Ebba Munck (1858–1946), his sister's lady-in-waiting, in a match that dismayed his parents and captured the hearts of the public. His father agreed to the union only if the Prince gave up his rights to the throne and married abroad. The Queen chose Bournemouth as the venue, a place she knew and loved from the days of the Empress Eugénie's visit. Crowds gathered outside St Stephen's Church on the big day to see the royal carriages come and go. The Mont Dore, cashing in on its position next door to the church, erected a grandstand for the convenience of guests. Some of the wedding party stayed at the Royal Bath, including Princess Helena, Duchess of Albany (1861–1922) – the widow of Queen Victoria's haemophiliac fourth son, Prince Leopold (1853–1884). Miss Munck spent her last night of

33 An invitation to the Japanese Drawing Room. The use of 'Cotes' suggests it was printed soon after the couple returned from their travels in 1886. Merton was styling himself 'Russell Cotes' by the time he received his fellowship of the Royal Geographical Society in the autumn of that year. (Russell-Cotes Art Gallery and Museum)

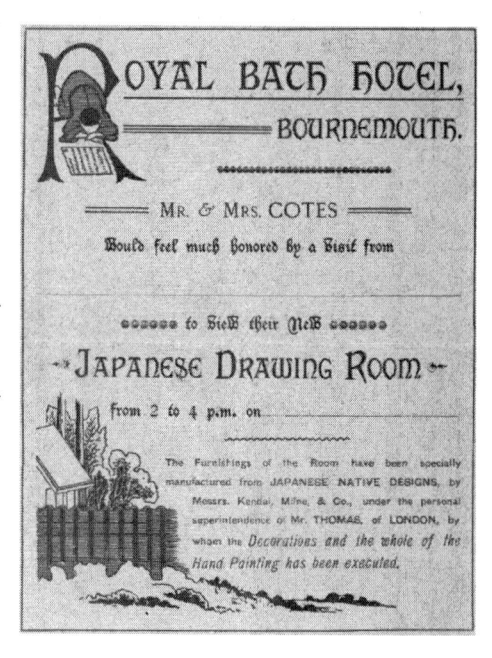

freedom at the Boscombe Chine Hotel, a newly refurbished establishment intent on luring Merton's clientele away from the town centre. Even so, the presence of the Queen's daughter-in-law at the Royal Bath guaranteed the hotel a prominent place in press reports of the wedding.

What he gained in publicity from the Swedish marriage, Merton lost to Henry Newlyn when Elisabeth, the Empress of Austria (1837–1898), came to town a month later. One report described the visit as 'exasperating, almost to a frenzy, the antagonism between the two rival hotels.' [8] A notoriously eccentric beauty, the Empress always carried a large fan to shield her face from the common gaze. Her luxuriant tresses, falling well below the waist, were said to require three hours of care every day. With privacy a priority, her entourage took over the whole of the Royal Exeter, bar one room on the top

34 Merton's refurbishments at the Royal Bath received a glowing write-up in an 1889 edition of The Architect, *which included this sketch of the Wedgwood Drawing Room. 'The hotel will shortly be lighted throughout with electric light,' the magazine reported, 'which will greatly enhance the beauty of the decorative work.'* [9] (Author's collection)

floor occupied by an elderly spinster. Three large vans were needed to shift the imperial luggage, and the Empress insisted on being chaperoned by Newlyn's wife whenever she went out for a walk. The press coverage more than paid for the upheaval, while Mrs Newlyn received – à la Eugénie – a valuable ring from their guest for her trouble. If all this seems excessive for a one-week stay, then the Empress's idiosyncrasies cannot be dismissed as paranoia: an anarchist stabbed her to death outside a Geneva hotel in 1898.

With hindsight, the Swedish and Austrian royal visits crowned Bournemouth's halcyon days as an elite resort. At the time, however, some in the town believed the best was yet to come. *Truth* magazine picked up grumblings about the 'neglect of that thriving watering place by English royalty.' [10] Written under the strapline 'The Season at Bournemouth', the article showcased the town's position as a refined winter retreat. It would take until the Great War to tip the balance, but the top hotels already faced a challenge from growing summer crowds. Merton, as always, was eager to express an opinion about what to do. 'I say that Bournemouth cannot hold its own against other competing winter health resorts until it possesses the same accommodation, attractions and conveniences as they do.'[11] Written in 1905, these remarks show how, even at that late stage, he saw the winter trade as paramount. The comments explain why he lobbied so hard for facilities, such as the undercliff drive, that were bound to attract the masses. As long as the nobility and gentry could take a bracing winter carriage ride, then he was willing to fight to control the summer hordes.

Merton and Annie took frequent holidays in other resorts, often timing their departure to avoid the height of Bournemouth's winter season. They could leave town with confidence knowing that Franz Kuntze and Arthur Painter were running the hotel. The couple's next long trip abroad, a three-month tour of South Africa, began in February 1889. Although Ella accompanied them, Clarie and Bert stayed at home on this occasion. Clarie never joined their later travels – she married in 1891 – but the reason for Bert's absence is not clear. Now eighteen and an alumnus of the prestigious Highgate School in London, he shared his mother's love of music and dreamt of becoming a singer. Merton, so the family story goes, wanted him to become a lawyer.[12] The school's magazine gives no hint of this dilemma, recording only a victory in a quarter-mile handicap race and form prizes for divinity and history. His father's career choice prevailed, so taking the first steps in that direction may be why Bert missed out on seeing South Africa.

In *Home and Abroad*, Merton uses his account of the trip to draw attention to a claimed friendship with Cecil Rhodes (1853–1902). While not saying how or where they met, some of his opinions of 'the greatest of great men of the Victorian era' are culled straight from an article in *The Times*.[13] As for South Africa, Merton has little positive to say about it. He found Cape Town dull, Ceres God-forsaken, the hotels dire, the trains stifling and the ships rat-infested hulks. A supply of ants' eggs for use as gifts was one of the few redeeming features. He also admired the sunny disposition of the locals and the magnificent physique of the Zulus. 'With education and sound, pure, simple Protestant instruction,' he wrote of the latter, 'they would become a most intelligent and highly cultured people.'[14]

The real saving graces came on the voyage home. They were befriended by Edward Stebbing (1858–1937), the ship's master, with the unmarried Ella becoming the main focus of the captain's attentions. Romance blossomed, although a dozen years would elapse before it reached full flower. Merton recalls how Stebbing granted them permission to go ashore when they called at St Helena. 'He begged us not to mention it to anyone on board,' he wrote, 'because if the other passengers got to know they would all want to go.'[15] They saw Longwood House – the converted farmstead used by the exiled

Napoleon – and visited the Emperor's tomb.[16] Merton says they took cuttings from a willow overhanging the grave, which they took back with them to plant in their garden. Great trees grew from these small beginnings, but their provenance is doubtful. Street traders on St Helena were well known for waiting at the harbourside in their droves ready for ships to disgorge gullible tourists. As *Gardener's Monthly and Horticulturalist* observed: 'They seem to have a large stock of well-rooted plants growing in jars, cigar boxes, paint kegs, etc., in readiness for the siege.' [17]

By the time they returned to England in May, the prospects for Bournemouth's incorporation were looking up. Few now doubted its benefits, and there was much rejoicing when the government agreed it in principle that summer. It was the culmination of seven years of attrition. Joseph Cutler, who had regained his seat on the board of commissioners, could bask in the glory of having been the first to speak up in its favour. While this suggests a progressive thinker, Cutler rode in the vanguard of resistance to spending money on the seafront. Opposition continued to dog the undercliff drive, while Boscombe pier – opened by the Duke of Argyll in July 1889 – came to fruition only through private enterprise. Merton may, then, have been irked to discover that a group of tradesmen planned to celebrate Cutler's contributions to the town. At a dinner in his honour, the eccentric builder stood before his peers to blow his own trumpet. He spoke of his fight for better rail facilities, his revival of the town's regatta and his role in saving the steam packet company after its ship came to grief at Portland. Cutler, just as Merton later did himself, was busy trying to create a legacy.[18]

Merton soon seized his own chance to shine. It came with the opening of the Royal Victoria Hospital in January 1890, a project begun three years earlier to honour the Queen's golden jubilee. Merton had been one of the first to subscribe to the huge fundraising effort needed to build it.[19] When it was announced that the Prince of Wales would perform the official opening, it became the most eagerly awaited event in Bournemouth's short history. The Prince planned to spend an hour in the town – just long enough to do the deed. All the same, an appeal went out to raise £2,000 for the celebrations, and Merton offered to host a civic banquet after the Prince's departure. The commissioners, mindful of the kerfuffle over the pier opening, approached the idea with caution. Henry Newlyn thought it disgraceful even to consider the proposal. Why, he asked at a board meeting, should Mr Cotes be treated as a person of great distinction? What had he done for the town that they should accept his invitation? Others agreed, with some in no doubt that the banquet's main purpose was to advertise the Royal Bath.

After much debate, the board voted for compromise and allowed individual commissioners to attend or not as they saw fit. Thomas Beechey, Henry Newlyn and Thomas Hankinson were among those who declined the

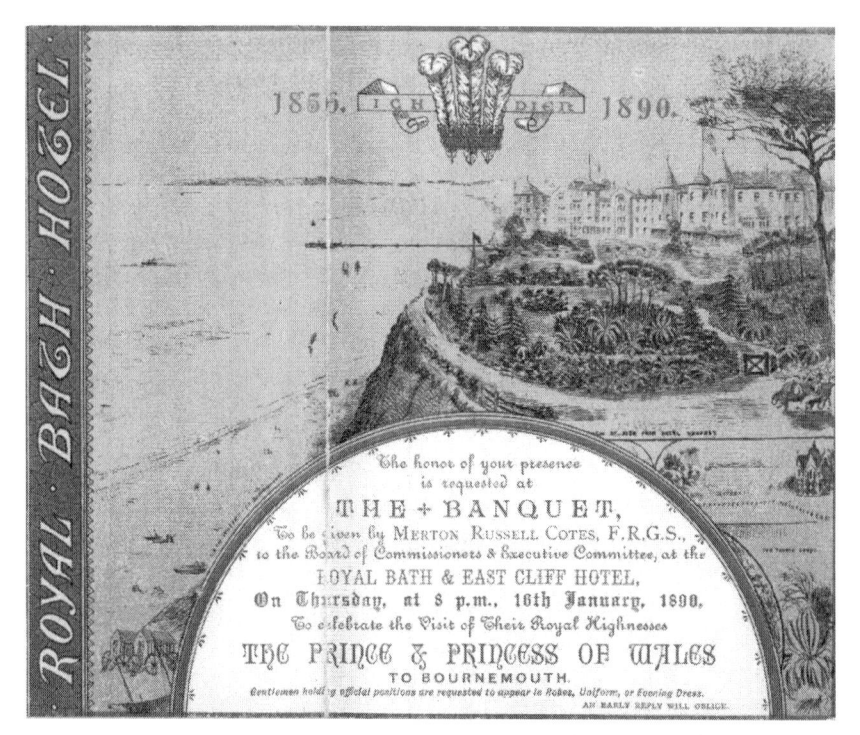

35 The fact that as many improvement commissioners accepted this invitation as declined it shows how Merton still divided opinion in Bournemouth. Note the use of 'Royal Bath & East Cliff Hotel', a variation of the name that featured regularly from this point onwards. (Russell-Cotes Art Gallery and Museum)

invitation. Joseph Cutler decided to accept. Any awkwardness around Enoch White's attendance was avoided when he died suddenly a fortnight before the Prince's visit. And yet, even in death, White managed to steal some of his old foe's thunder. Whereas Merton gained praise for a gift of eleven Alpine landscapes to adorn the walls of the new hospital, White had already donated a tree for their royal guest to plant in the grounds.[20]

While Merton's banquet led to some soul-searching, the route of the Prince's carriage procession caused a much bigger headache for the commissioners. A month before the opening, the board went through the options with Lord and Lady Wimborne, who were to host the Prince at their Canford Manor estate. The Wimbornes were Ivor Guest (1835–1914) and his wife, Cornelia (1847–1927), who had recently gifted land for a public park in Poole. The idea was for the Prince to open the Royal Victoria Hospital on a Thursday, go shooting the next day, then open Poole Park on the Saturday. Merton offered to host the banquet as soon as discussions started about the Bournemouth part of the itinerary, fully expecting the procession to pass the Royal Bath at some point. When it emerged otherwise, Lady Wimborne made

THE ART OF A SALESMAN

a surprising plea to the board's organising committee on his behalf. She feared he would be 'extremely disappointed' if the Prince's carriage failed to pass the hotel on its way through the town.[21] The committee agreed to change the route to oblige her, sparking a heated row when the news reached the main board. Henry Newlyn objected in the strongest terms, but the Prince, so he was told, had already approved the new route.

On the day of the opening, dense crowds watched the procession make its way through a blaze of flags, banners and bunting. Fourteen triumphal arches marked the way, one of them an enormous model of the Eiffel Tower. The Prince rode in the lead carriage alongside his eldest son, Prince George (1865–1936), together with Lady Wimborne and her brother, Lord Randolph Churchill (1849–1895). The town was witnessing history, both current and in the making. Two future monarchs were riding in that carriage, along with the man whose son would become the country's most revered Prime Minister. If the Prince of Wales remembered anything of his boyhood visit to Bournemouth, then the houses and shops along Old Christchurch Road provided ample proof of how much it had changed. Westover Road, lined with the original villas built by Sir George Gervis, would have been more familiar.

At around half past twelve, the procession came to a halt outside the Royal Bath. All Merton's planning depended on this precious pause. The band of the Grenadier Guards struck up the national anthem, encouraging the Prince to look out of the carriage window. He could hardly fail to be impressed by the hotel's extraordinary decorations. The main flagpole flew the Royal Standard, while the masts at each end bore pendants bearing the words 'Royal Bath Hotel'. Green lamps on the roof pinnacles displayed the years '1856' and '1890', marking the Prince's two visits to the town. More lamps, ready to be lit for the banquet, framed the outline and entrance of the building. A giant crystal medallion, topped by a crown, formed the centrepiece, with the motto 'God Bless Them' appearing underneath. On each side stood a large letter 'A' – one for Albert, the other for Alexandra – both fashioned out of white and green crystal. Only this last part fell flat, as an eleventh-hour illness had confined the Princess of Wales to bed. The rest of the extravaganza made its point with triumphant exuberance. In case of doubt, Lady Wimborne explained everything to the Prince as they waited for the carriage to move on.

The rest of the visit flew by. The royal party made a short stop in the pleasure gardens for a civic welcome in a grand pavilion, then made its way to the hospital for the opening. After using a spade of ebony and silver to plant Enoch White's tree, the Prince left town to have lunch with Lord and Lady Wimborne. Merton, without an official role in the proceedings, contented himself with the Prince's admiration for his paintings, passed on to him by a friend on the reception committee.

That evening, local dignitaries and executives from the London and South Western Railway gathered for Merton's banquet to reflect on the day's events. Wyndham Portal heaped praised upon their host, emphasising his role not only in the Prince's visit but also in the pier opening and the promotion of better rail facilities. These comments highlight how Merton's relationship with Portal and his colleagues was built upon the receipt of mutual dividends. The railway company used him as their advocate in Bournemouth, while Merton could rely on their support whenever needed. Indeed, he may have used these connections when presented with the original route of the royal carriage procession. As well as Portal, the attendees of the banquet included Charles Scotter, Merton's old Altrincham acquaintance. Now the company's general manager, Scotter provided a channel into Arthur Guest, who sat on the board of directors. Guest (1841–1898), as luck would have it, happened to be Lord Wimborne's brother. When the proposed route put Merton's plans in jeopardy, an appeal to the Wimbornes via Scotter and Guest was the best way to avoid disaster.

Merton's railway connections paid off again in the spring when the London and South Western ran its first luxury carriages over the direct line. The company's directors invited the Duchess of Albany on board to gain a royal seal of approval. They entertained her to lunch at the Royal Bath, where she admired the paintings and viewed the Japanese Drawing Room. In *Home and Abroad*, Merton gives the impression of hosting the visit himself, but it was Clarie Cotes, in a rare public outing, who attended to the Duchess's needs on this occasion. Merton and Annie were out of the country by then, reviving the journey sacrificed to the cause of Annie's ankle back in 1885. Thanks to the visit of the Prince of Wales, they left England with Merton's personal stock on the rise. Unlike the pier opening ten years earlier, accusations of self-interest were confined to the build-up, and there was no unpleasantness afterwards. Merton still had his critics, but his lavish banquet and stunning decorations brought a certain sparkle to Bournemouth's day in the spotlight.

Notes:

1. Merton names Sir Clements Markham, the secretary of the Royal Geographical Society, as the prime mover in his election, but he is not listed on the nomination form.
2. Tettenhall was in Lindsay Road, Poole, and is now the site of a supermarket. Another property called Tettenhall – in Norwich Avenue, Bournemouth – appeared in street directories in the 1890s. If Merton owned it, there is no evidence of him living there.
3. The Imperial was at the Lansdowne, on the junction of Bath Road and Meyrick Road. It was demolished in the 1960s.

4. Pugh, *The Royal Bath*, pp. 22–24, quoting *Plumber and Decorator*, July 1889.
5. John Thomas may also have provided the illustrations for *Westward from the Golden Gate*.
6. The restriction came to light in 1893 when attempts to circumvent it led to prosecution. The Imperial's proprietor also owned the Belle Vue Hotel, which held a licence. Drinks were supplied from there and billed separately, but officials caught The Imperial keeping its own stocks.
7. On p. 62 of *Home and Abroad*, Merton says he was not known as the instigator of the route of the direct line until the chairman of the LSWR referred to it in a speech in 1908. However, the *Bournemouth Guardian* mentions it in a potted biography published in 1891.
8. *Sandusky Daily Register*, 7 July 1888.
9. *The Architect*, 29 November 1889.
10. Quoted in the *Southern Echo*, 3 January 1889.
11. *Home and Abroad*, p. 183.
12. This is according to an interview given by Phyllis Lee-Duncan to Shaun Garner, the former curator of the Russell-Cotes Art Gallery and Museum.
13. *The Times*, 24 May 1916 and *Home and Abroad*, pp. 584–85.
14. *Home and Abroad*, p. 595.
15. ibid., p. 596.
16. This refers to Napoleon's original grave, as his body was moved to France in 1840. Merton later bought a wine cooler and octagonal table used by the Emperor at Longwood.
17. *Gardener's Monthly and Horticulturalist*, Volume XXV, 1883.
18. Merton is not listed in reports of Cutler's dinner, but Arthur Painter did attend.
19. The hospital was in Poole Road, between the town centre and Westbourne.
20. In moving a vote of condolence at a commissioners' meeting, Thomas Hankinson said of White: 'He had a very strong personality and impressed the board very much with it at times, and perhaps some of them felt that he trod on their corns a little vigorously.' (*Bournemouth Guardian*, 11 January 1890)
21. *Bournemouth Observer*, 8 January 1890.

9

PROGRESSIVE

Merton and Annie, joined by Bert this time, left England soon after the announcement of the Duchess of Albany's visit. The couple were recovering from a bout of influenza and planned to take the eastward route across America scuppered by Annie's stumble on Kilauea five years earlier. They had to reach the Pacific first, which meant crossing the isthmus of Panama without a canal to ease their way. The French abandoned the workings the year before in the face of spiralling costs and a rising death toll from accidents and disease. Merton recalls how they were obliged to remain on the Atlantic side for two nights before catching a train to join a new ship in the Pacific port of Panama City. With yellow fever prevalent, they decided not to explore the area and went on board at the first opportunity. As they sailed northwards towards the Gulf of California, a sudden drop in temperature aggravated Bert's asthma. It triggered an attack so severe that he had to be carried off the boat when they reached San Francisco. This meant staying longer in the area than they intended, but Bert did not suffer alone. In Los Angeles, Merton was smoking at the front of a tramcar when the conductor ordered him to go to the back. Getting there meant shuffling along the footboard outside, and he slipped and gashed his shin. The wound turned ulcerous and he was soon struggling to get about. While Bert recovered and went riding, Merton had enough time on his hands to spend $1,200 on a plot of land in Pasadena. The property was once again vested in Annie's name, but what became of this potentially valuable piece of real estate is a mystery.

The three of them caught an eastbound train when they were all fit again, stopping for a few days in each city as they made their way across the States. Merton punctuated the trip by giving interviews to the press. Journalists scouring hotels for newsworthy visitors were delighted to find that an F.R.G.S. had come to town. The four letters featured in many of their reports, along with a willingness on both sides to make the most of them. A Pasadena reporter believed that he was an explorer and one of the best-known men of science in England. In Denver, he was said to have known Henry Morton Stanley (1841–1904) for sixteen years. This allowed him to pass comment on Stanley's forthcoming nuptials and dismiss 'absurd' rumours about his use of hair dye. *The Kansas City Times* described how Merton had entertained the Prince of Wales at 'one of the most magnificent banquets ever served in the kingdom.' [1] Later, he was touted as the Prince's friend. In Chicago, Merton revealed that Belgium was on the verge of ceding the Congo to the British, who would then set about clearing the jungles. 'This will probably take from fifteen to twenty years,' he explained, 'but the riches of the territory in ivory and lumber will make ample return for the outlay.' [2]

As well as these weighty issues, Merton shared his opinions of American hotels. He praised their modernity but deplored the tipping culture and the vast amounts of wasted food. En suite rooms also came in for criticism, which he considered unsanitary and no substitute for tin baths and chamber pots. He also disliked the inclusive rates charged by the Americans, which forced him to pay for things he never used. His policy was to bill everything separately back home, even down to the lights, baths and fires in the hotel's bedrooms. These comparisons allowed him to bring Bournemouth and the Royal Bath to the attention of any Americans contemplating a trip to the old country. One Washington newspaper called the hotel 'the most exclusive house at the most fashionable resort in England.' [3]

Interviews with the press aside, Merton's somewhat tame account of the trip suggests they did much the same as other tourists. They met George Pullman (1831–1897) of railroad car company fame at the American Derby, but that came courtesy of some old friends in Chicago. Washington delivered the most exciting moments, thanks to calling cards provided by the British consulate. These, according to *Home and Abroad*, gave them the 'entrée everywhere'.[4] They used the cards to visit the Senate and the Congressional Library, and to listen to a debate at the House of Representatives. Merton even claims to have met President Benjamin Harrison (1833–1901), who stopped for a chat, signed an autograph and threw a guided tour of the White House into the bargain.

After a short trip to eastern Canada, they returned to England from New York in August 1890. In their absence, the news filtered through that the Queen had at last granted Bournemouth's charter of incorporation. This was a defining moment in the town's history. It meant replacing the improvement commissioners with a mayor, a council, electoral wards and all the other trappings of a municipal borough. Merton, while pleased with the outcome, found himself on the fringe of these changes. Much of the debate had taken place during his various travels and yet, despite the glamour of his F.R.G.S. and the Royal Bath's success, his standing remained ambiguous. Many would have echoed Henry Newlyn's view – 'What had he done for the town?' – as Bournemouth celebrated its new status. From this point onwards, however,

36 Bournemouth's last board of improvement commissioners, 1890. Thomas Beechey (far left), Henry Newlyn (fourth left), Thomas Hankinson (standing) and Joseph Cutler (far right) had already crossed swords with Merton. J. H. Moore (seventh left) would later play a leading role in his biggest controversy. (Bournemouth Library)

the town heard his voice more often, and more loudly, on many key issues.

With only 4,000 people entitled to vote – about a tenth of the population – the first elections that November fell short of full democracy. Familiar names saw mixed results at the ballot box. Joseph Cutler failed in his bid to gain a seat on the new council, as did Thomas Beechey of the lamp post affair. Henry Newlyn was successful, along with Thomas Hankinson – the man who triggered the row over the Lord Mayor's banquet. Hankinson, a successful estate agent and a champion of incorporation, took the honour of becoming the town's first mayor. Merton was left on the sidelines as these events unfolded but made an entrance with his usual good timing. At the first full meeting of the new council, it was announced that he and Annie had offered to donate a mayoral mace and badge to the fledgling borough at a cost of 150 guineas. It was a bold statement of the couple's wealth and importance. Moreover, by giving the badge in Annie's name and the mace in his own, he set the precedent for their future philanthropy. On the same day, and with more than a hint of choreography, the Royal Bath hosted a luncheon at which Merton himself was the guest of honour. While not an official council function, a group of influential friends gathered to present him with an illuminated address of thanks for his contribution to the visit of the Prince of Wales. Written on vellum and with the appearance of a page from a monastic Bible, addresses of this kind were a favoured way of expressing civic gratitude. It was the first of many received by Merton. Sewn into an album

37 The reading of Bournemouth's charter of incorporation at the pierhead by the town clerk, 27th August 1890. The London and South Western Railway had laid on a special carriage to bring the charter from London that same morning. (Bournemouth Library)

of Russian leather, this example contained sketches of the Royal Bath Hotel, the new hospital, Old Harry Rocks and other local landmarks. Hankinson, although unable to attend the presentation, sent a letter of thanks as an olive branch to ease old tensions.

Merton took great care over the design of the mace and badge. He modelled the former on the one given to the borough of Wolverhampton by George Thorneycroft, the father of the eccentric colonel. Merton's version introduced an innovative twist – a loving cup hidden beneath the crown and accessed by unscrewing the shaft. The badge, in eighteen-carat gold and enamelled with Bournemouth's coat of arms, bore the town's new motto, *Pulchritudo et Salubritas*. Meaning 'beauty and health', the council preferred it to *Hic Odor et Sanitas*, a suggestion intended to mean 'perfume and health'.

The couple handed over their gifts in a ceremony at the Royal Bath in March 1891. Among the attendees were Charles Scotter and the Earl of Portarlington (1832–1892), an Irish peer with a house in the town who could be relied upon to add weight to civic occasions. In accepting the mace and badge on the town's behalf, the mayor hinted at the delicacy with which he had handled Merton's offer when raising it with his colleagues. He told them only that he had received a letter from 'a gentleman', thus avoiding any temptation for councillors to decline the gifts based on bygone hostilities. In his own speech, Merton alluded to the health problems that dogged him as a commissioner, claimed credit for little and spoke only in vague terms of old quarrels. Passing round the loving cup, he hoped that 'instead of envy, malice and all uncharitableness, they would have shining forth in the future a most kindly and dovelike affection.' [5] This was a new, almost statesmanlike Merton, using this very public occasion to acknowledge the past without raking over it. Seizing the moment, he urged the assembled council to be bold in their ambitions and press ahead with the undercliff drive. His remarks were well timed: this latest attempt to resurrect the scheme came two days after Sir Joseph Bazalgette's funeral.

The couple's gifts received a great deal of publicity, with the donors, naturally, at the centre of the fuss. A Wolverhampton newspaper printed a potted biography of Merton, which soon found its way into the *Bournemouth Guardian*. It refers to his ironmaster father, his aborted medical studies and his stint in Batley but makes no mention of the Scottish Amicable. It also contains the first known statement of his links to the Shropshire Coteses, bringing an extra shine to the mace and badge. The piece has all the hallmarks of Merton trying to consolidate his back story, but it needed some refinement for inclusion in *Home and Abroad*. The reference to Batley is dropped, while his relationship to the Shropshire Coteses is changed from 'cousin in a direct line' to the more generic 'kinsman'.[6] As it so happened, a distant relative of that family came to Bournemouth twice in 1891. Rev. Charles Cotes (1848–1896), a fourth cousin once removed of the Woodcote squire, attended Bert's twenty-first birthday dinner in September and Clarie's wedding three months later. While his presence adds a layer of intrigue to Merton's claims of descent from the gentry, it may have started as no more than his namesake checking into the Royal Bath as an everyday guest. It is easy to imagine a conversation about shared ancestry, although there is little to suggest that the Shropshire squire ever confirmed the family connection.[7]

With Bournemouth in a state of incorporation euphoria, a chance soon arose for Merton and the council to display their new-found rapport. The town's doctors, themselves swept up in the mood, had agreed to host the British Medical Association's 1891 conference. It was an opportunity for the borough to show off, albeit at the risk of playing to its own stereotype. 'We have no staple article in Bournemouth except the medical profession,' Merton once said of what was often a mixed blessing.[8] While the town's hotels profited from wealthy health seekers, some of them loved the place so much that they made it their home. Furthermore, these incomers expected things to stay as they found them and often put up the strongest resistance to change. Merton had no truck with that: 'One of the remarks frequently made was that, by my suggested improvements, I should drive all the invalids away. Well, a very good job, too, as it was not invalids that were wanted in particular.' [9] Regardless of the pros and cons, Bournemouth's reputation made it a good place for a thousand doctors to discuss ailments and cures.

The town faced strong competition, with Portsmouth, Scarborough and

Torquay all trying to woo the BMA their way. Some saw Bournemouth's triumph as a reward for pushing ahead with incorporation, but the new railway also helped. Overjoyed, the council gave the doctors their full backing. Venues were booked, banquets organised and garden parties arranged, as the town worked hard to make the conference a success. Merton, who was one of the first to spot the opportunities on offer, donated 200 guineas to an appeal fund set up to support the event. Once again, he left no one in doubt about the extent of his wealth. To avoid a repeat of earlier disputes, the council asked the Royal Bath, the Highcliffe Mansions and the Mont Dore to submit tenders for a civic reception. The Mont Dore won the business, an apt choice given its status as the hydropathic hotel par excellence. As if to salve Merton's disappointment, the council voted to reopen the undercliff drive debate on the same day as awarding the contract.

The Royal Bath held a garden party during the conference and hosted the BMA's official banquet. The latter boasted a series of *tableaux vivants* arranged by Bert. The garden gathering, although dampened by rain, featured a giant pavilion decorated with Merton's usual panache. While doormen dressed as beefeaters kept gate-crashers at bay, the delighted doctors were treated to singing, poetry and the band of the Grenadier Guards. Several fringe meetings took place at the hotel, too. At one of them, mind-reading artiste Alfred Capper (1858–1921) submitted his skills to the scrutiny of medical science. Capper liked to call his subjects 'mediums' but laid no claims to conversations with the dead. Merton counted him as a friend yet could see no point in a gift that went little further than finding pins hidden in clothing. Capper demonstrated the feat to the family several times, with Ella the most susceptible to his probing. The doctors' verdict was not made public.

The BMA's visit was Bournemouth's first serious venture into the conference market. Hotels enjoyed a bumper four days, boosted by a large contingent from the London press. *Punch* magazine made hay with the event, placing a thinly disguised Merton at the heart of a comic caper in which their reporter plays a bewildered tourist. Arriving in town with the conference in full swing, the *Punch* man is mistaken for an eminent doctor when he turns up at the Royal Bath. The manager, grovelling and attentive, shows him upstairs to one of their best rooms, but the proprietor is summoned after a confusion about luggage. Enter Mr Norfolk Capes, F.R.G.S., P.R.B.H.[*], who also mistakes the unwitting guest for their expected VIP. Capes fawns in apology and offers free tickets for an evening concert and a private table in the *salle à manger*. The dinner is superb – Christchurch salmon, Poole pickles, Boscombe beef and Bournemouth beans, all washed down with Corfe Castle coffee. Only when the guest is introduced to a group of real doctors does the mix-up finally resolve itself.

---

[*] P.R.B.H = Proprietor of the Royal Bath Hotel

38 Merton, in the guise of Norfolk Capes, takes care of an 'un-illustrious visitor' in these cartoons from Punch. *The use of 'Welcome the coming, speed the parting guest' predates its appearance in Bram Stoker's* Dracula *by six years. Stoker stayed at the Royal Bath in 1898 – a year after his most famous book was published – but it is not known if he did so beforehand.* (From *Punch*, 8 August 1891)

Although Merton's pretensions are the butt of the joke, the article does him no great harm. Capes allows the visitor to keep his room for the night and accepts his explanations with good grace. The flimsy alias suggests that many *Punch* readers knew of Merton's foibles, a point underlined by an illustration showing the impeccably dressed Capes standing in front of a clutch of paintings and statues. Those who spotted the parody would have smiled at the string of letters after his name, but it did nothing to dim the real-life hotelier's love of them. A few months later, he became one of the first members of the Japan Society, a body founded to promote the country's culture. His interest in Japanese art made him a natural choice for membership, which came with the letters 'M.J.S.' to use whenever required.[10]

The *Punch* caricature confirmed Merton as the familiar face of Bournemouth's best-known hotel. With respect for him riding high, Clarie's wedding took on the air of a civic gathering.[11] Sir George Meyrick sent a gift – a clear sign of status – and the mayor, ex-mayor and other notables mingled with family and friends at the reception. The presence of Merton's sister Clara is proof, too, of their ongoing bond. Even brother Samuel sent a pair of china figures to the happy couple, the only evidence of any contact with Merton after his move to Bournemouth.[12] All seemed set fair as Clarie embarked on married life. Her husband, Joseph Drew (1861–1919), served as a lieutenant in the Middlesex Volunteer Regiment and was the son of a police superintendent. His uncle had interests in the hotel trade, further cementing the bonds between the two families. And yet, despite these good omens, the marriage was to end in disaster.

For Merton, things were going well for the time being. The Royal Bath continued to welcome the great and the good by the dozen, with Prince Albert of Belgium (1875–1934) and Sir Charles Hallé (1819–1895) among its guests in the early 1890s. Oscar Wilde (1854–1900), who stayed at the hotel during the first run of *Lady Windermere's Fan*, reportedly left a glowing review in the hotel's visitors' book: 'You have built and fitted up, with the greatest beauty and elegance, a palace and filled it with gems of art for the use and benefit of the public at hotel prices.' [13] While a magazine article valuing the artworks at £300,000 is fanciful, Wilde was one of many to admire the collection. That said, a letter written from the Royal Bath by Pre-Raphaelite founder and Royal Academy president John Everett Millais (1829–1896) made no mention of its paintings. He saved his praise for Lady Hallé's violin playing, heard through an open window while strolling in the hotel garden.

Of all Merton's guests, the actor Henry Irving was by far the most important to him. He claims to have known him since the 1860s, when one was an aspiring thespian, the other an ambitious salesman. Irving's first known visit to the Royal Bath came in the spring of 1892, which Merton missed due to a holiday in the Caribbean. The actor was joined on that occasion by Ellen Terry, his best-known leading lady, whom Merton considered an even better actress than the illustrious Sarah Bernhardt (1844–1923). Yet this is faint praise compared to his adoration of Irving. 'A friendship such as existed between us is exceptional as between two men,' he wrote in the chapter of *Home and Abroad* devoted to his idol. Its fifty pages rejoice in 'the wizard depth of his lambent, searching eyes' – Irving was famously myopic – and his 'captivating smile'.[14] Merton refers to the Royal Bath as the actor's 'harbour of refuge and rest', but the Bournemouth climate did the great man little good during his stay in 1892. He caught a cold, lost his voice and ended up in Hastings to recuperate. Even so, his patronage added to the glow of prestige radiating from the hotel.

The Royal Bath's reputation as the haunt of celebrity gave Merton a platform to express his views. He targeted the town's Winter Gardens, a failed venture derided by some locals as 'the cucumber frame'. The council wanted to buy it for use as a concert hall and tourist rendezvous, but Merton demanded something better. 'Its position is in a hole,' he declared, 'and its entire surroundings are lugubrious and distressful.' [15] He proposed a new pavilion near the pier that would 'out-rival every other seaside resort in Europe.' Some might have questioned his motives – the Winter Gardens were next door to the Royal Exeter Hotel – and yet he was joining a debate that would drag on for more than a hundred years. When a public vote came out against the purchase, the council decided to lease the building instead as a venue for its planned municipal orchestra.[16] The outcome left the trickier pavilion question unanswered. As with the undercliff drive, the scheme was forced to compete for time at council meetings with debates about stray dogs and rogue cabmen. Incorporation may have meant more power, but some detected a lack of vigour in wielding it.

After returning from a summer break in Switzerland and Italy, Merton threw himself into the debate about the town's future. He came back in the middle of the posturing leading up to the 1892 council elections. With no thoughts of standing himself, he agreed to support the candidature of Nelson Jenkins (1850–1932), a local builder who, as a Liberal, did not share his opinions on national politics.[17] The two men did, however, hold similar views on the pavilion and undercliff drive. The fact that Jenkins chose to stand in the same ward as Joseph Cutler may also have swayed Merton's decision. His old adversary, a vocal opponent of the drive, was making his first pitch for a council seat since his loss in 1890. After threatening to quit Bournemouth in the wake of that humbling, he changed his mind, wrote his memoirs and donated an inscribed copy of the same to a bemused council.

In the run-up to the poll, a leaflet backing Jenkins, signed by 'A Consistent Conservative', began to circulate in the town. One person, calling themselves 'A Sorrowful and Disgusted Tory', was in no doubt that Merton was its author.[18] They wrote to accuse him of making a pitch for the mayoralty and of endorsing Jenkins' candidacy in return for securing his support. Cutler, a committed Conservative himself, might well have agreed with these sentiments, but Merton brushed them aside. He wrote to a local newspaper to deny the claims and press the case for a united approach to tackling the issues facing the borough. 'We ought not to recognise Conservative, Radical, Protestant, Non-conformist or Roman Catholic in the town council,' he proclaimed. 'We should speak with one voice, and as one man, and utter one word, and that word should be *Advance Bournemouth*!' [19]

This rousing rebuttal made no comment about his alleged mayoral ambitions. They must, in any case, have seemed hopeless to those unfamiliar with the finer points of civic legislation. Councils, by custom, chose a leader from within their own ranks, but there was no rule to say that a mayor had to be an elected councillor. Indeed, Merton says he was invited to take on the role in 1891 and 1892, declining only when the council refused to cooperate with him on the undercliff drive. He reveals none of the details surrounding these invitations, but his name was never discussed in public. Besides, the council chose Henry Newlyn in 1892, a benign figure with a track record of dependability. Nelson Jenkins, meanwhile, triumphed over Joseph Cutler, leaving the latter to gain a seat a year later via an uncontested ward. Jenkins, for his part, felt no obligation to Merton for supporting his election efforts that year. He claimed to be one of the few men in Bournemouth prepared to stand up to him and once threatened to remove his scaffolding from the Royal Bath after a dispute about an estimate.[20]

While it must have been galling to see Henry Newlyn wearing the mayoral

THE ART OF A SALESMAN

badge donated by Annie, Merton could have found little fault with his rival's maiden speech. Newlyn stressed his support for the undercliff drive, even though his many years as a commissioner and councillor had seen much talk result in little action. Merton offered the new mayor clear-sighted advice from his vantage point outside the council. He sent a string of letters to the newspapers, using 'Advance Bournemouth' as his two-word slogan. These included a swipe at 'the well-meaning persons who come here for their own health and pleasure and, after settling down, seem to imagine that Bournemouth and all its natural beauties were made expressly for *them*.' The masses, he made clear, did not feature in his vision for the town. Weymouth, Margate, Southend and Blackpool would do for them. He went on: 'The tradesmen of Bournemouth do not and never did cater for *visitors* (I don't refer to *residents*) otherwise than the elite. Certainly not for "cheap trippers". It is like trying to mix oil and water – they won't mix!' [21]

The substance of his letters sum up Merton's life philosophy: success demands investment, while stagnation awaits those who sit back and do nothing. The council, he argued, needed to spend money on a promenade, a pavilion and on public parks. Sir George Meyrick, the landowner most affected by these ideas, was said to be ready to negotiate. As Merton urged the ratepayers to catch the wind of this goodwill, his letters brought forth a rush of indignant replies. Others saw wisdom in his thinking and were willing to voice their support. 'We want such men of ideas to represent us as Mr Cotes,' wrote one. 'A thousand pities for Bournemouth he is not the chairman of some council committee.' [22]

39 Henry Newlyn wearing the mayoral badge given to the borough by Annie. The chain was made up of individual links donated by Bournemouth's first councillors. Newlyn had been the manager at the Guards' Club in Pall Mall before taking over the Exeter Hotel from his father – a former mayor of Christchurch – in 1876. Merton arrived at the Bath Hotel a month later. (Bournemouth Library)

Merton's high profile and skilled letter writing saw him emerge as the uncrowned cheerleader of the town's progressives. Yet he remained an outsider at a time when there was a new mayor committed to delivering change. The early signs for Newlyn were good, as the council sought powers to extend the pier and build a pavilion at its shore end. Better still, Sir George Meyrick, who owned a large stretch of the Bournemouth foreshore, was said to be in favour of the undercliff drive. With much of his property close to the unstable cliffs, he had a vested interest in its completion. The drive's supporters, pointing to a recent collapse, played on its value as a cliff protection measure. Its opponents claimed that water from above was causing the problems, and that, by scouring the drive, the sea would dump shingle on the sands.

Matters moved ahead regardless. By the late summer of 1893, the borough surveyor had drawn up proposals for a drive costing £60,000. The council sent the plans to the landowners, but Newlyn's mayoralty ended with no further progress. Merton says he refused another invitation to become mayor that year, citing the same reasons as before. Dr George Hirons (1844–1927), an undercliff drive agnostic, got the job instead, and the project soon became entangled with the council's bigger ambition to gain control of the cliffs. By doing that, they could build drives and footpaths on the overcliff and create public open spaces. Meyrick, however, refused to grant them a lease without a firm commitment to build an undercliff drive. When talks reached an impasse, a council committee recommended abandoning the project. By the beginning of 1894, the scheme was once again teetering on the brink, but Merton was then in no position to fight for the cause. He and Annie were heading for the Mediterranean, ready to write the next instalment of their travel adventures.

Notes:

1. Taken from Merton's scrapbooks.
2. *Evening Star* (Washington), 5 July 1890.
3. Taken from Merton's scrapbooks.
4. *Home and Abroad*, p. 560. The cards were day passes to the diplomatic galleries at the US Congress.
5. ibid., p. 74.
6. *Bournemouth Guardian*, 18 April 1891 and *Home and Abroad*, p. 68.
7. On p. 945 of *Home and Abroad*, Merton transcribes a letter from Rev. W. Eastwick Cotes, who – like Rev. Charles Cotes – was a fourth cousin once removed of the Woodcote squire. It reads: 'I well remember my cousin, Charles Cecil Cotes [the incumbent squire], speaking of you in terms of eulogy.' As the two clergymen were first cousins, one suspects that Merton added 'Cecil' to his transcription to enhance his links to the Shropshire family.

8. *Home and Abroad*, p. 74.
9. ibid., p. 133.
10. Merton was one of c. 100 original members of the Japan Society, not 'one of the eight original promoters' as stated on p. 296 of *Home and Abroad*. Annie was elected as a member a few months later.
11. Laura Cotes, the 8-year-old daughter of Rev. Charles Cotes, was one of Clarie's bridesmaids.
12. Samuel was sixty-eight and 'living on his own means' in Birkenhead at the time of the 1891 census. In 1881, he was working as a draper's assistant in Liverpool.
13. This oft-repeated quote comes from a syndicated article written by the journalist Phebe Lankester in 1893. Wilde stayed at the Royal Bath on at least three occasions, the earliest in 1878 while a student at Oxford. In 1891, he entered only his name and address in the visitors' book, while in 1892 he wrote: 'All charmed at the beauty and comfort of the hotel.' Mrs Lankester may, then, have been referring to another visit at an unknown date.
14. The Irving chapter covers pp. 757–811 of *Home and Abroad*.
15. *Bournemouth Guardian*, 21 November 1891.
16. The municipal orchestra, under the baton of Dan Godfrey, later became the Bournemouth Symphony Orchestra. Godfrey's father conducted the band of the Grenadier Guards when it played outside the Royal Bath during the visit of the Prince of Wales in 1890.
17. Jenkins carried out the building work at the Royal Bath in 1887/8.
18. Taken from Merton's scrapbooks.
19. *Bournemouth Guardian*, 5 November 1892.
20. This is according to Carl Jenkins' history of his family's building firm. He wrote: 'Sir Merton Russell-Cotes ... liked to see himself as a demi-God, and Nelson was one of the few who never feared him.'
21. Taken from Merton's scrapbooks.
22. ibid.

10

MAYOR

The couple's latest trip abroad began in February 1894, lasted four months and took them to Egypt and the Holy Land. Now in their late fifties and grandparents – Clarie gave birth to a daughter in September – the itinerary brought the usual discomforts. Annie bore the brunt, with a fall from her horse forcing them to curtail part of the tour.[1] Merton went down with liver congestion on the Nile and a bronchial cold in Jerusalem but still managed to camp in the desert and ride through a sandstorm. Egypt was not to his liking, where heat, haggling and an overdose of tombs coloured his opinions and depressed his spirits. Constant demands for backhanders – the ubiquitous 'baksheesh' – also annoyed him. He put his cash to better use by acquiring 'an historical and invaluable' lapis lazuli necklace from a museum in Cairo.[2]

When they reached the Holy Land, places familiar from cherished Bible stories began to stir his interest. A contemporary fascination with biblical archaeology seeps into *Home and Abroad*, most notably in his account of a visit to the Garden Tomb in Jerusalem. With no doubts that Christ had been laid to rest there, he and Annie had subscribed to a fund set up to buy the site in the months before their departure. Seeing the tomb at first hand was one of the highlights of the trip. Elsewhere, although awestruck by the grandeur of the Muslim shrines, many of the sacred Christian sites left him in despair. Christ's birthplace, he complained, 'is reduced to little better than a penny peepshow or a farcical grotto.'[3]

As always, Merton wanted to share his experiences with people back home. While laid up with his cold, he wrote a piece for *The World* magazine about the ceremony of the Holy Fire in Jerusalem. An annual spectacle witnessed by thousands, the event sees a burst of flame emerging from another tomb claiming to be that of Christ. According to *Home and Abroad*, the magazine's editor described his account as 'one of the finest pieces of word-painting that I have ever read.'[4] That may be so, but its mere publication cemented Merton's reputation as a traveller. He emphasised the point by sending a letter from Constantinople to the Bournemouth press on their way back. 'We were received as guests of the Sultan,' he wrote – at once demonstrating his importance and heralding their imminent return to England.[5]

The couple arrived home in July 1894 after a brief stay on Anglesey. Nothing had changed on the undercliff drive in their absence, with the scheme now on indefinite hold while the council looked for other ways to protect the cliffs. To add to the frustration, Scarborough was soon to vote in favour of a more expensive drive than the one proposed for Bournemouth. Wyndham Portal bemoaned this latest delay: 'I hear expressions of great disappointment from visitors of distinction at finding the impracticality of driving along the sea coast. I am told that the number of carriage gentry is very few, comparatively, at Bournemouth. My astonishment is that, as matters now are, there are so many.'[6]

Portal's remarks reflect the commercial imperatives faced by his company. The London and South Western had committed £10,000 towards the cost of the drive as it sought to maximise its return on the direct line. Such an outlay needed more than carriage gentry travelling on trains to pay dividends, but some visitors felt the town was already suffering from a railway influx. One hotel guest wrote to Merton to air his disgust: 'This year I find all the amusements of a low-class fair upon the sands – merry-go-rounds, swings, dancing platforms, besides booths of all sorts. I cannot think that the advent of 'Arry and 'Arriet will be conducive to the prosperity either of your hotel or of your town.'[7] Sir George Meyrick pressed the council for byelaws to control a situation that was threatening to get out of hand. Merton, with the problem on his doorstep, backed his landlord to the hilt as they worked in tandem to find a solution. The answer they came up with would, in time, prove embarrassing for Meyrick and calamitous for his tenant. In the short term, with the town ignorant of their intentions, the mayoral stars were aligning very much in Merton's favour.

With Portal's comments raising doubts about his firm's investment in the undercliff drive, the town's progressives took matters into their own hands. After years of fruitless talking, they wanted a man of action to lead the council. They also needed someone who was trusted by the railway company and who had the ear of the landowners to revive the seafront negotiations. Merton kept to the sidelines of these discussions but remained alert to the opportunities on offer. A month before the council elections, he sent a seemingly innocuous letter to *The Times* in response to an item about growing desert shrubs in the mild climate of Swanage. Describing the same – but bigger – plants in his own garden, he crammed his reply with marketing soundbites for Bournemouth and the Royal Bath. In the space of 200 words, he threw in the hotel, the pier opening, the BMA visit, his trip to California

40 Beach amusements near Bournemouth pier, 1890s. The summer season became increasingly important to the town, helped by fast and cheap rail access from London. However, carts parked by beach traders near the Royal Bath forced Merton to take drastic action to prevent disturbance to the hotel. (Bournemouth Library)

and a sly plug for a local photography firm.

This relentless promotion, once the cause of so much controversy, now gave him an advantage. If the town needed to sell itself to prosper, then here was a man with a proven ability to do exactly that. Many now arrived at the same conclusion: with Merton as mayor, Bournemouth stood the best chance of competing with Brighton, Scarborough, Torquay and the rest. Doubters may have pointed to recent events elsewhere as a warning to choose a safer pair of hands. In Weymouth, after a row over the use of public money for entertaining, the mayor had resigned in a fit of pique in the heat of a council meeting. Bournemouth, though, was unlikely to have that problem. The council wanted someone who would part with his own money, not theirs, and Merton was always willing to do that.

The deal was done in the run-up to the mayoral anointment in November. A group of councillors met a week earlier – 'a secret conclave', some called it – to ensure they had enough support.[8] Merton had already agreed to accept the role subject to what he called 'qualified conditions necessitated by the circumstances of his own health.'[9] He waited in the wings of the municipal chamber while the council went through the process of proposing, seconding and voting. Councillors spoke of how he had done his duty as a commissioner until his health broke down, and how he entertained the Lord Mayor of London and the BMA at his own expense. He was a man, they said, who had brought Bournemouth to the attention of the world. They cited the Marquess of Bute and the Earl of Warwick as distinguished, unelected residents who had served as mayor in other towns.

The vote was unanimous, a coronation not an election. Now was the time for council unity, a public show of support for the man carrying the hopes of many. Some councillors, without doubt, privately questioned the wisdom of the appointment, as did many outside the chamber. One resident vented his anger in the *Bournemouth Observer*: 'Is it not a shame and a disgrace to the town council itself, and an insult to the ratepayers as the electing body, that out of twenty-four elected representatives, there is, by implication in this transaction, not one capable of holding the chairmanship of our own local government?' [10] Merton's poor health and mediocre record as a commissioner also counted against him, concerns he tried to address in his acceptance speech. He harked back to his work on the sanitary hospital, the opposition against it and the poor health he endured as a result. For that reason, he had been reluctant to accept an office that he felt 'almost incompetent to fulfil.' [11]

So began what Merton describes as one of the most active years of his life. In an inspired move, he chose Henry Newlyn as his deputy – not a natural ally, but a man with ample experience of council machinations. Previous incumbents had chosen the outgoing mayor for the role – meaning Dr Hirons in Merton's case – and it is not clear why he preferred to appoint his business rival instead. Perhaps he kept Newlyn close in the hope of making life less difficult for himself. In any event, the press greeted the new dawn with optimism. 'It may be expected,' wrote *Truth* magazine, 'that during the next year or two Bournemouth will go ahead conspicuously.' [12]

One of Merton's first duties was to take his seat as chief magistrate of the borough's petty sessions. In a sign of the health conditions under which he took office, he offered the position to the most senior magistrate on the bench when he entered court for the first time. The day's proceedings included a charge against a member of the town's regatta committee, who stood accused of wounding the manageress of the Belle Vue Hotel while fooling around with a starting pistol. Bizarre though it was, the case set a bar of normality that Merton's mayoralty seldom reached. A storm swept across southern England over the next few days, claiming lives and damaging buildings from Cornwall to Kent. A large section of the cliffs collapsed near the Royal Bath in a portent of the misfortune that, quite literally, lay just around the corner.

A handful of long-term projects came to fruition in Merton's early weeks in the job. November saw the opening of Meyrick Park, the first of Bournemouth's commons to be converted to leisure use. The result of more than a decade of effort, it featured the town's first public golf course. Merton put on a show to fit the occasion and catered for a host of reporters at his own expense. Meyrick's daughter-in-law performed the opening and struck the first ball but may have squirmed when Merton slipped the undercliff drive

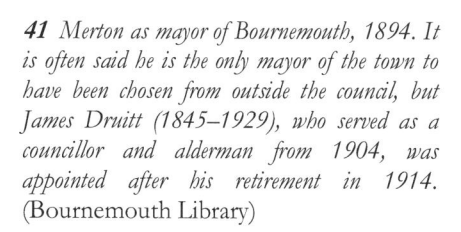

41 Merton as mayor of Bournemouth, 1894. It is often said he is the only mayor of the town to have been chosen from outside the council, but James Druitt (1845–1929), who served as a councillor and alderman from 1904, was appointed after his retirement in 1914. (Bournemouth Library)

into his address of thanks. Still, the day went off with enough razzamatazz to suggest that the council had acted wisely in choosing the new mayor.

Merton started to tackle the burning issues in early December, forging ahead on two fronts. Efforts to secure support for a carriageway through the pleasure gardens soon stalled, but he managed to set up an Undercliff Drive Committee as a first step towards achieving his main objective. Already plagued with anonymous letters from the scheme's opponents, the last thing he needed at this point was a distraction. One arrived in mid-December with the news that Samuel Coates had died in Liverpool's Mill Road infirmary – a hospital run by the local Poor Law guardians. He was seventy-one. How much it affected Merton is hard to tell, but his brother's passing coincided with the disastrous error of judgement that came to dominate his mayoralty. It stoked a controversy to eclipse all that had gone before.

The issue centred on an unremarkable byway called South Road adjacent to the Royal Bath. Earlier that year, Merton had bought the leases to Rothesay, Kildare and Lynwood, three upmarket guest houses running down the hill from the hotel. He changed the name of Rothesay to East Cliff Hall and decided to use it as his main residence. South Road, which ran from the main highway to the overcliff, separated his new home from the Royal Bath. A cul-de-sac for vehicles, it featured a barrier at the sea end to stop unwary carriage drivers from plunging over the cliffs. Others used the road simply to admire the view. With level access to the clifftop from Invalids' Walk, it was the highlight of a pleasant stroll for the able-bodied or an easy trundle for those with bath chairs. About two hundred feet long and thirty feet wide, this tiny road soon became infamous.

In December 1894, and without the council's consent, a drastic

THE ART OF A SALESMAN

42 Lynwood, Kildare and Rothesay, seen here from left to right, were built in the early 1870s. The barrier at the end of South Road is also shown. Rothesay was named after one of the titles of the Prince of Wales, not the home town of Merton's sisters on the Isle of Bute. All three houses were demolished in the 1970s to make way for a car park. (Bournemouth Library)

redevelopment of South Road took place. It reduced its width to seven feet – wide enough for two people walking side-by-side but awkward for a U-turn in a bath chair. The remaining twenty-three feet ended up in the garden of East Cliff Hall. An earth bank bedecked with flowers and shrubs marked the new boundary, topped off with a summer house made of varnished pine and tinted glass. A council lamp post, half buried in the haste to finish the work, protruded from the new rampart like a stunted iron flower. These changes soon attracted notice. Amid discontented murmurings and the rustling of old maps, the council sent the borough surveyor along to investigate. It transpired that Sir George Meyrick had given the go-ahead for the work, with Merton suspected of putting it into effect. South Road was a nuisance for both men, as it had become the focal point of complaints by the Royal Bath's guests about the behaviour of 'Arry and 'Arriet. Beach traders parked their carts in the road overnight, while some people, so it was alleged, were using it as a hidey-hole for all sorts of nocturnal shenanigans. The narrower road was too small for carts, but some observers pointed out that the more secluded layout made the shenanigans a lot easier to carry out. Meyrick distanced himself from the debate as the clamour grew louder, leaving Merton in an awkward position. With a bigger garden and less disturbance to his guests, many believed he had abused his position by commandeering a public right of way.

If his brother's death caused Merton to lose sight of the potential impact of South Road, then the issue made it all the more difficult for him to focus on his goals. With no one willing to compromise, the council had no choice but to instruct its lawyers to consider the legalities of the situation. As a result, when Merton convened the first meeting of the Undercliff Drive Committee, a difficult task became almost impossible. The opposition came prepared to disrupt the process, first by proposing Joseph Cutler as the committee's chairman, then by calling for its immediate dissolution. As paralysis loomed, Merton sought help from Charles Scotter, who was staying at the Royal Bath over Christmas. Scotter suggested that dialogue might work in the scheme's favour and proposed a joint committee of councillors and ratepayers. The railwayman's knighthood in the New Year's honours list added weight to his opinions, but South Road was to block any hope of progress in the months ahead.

Scotter's intervention allowed 1895 to begin in conciliatory mood. After laying on lunch for the council, Merton opened the town's first public library in Old Christchurch Road. This was another project many years in the making. He borrowed the first book – a history of Japan – and urged users to read Shakespeare, Chaucer and Ruskin or, for something lighter, Scott, Dickens and Thackeray. 'Avoid as poison,' he warned, 'the ephemeral and impure literature which at present is emanating from the press.' [13] He opened the Boscombe branch of the library later that day, where budget constraints restricted the offering to a selection of newspapers.[14] While the prestige of these openings offered some relief from the spectre of South Road, another spate of anonymous letters forced Merton to announce that he would burn any received. The council, meanwhile, emboldened by legal opinion that South Road was a right of way, voted to seek redress from Meyrick. As an interim measure, they ordered the surveyor to draw up plans to widen the road to accommodate bath chairs. Matters drifted into abeyance when Meyrick failed to respond.

Merton's opponents now redoubled their efforts to besmirch his reputation. In mid-January, he and Annie hosted a children's fancy dress carnival at the Winter Gardens, a charity event that ought not to have caused any problems. Merton, dressed in his civic finery and enthroned on his official chair, watched a procession of fairies, witches and pirates file past his podium. He smiled when one awestruck little girl mistook him for a king, but in other circumstances he could be pernickety about titles and forms of address. In one of his first acts in office, he asked the town clerk to find out if other boroughs addressed their mayors as 'His Worship', 'The Right Worshipful' or some variant of the two.[15] The earnest and conflicting answers received from Canterbury, Dover, Liverpool and Manchester caused some hilarity when read out at a council meeting. Dr Hirons, the jilted deputy, suggested that the people of Bournemouth would have no such doubts about the mayor's appellation. 'I am sure they know how to address the chief magistrate of this borough,' he remarked.[16]

Those who attended the carnival agreed that it was a great success. Others, including Dr Hirons, were less concerned with the children's enjoyment and more with the mayor's alleged misuse of the Winter Gardens. Merton had booked the venue until seven o'clock, leaving no time for the staff to prepare for a concert scheduled for that same evening. The manager had spoken to his contact on the council, who advised him to cancel the concert provided he received ten pounds to cover the costs. Merton paid up and the carnival went ahead, an arrangement seized upon by his detractors. They argued that he had again exceeded his powers by failing to seek formal approval for the cancellation. Moreover, they objected to his handling of the entrance fee levied on parents to watch the carnival from the gallery. Merton had sent the money to local hospitals, but only after deducting the ten pounds paid to the council.

Petty quibbling or point of principle, the carnival affair divided opinion. Merton, overwhelmed with the stress of it all, stayed away from the council chamber on doctor's advice but left a moral dilemma behind him. A row broke out over the fate of the money at the next council meeting, with the debate taking on a significance far beyond that of the ten pounds. It became a de facto vote of confidence in the mayor. Merton's supporters, thinking him hard done by, wanted the cash to go to the hospitals as he intended. His critics thought that to do so would exonerate him from blame by giving the impression that it was wrong to charge him in the first place. Nothing separated the two sides when it came to a show of hands. It was left to Henry Newlyn, as the deputy mayor, to settle the issue with his casting vote. He sent the money to the hospitals. Even so, it did little more than paper over the cracks of the growing strength of feeling.

In mid-February, suffering from what he called a 'severe nerve breakdown', Merton sought respite from his troubles by taking a three-month break in Germany and Italy.[17] His absence meant missing out on Henry Irving's latest visit to the Royal Bath, which came just a few weeks before the actor received a knighthood. Merton wrote to congratulate him as soon as he got back, but this was one of the few pieces of good news that greeted his return to Bournemouth.[18] Progress on the undercliff drive had stalled again, and the council's patience on South Road had run out. They issued Meyrick with an ultimatum: either meet to discuss a compromise, or the council would take steps to restore the road to its former width. As weeks went by with no resolution, some councillors demanded a deadline to bring the affair to an end.

Merton resumed his mayoral duties in early June with the issue still unresolved. He returned in time to lead the civic welcome for the Royal Counties Agricultural Society, which was holding its annual show in the town. It was an event on a par with the BMA conference four years earlier. The council set aside a 27-acre site near the main station, a sign of the large pockets of land still undeveloped in Bournemouth at the time. Over a thousand competitors paraded their livestock and farming inventions before the judges, and many thousands more came to watch the show over the course of its four days. The occasion demanded that the mayor and his councillors presented a united front, as Prince Henry of Battenberg (1858–1896) – husband of the Queen's youngest daughter, Princess Beatrice – was to visit the show. For Merton, briefly free of troublesome distractions, it saw a return to form.

The Royal Bath hosted a civic lunch and the Society's formal dinner, both of which Prince Henry attended. Merton established a good rapport with his guest. The Prince took tea with him in private, planted an oak tree in the hotel grounds, posed for a photograph and engaged in surprisingly candid conversation. 'It is marvellous how the Anglo-Saxon race have colonised the world,' Merton remembers him saying in an unguarded moment. 'Not only that but the way in which they have done it, the justice, equity, and good results that have appertained to their colonisation. This, Germany has never accomplished and never will. The Germans do not understand how to colonise.'[19] If these remarks seem odd coming from a former officer in the Prussian army, then they came with a keen sense of irony. When Merton

43 Merton (back left) and Annie with Prince Henry of Battenberg (seated) and his aides. The Royal Counties Agricultural Society, of which the Prince was president, agreed to hold its show in Bournemouth during the previous mayor's tenure. The town also hosted the show in 1888. (From *Home and Abroad*)

expressed the town's heartfelt affection for their royal guest, the Prince's reply surprised him: 'I am afraid, Mr Mayor, that perhaps it is because I am the son-in-law of the Queen more than for myself.' [20] Six months later, Merton felt confident enough in his bond with the Prince to implore him not to join the campaign against the Ashanti in West Africa. 'I wrote to him at Balmoral, pointing out to him the awful dangers and risk accruing for a European from jungle fever.' [21] The Prince replied saying that duty compelled him to go.

A week after Prince Henry spoke about the mayor's popularity, the men of the council were sharpening their knives ready for an attack on South Road. Alderman J. H. Moore (1842–1898), a civil engineer and the chief belligerent, declared that Meyrick had 'stolen' it and was now playing them for fools.[22] In a febrile atmosphere, he backed a motion to restore the road to its old width if Meyrick failed to meet a council deputation within one month. Stuck in a vice between the council and his landlord, Merton panicked. He refused to put the motion to a vote and begged his colleagues to put themselves in his position. The alterations to the road, for which he now admitted responsibility, were no more than an attempt, he said, to curb the nuisances affecting his business. He asked them to consider making a new road further down the hill and warned of legal action if they acted without Meyrick's consent. Firm in his refusal to consider the motion, Merton tried to vacate the chair in Newlyn's favour. The town clerk intervened, pointing out that no one else could chair the meeting while the mayor remained in the chamber. Merton stormed out in disgust. As some councillors moved to adjourn the session, Newlyn insisted on pressing the vote as a point of order. The motion carried, leaving Meyrick with one month to respond.

The *Bournemouth Observer* delivered a damning verdict on the proceedings: 'It is more than childish for the mayor to throw at the heads of the council the threat of protracted litigation and the implied threat of so influencing the mind of Sir George Meyrick that he will probably cease to be the liberal benefactor which, as our principal ground landlord, times past have declared him.' [23] Merton, trying to head off the furore, gave his side of the story in the next edition. 'Neither can I, nor will I, put a resolution having for its object a direct censure upon the lord of the manor for the action he has taken in protecting his own property, and also his lessees, from a repetition of intolerable and immoral nuisances.' [24] Alderman Moore sent a stinging rebuttal homing in on Merton's inconsistencies. 'Previous to the last council meeting,' he wrote, 'the mayor stated he had nothing whatever to do with taking possession of this land and that it was all the work of Sir George Meyrick. At the late council meeting he completely changed his front and said he had more to do with it than Sir George. Indeed, he was at the bottom of it all, and I doubt not he had good reasons which compelled him to disclose this fact and accuse himself of the worst of municipal sins.' [25]

Stung by the attack, Merton referred the matter to his solicitors just as Meyrick signalled his willingness to negotiate. The council set up a committee to consider the issue, including ideas for alternative access to the East Cliff. The ratepayers, insisting on a swifter outcome, demanded a public meeting. Merton's refusal even to consider their request failed to stop the Town's Interest Committee calling one themselves. He chose not to attend but sent a letter defending his position and outlining his own proposals. It was met with loud hissing when read out. Many of those present urged the council to restore the road to its former width and threatened councillors with retribution at the ballot box if they failed to do so. As speaker after speaker rose to condemn Merton and demand action, one of them summed up their overwhelming message to the council: 'Take your men and carts down there and remove the obstruction.' [26]

Merton left for Scotland, his nerves shredded. Meyrick declared South Road to be more trouble than it was worth but was reluctant to undo the work already carried out. The Town's Interest Committee then landed a killer blow. They unearthed an old map denoting the road as a public highway, removing all doubt that the council should act. Merton, deluged with spiteful letters, sent an impassioned plea to the council from Girvan, where he had taken refuge with Annie. He said he wanted to find a solution and offered a slice of the Royal Bath's garden as a sweetener. Newlyn urged his colleagues to meet him halfway, but Joseph Cutler was in no mood for compromise. He tabled a motion to restore South Road to its former state at once. Ten councillors voted in favour, nine against. But for one abstention, Cutler's proposal would have been thrown out on Newlyn's casting vote. As it was, the council had chosen to humiliate their mayor by sending in the men and carts. Having made their decision, they wasted no time in carrying it out.

Notes:

1. Ella and Bert joined their parents for part of this trip. They planned to travel from Jerusalem to Beirut via Palestine, but Annie hurt her wrist in the fall soon after they started. She and Merton returned to Jerusalem and made the journey to Beirut by rail and sea.
2. *Home and Abroad*, p. 600.
3. ibid., pp. 601–2.
4. An item in the *Bournemouth Graphic* of 14 February 1907 stated that William Holman Hunt based his painting *The Miracle of the Holy Fire* on Merton's description of the ceremony. No other source has been found to back up this claim.
5. *Home and Abroad*, p. 631.
6. *Bournemouth Observer*, 25 August 1894.
7. *Bournemouth Guardian*, 1 September 1894. The writer was a lawyer with Morten,

Cutler & Co., the firm Merton describes as 'my solicitors' in the case of *The Watchers Asleep*.
8. *Bournemouth Observer*, 10 November 1894.
9. ibid., 7 November 1894.
10. ibid., 10 November 1894.
11. ibid.
12. Quoted by the *Birmingham Daily Post*, 15 November 1894.
13. *Home and Abroad*, pp. 104–8. The first library was in a building leased from Joseph Cutler.
14. Some sources state that Merton opened the new School of Science and Art at Poole Hill in January 1895, but he was there to present prizes. It opened in September 1893, when he was one of several people to lend pictures to an inaugural art exhibition.
15. *Home and Abroad*, p. 83.
16. *Bournemouth Guardian*, 9 February 1895.
17. *Home and Abroad*, p. 124.
18. Merton's letter to Irving is held by the V&A Theatre and Performance Archives. It puts his absence down to 'the accursed "Grip"' (i.e. the effects of influenza), rather than the nerve problems referred to in *Home and Abroad*.
19. *Home and Abroad*, p. 348.
20. ibid., p. 346.
21. ibid., p. 347.
22. *Bournemouth Observer*, 19 June 1895.
23. ibid.
24. ibid., 22 June 1895.
25. *Bournemouth Guardian*, 29 June 1895.
26. *Bournemouth Observer*, 27 July 1895.

11

EXHIBITOR

With Merton still in Scotland, the council put its plans into effect within hours of the vote. It left no time to mount a legal challenge to stop them. In the hope of avoiding a circus, the assistant surveyor gathered his troops on the East Cliff at half-past two in the morning. They were blessed with a still night and a bright moon, its light boosted by the rays from the half-buried lamp post. A handful of spectators arrived expecting a confrontation, but no one from the house or the hotel bothered to stir at such an ungodly hour. Fifty-six men, along with a dozen horses and carts, set to work on the earth bank with their picks and shovels. The first cartload of earth went tumbling down the cliffs as the pier clock chimed three. The men uprooted Merton's plants and took them away to use in the pleasure gardens; they loaded his summer house onto a trolley and wheeled it to the council yard; they even ripped out the gates of East Cliff Hall when they were found to lie within the confines of the old road. As dawn broke and word spread, a crowd formed on the clifftop. People going about their daily business went out of their way to witness the scene. To a host of jeers, a policeman turned up and started to take the workers' names. The men carried on regardless, but the operation took much longer than expected. At ten o'clock, after checking and re-checking the road's width, the assistant surveyor declared himself satisfied. It was the cue for some onlookers to break ranks and march up and down the restored highway. Others organised a whip-round for the exhausted men. A mood of celebration hung in the air, as the townsfolk revelled in their glorious victory.

From Dublin to Dover and from Glasgow to Guernsey, newspapers reported the final act of the South Road farce. From a distance, the tale of civic embarrassment, popular revolt and mayoral come-uppance made for light relief. 'Extraordinary Scene at Bournemouth,' ran one headline. 'Destruction of the Mayor's Summer House,' crowed another.[1] Meyrick's solicitors preferred to call it a 'moonlighting expedition', but their client let

44 Aside from the parked cars, this 1962 photograph shows the area around South Road much as it would have been in Merton's day. The Royal Bath's garden is in the foreground, with the hotel to the right. Rothesay – or East Cliff Hall as it was known in 1895 – is the first house beyond the cars. (Bournemouth Library)

the matter drop amid widespread support for the action.[2]

South Road, the road to nowhere, proved terminal for Merton's mayoralty. He never returned to the council chamber, but the erratic nature of his occasional contributions from beyond it offers a clue to his mental strife. On the one hand, he donated a silver cup for an annual bicycle race in aid of the Royal Victoria Hospital; on the other, he pledged only one guinea to the Boscombe regatta. In a letter to the organising committee apologising for the small sum, he pointed to the hundreds of pounds he had already spent on functions, prizes and gifts. 'This, I do not mind – I mean the expense – but to be treated like some low, common adventurer, and get no thanks for the good I have tried to do, is more than flesh and blood can stand. I hope the next mayor will be more to their mind.'[3]

If the snub to the regatta seemed churlish, Merton roused further ire in the town by voicing his opinions on national affairs in the London press. One observer saw the irony: 'It is, indeed, with an increased sense of self-importance that I, as a resident in Bournemouth, read in the *Daily Telegraph* that the mayor approves of the proposal that there should be a royal residence in Ireland. It must give to Lord Salisbury and to Mr Arthur Balfour a feeling of strength and conviction when they realise that it has the sanction of one so eminently fitted to express an opinion as the present municipal head of Bournemouth.'[4] As his mayoral year fizzled out, the council expressed its regret that ill-health had prevented Merton from fulfilling his duties. He left it until mid-October to announce his formal exit, but his mayoralty was as good as over when the workmen moved into South Road. The council's gamble had failed, and he remains the only mayor in the town's history never to have served as an elected councillor.

In *Home and Abroad*, Merton gives an upbeat assessment of his tenure. Official functions dominate his narrative, and he mounts a strong defence of his conduct over the children's carnival. 'One has to contend with much criticism about comparatively small matters,' he remarked.[5] South Road is omitted from the account, thereby missing the chance to put his own side of the story. In any case, the affair spelled disaster for the policy issues the council's progressives wanted him to advance. Civic functions aside, he could point only to a doubling of the pier tolls as a mark of his influence. The undercliff drive – the real prize – made no progress during his time in office. His downfall served only to rally its opponents.

South Road embodies how Merton's single-mindedness attracted controversy. That trait, so often an asset in business, made it hard to press his agenda in the council chamber. He observed that, to some people, 'everything was objectionable which had the slightest tendency to coincide with my views upon any subject.'[6] A local historian took a more balanced view of the matter: 'It is not as a member but rather as a friend of the local authority that his chief work for Bournemouth has been accomplished. He has been a buttress rather than a pillar of civic administration.'[7] In other words, Merton was most effective when he sat outside the council chamber and cajoled those within it.

After its restoration, the council adopted South Road as a public highway. Nowadays the entrance to a car park, it forms an unlikely scene for a key moment in the relationship between the town and its lord of the manor. Meyrick's influence was waning, and South Road proved it. For Merton, the men in carts left a question behind when they took away his summer house. If Bournemouth felt so little love for him, why should he love Bournemouth? He thought about leaving. Talks started with the Gordon Hotels group, a chain with a presence in a string of resorts, including Brighton, Margate and Monte Carlo. News emerged in November, based on 'excellent authority', that the firm had bought the Royal Bath for £80,000. 'It appears that Mr Cotes has been thoroughly disgusted with Bournemouth,' ran one report. 'He will be missed at the handsome hostelry which he has brought into such prominence, but the Gordon Company may be congratulated on obtaining a great bargain.'[8] How close he came to finalising the deal is unclear, but the timing of the announcement was ironic. News of the sale appeared in the same week that Henry Newlyn replaced him as mayor, but it was never mentioned again after the initial flurry of reports.[9]

A holiday in the Canaries in January may have put Merton's woes into perspective. On reaching Las Palmas, he learned that Prince Henry of Battenberg was dead. 'The news fell upon us like a thunderbolt,' he wrote, 'and for a few minutes we stood speechless from emotion.' [10] As he feared, the Prince contracted malaria during the campaign against the Ashanti and died on his way back to England. While doubtful to suggest it influenced his decision, the Prince's death preceded a heart-warming moment in Merton's troubled relationship with Bournemouth. When the couple returned home, the children's carnival committee presented Annie with an album of photographs more than a year after the event. The gift came as a reminder that many in the town were still on their side.

Merton kept himself busy by arranging the loan of part of his art collection to the Mappin Gallery in Sheffield. While therapeutic to indulge his hobby at a difficult time, selling the hotel would have left him short of storage space. Sending paintings away makes sense in that context, but his own explanation for the loan is caught up in another muddle about dates. According to *Home and Abroad*, he had built up a large store of pictures at the Walker Gallery in Liverpool. The result of frequent purchases at their autumn exhibitions, nothing happened to them, he says, until his trip abroad in 1884.[11] The curator put the paintings on display in his absence, a fact unknown to Merton until he visited the gallery on his return. This welcome surprise gave him an idea: 'Knowing personally the chairmen and curators of most of the corporation art galleries in the various large cities, I wrote to several, and the replies accepting my offer of loaning this collection were instantaneous.' [12] This gives the impression that he established the loan collection soon after returning from his world travels in 1886. In fact, the Mappin exhibition – in the spring of 1896 – was the first to include large numbers of his pictures.[13] The timing suggests that the loan is connected to his disillusionment with Bournemouth, but there was also the simple pleasure of basking in his artistic credentials. Many of the same paintings had featured a year earlier in a series of articles in *The Art Journal*, confirming Merton as a serious player in the art market. Regardless of his intentions, the Mappin exhibition received much acclaim. 'Mr Russell Cotes,' said the *Sheffield Daily Telegraph*, 'has conferred a benefit on the city which the citizens will not be slow to appreciate.' [14]

Part of the collection moved to Leeds in 1897, the second in a sequence of loans that lasted until 1904. It earned Merton a string of illuminated addresses from grateful town councils. His aim, he says, was to educate the public in the art of their own country, but the loans came with another important advantage. An exhibition tends to boost a painting's value – a useful side effect for those who bought for profit as well as pleasure. Merton, as a regular client of the London auction houses, certainly fell into that category. *Home and Abroad* abounds with stories of his connections to leading figures in the art world. A typical tale describes how he bought a painting by

Solomon J. Solomon (1860–1927), an artist who later turned his talents to the development of military camouflage. Believing it could be improved, Merton sent the picture to Solomon with some suggested alterations. The artist made the changes without quibble or payment, a sure sign that he knew the reputation of the man he was dealing with.

If Merton did make any financial gains from the exhibitions, then he was seldom short of things to do with them. His decision to remain in Bournemouth heralded a burst of activity, as he sought to secure his business interests and safeguard his future. Dates on the Royal Bath's title documents indicate that the hotel's lease expired in the summer of 1896, some three months after the death of Sir George Meyrick.[15] His heir, another Sir George (1855–1928), considered selling the freehold to Merton, but a rare surviving letter from Annie to Bert reveals a fraught negotiation lasting many months. Meyrick was also willing to part with the freehold of the Belle Vue Hotel, which stood on a prime site facing the pier. It gave Merton a golden opportunity to add to his collection of seafront real estate. Meyrick wanted £55,000 for the two freeholds, a figure that proved to be a sticking point. Rival bids for the Belle Vue also clouded the issue. Annie's letter describes Merton's final attempts to revive the deal, and it can be no coincidence that the parties agreed a backdated lease of the Royal Bath a few months later.[16]

What is clear from the paper trail surrounding these discussions is that, in June 1896, Meyrick agreed to grant Merton a 99-year lease on a plot of land next to the Royal Bath. It lay on the opposite side of the hotel to South Road and came with a commanding outlook. This land provided the foundations for the project that was to consume the greater part of the couple's time and money for the rest of their lives. Merton explains it like this: 'For many years, I had it in my mind that, some day, I would build a house after my own heart as an offering of love and affection to my wife.' [17] Romantic gestures aside, the planned house also proclaimed Merton's intention to remain in Bournemouth despite what some people thought of him. By building it in such a prominent position, it spoke of status, power and a determination to face down his critics.

The earliest plan of 'the chalet', as the house was first called, dates from July 1896 and shows a building of middling architectural ambitions. With a conventional outline, red-tiled roof and a mock-Tudor facade, it was little different from many other villas springing up in Bournemouth at the time. Its standout feature – an imposing central tower – gave it impact but also presented the greatest problem: the planned building lay in the eye-line of anyone looking out to sea from the houses to the rear. Although Merton talks only of 'spoiling various plans', objections to the tower from his neighbours may account for at least some of these redrafts.[18]

As the plans for his dream house progressed, Merton's relationship with the council remained as fraught as ever. They turned down his application to

THE ART OF A SALESMAN

45 A section of the first plan of 'the chalet', which is unrecognisable from the completed house. Merton's annotations include: 'Plan showing conservatory prepared for Sir George per Mr English [Meyrick's agent], July 1896.' (Russell-Cotes Art Gallery and Museum)

plant shrubs at the edge of the revamped South Road, an outcome as unsurprising as the request was hopeful. Unruffled, in March 1897 he offered to donate a clock and drinking fountain to the town in honour of the Queen's diamond jubilee. The council welcomed the idea to begin with and sent a delegation to meet him in the Square – Bournemouth's commercial heart – to discuss the details. Merton left the scene believing that his gift would soon be erected there, but the councillors came away with a different view. They thought the clock would be better placed at the Lansdowne, more than half a mile away. At twenty-four feet high, they claimed it would look more imposing where there were fewer tall buildings. Merton was not happy when he found out. If his clock was not good enough for the Square, he argued, then foisting it on the residents of the Lansdowne was an insult to them and to him. In a letter to the press, he explained that he had based the design of the clock tower on one given to the town of Rothesay by its local MP. If anyone wondered what relevance a clock on the Isle of Bute had to Bournemouth, then Merton himself provided the link. His three sisters had lived there at various points, with Mary and Georgina making it their permanent home.[19] Merton retracted his offer when the Bute precedent failed to win the argument, leaving both the Square and the Lansdowne without the means to tell the time. Although the council denied it, the ghost of South Road still haunted their dealings with the erstwhile mayor.

Merton's revised plans for his new house – the earliest recognisable as the final design – emerged around the time of the clock affair. The council rejected them again, with the building's height still the most likely point at issue. Many months passed before the next attempt, as Merton's attention turned to matters beyond Bournemouth. He lent paintings to galleries in Hull and Derby over the next twelve months, but family matters provided the biggest distraction. Clarie's marriage was now in serious trouble. The only one of the three children to have married up to this point, the distress was compounded by the involvement of her husband, Joseph Drew, in a well-publicised fraud case. The scheme was masterminded by Drew's uncle, who had made a fortune from a London butchery business and later expanded into groceries, laundry and coal. After buying into a hotel at Victoria station, he managed to acquire enough shares in the business to infiltrate the board with his nominees. He installed his nephew, a former assistant in his butchery firm, as one of the directors. According to the case against him, the uncle supplied the hotel at inflated rates from his own businesses, often charging for goods he failed to supply.

The case came to court in February 1898. Clarie's husband was a mere puppet in the scheme, but his uncle still felt compelled to brand him as a scoundrel during the hearings. Other witnesses supplied the details – stories of the younger Drew's gambling and drinking that echoed Clarie's experiences of his behaviour. She had petitioned for divorce by then, citing her husband's violence towards her, a threat to shoot her dead, and an affair with a woman he tried to pass off as his wife. The law still favoured the man when it came to marital breakdown, leaving Clarie no choice but to air these details in public. The divorce court granted her petition, while a judge in the fraud case awarded substantial damages against Drew senior.[20]

With the divorce finalised, Merton and Annie left for a one-month tour of Russia and Sweden in the summer of 1898. Annie wrote frequently to Ella while they were away, correspondence she published a decade later under the title *Letters from Russia*. While Bert appears several times in these letters, they make no mention of Clarie. 'How we do wish you and B. were with us!' wrote Annie, thus raising a question about the couple's ongoing relationship with their younger daughter.[21] Their actions answer it, as Clarie returned to Bournemouth to live at the Royal Bath for several years after the breakdown of her marriage. Divorce, while becoming more common, still carried a great stigma for everyone involved. That, and the high cost of obtaining one, suggests that the support of her parents helped Clarie through a traumatic time.

Merton's account of their Russian tour begins with an echo of his boyhood encounter with the Queen and Prince Albert at the Great Exhibition. As their ship approached St Petersburg, they passed the imperial yacht with the ill-fated Nicholas and Alexandra in clear view on the upper deck. 'The Czar stood up and saluted us,' wrote Merton, 'and the Czaritsa bowed.'[22] From St Petersburg, they travelled to Moscow and as far east as Nizhny Novgorod, the site of a vast annual trade fair. As usual, they bought up large quantities of art and curios, but Annie sometimes preferred to leave Merton to get on with it. 'Father and Serge [their guide] are off to shop,' she wrote to Ella from Moscow. '*I* am taking it easy.' [23] Her letters also reveal how Merton still suffered from debilitating bouts of ill-health. A bad cold laid him low for several days, while raucous street noise led her to wonder: 'How father's head stands it is a mystery.' [24]

Despite his vast sales experience, Merton portrays himself as a naïve buyer at one point on this trip. During their week in Stockholm, an antiques dealer persuaded him to buy a table lamp reputedly used by Napoleon. 'He assured me in the most conscientious and confident manner that it was really genuine,' Merton recalls.[25] The dealer failed to provide evidence to support its provenance, but that is not the main point of the story. Sir Henry Irving later admired the lamp during a visit to Bournemouth and wished he could have used it when playing the part of the Emperor. Annie makes no mention of the lamp in her letters, so its appearance in *Home and Abroad* may be no more than a prop to introduce an anecdote about Irving.

Another example of Merton and Annie's unique perspectives on their travels comes in their differing accounts of a trip to the Swedish royal palace. According to Annie, their guide had been part of the King's entourage during his visit to Bournemouth and so let them see the rooms normally closed to the public. Merton, on the other hand, provides a much grander account of how the private viewing came about. 'When the King and Queen of Sweden were at Bournemouth,' he wrote, 'we were invited by their Majesties, if we were ever in Stockholm, to call at the palace.' [26] The royal couple were away when they tried to take up the offer, so the household chamberlain gave them an extended tour to make up for the disappointment. Their guide even allowed them to keep some royal stationery as a souvenir and presented them with a painting of the palace on behalf of the King and Queen.

The couple returned to Bournemouth in September 1898 to more rave reviews of Merton's loan collection. The Derby corporation gallery had been pleased enough with its reception in the spring to put the pictures on display again in the autumn. These exhibitions enhanced Merton's standing in the art world at a time when he was once more on the fringes of affairs in Bournemouth. The *Derby Mercury* described the paintings as 'exquisite' and 'delightful' but gave little away about the man who lent them.[27] Only a few of the pictures received special attention, reflecting the collection's general conservatism. Even *The Dawn of Love*, a once controversial painting by William Etty (1787–1849), was referred to simply as 'a grand piece of work by this celebrated artist.' Featuring an expanse of exposed flesh, it depicts a Rubenesque Venus caressing the wings of a slumbering Love. Considered daring in its day, the boundaries of good taste had expanded – at least in Derby – in the half-century since Etty's death.

Whereas the people of the East Midlands took *The Dawn of Love* in their stride, not so the citizens of Glasgow when the collection moved north a year later. The painting prompted outraged letters to a local newspaper, a chain of correspondence reproduced in its entirety in *Home and Abroad*. Merton, it seems, was delighted with the fuss. One writer protested that 'in civilised life the Dawn of Love is seldom heralded in with clothes off.' Another questioned the wisdom of the entire exhibition. 'The object of this picture gallery, I presume, is to elevate the masses. The object may be commendable, although for my part I think a free circus or a boxing booth better suited to the present demands of the East End of Glasgow.' [28]

While these exhibitions were an end in themselves, they also offered a means to an end. His art collection may have uplifted the spirits of the common man, but Merton also benefitted in the shape of free and secure storage and the kudos of being the lender. Improved saleability of his paintings was another bonus. He put more than a hundred on the market after the Sheffield exhibition, including works by Edwin Long (1829–1891),

46 The Dawn of Love *by William Etty. The painting was called* Venus now Wakes and Wakens Love *when first exhibited in 1828 – a line taken from* Comus, *John Milton's work in praise of chastity. While admiring the skill of the artist, one contemporary reviewer remarked that the subject 'was handled in a way entirely too luscious (we might, with great propriety, use a harsher term) for the public eye.'* [29] (Russell-Cotes Art Gallery and Museum)

Henry Moore (1831–1895) and – so it was said – John Constable (1776–1837). It freed up cash to use on the chalet project. In turn, that building went on to form the centrepiece of Merton and Annie's most celebrated act of philanthropy. If all this speaks of a grand plan to erase memories of South Road, then things are unlikely to have been that simple. Merton craved status, influence and respect, all of which had suffered during his chaotic mayoralty. Everything he later did has to be seen in that light. Even so, his reputation for grand gestures made in a blaze of publicity is only partly justified. While self-interest plays a part in almost all giving, Merton's motives were often more complex than some critics liked to make out. His gift of a bust of George Washington to the American people is a case in point.

In 1899, Joseph Choate (1832–1917), the US ambassador to Britain, spent Easter at the Royal Bath. He and Merton got on well, with their mutual veneration of Sir Henry Irving providing a ready topic of conversation. Choate admired the hotel's art collection and took a great liking to a bust of Washington sculpted from black basalt. Almost a year later, Merton offered it as a gift to the American people to honour the 168th anniversary of the first president's birth. While straightforward on the surface, this offer came during a period of strained relations between the two countries. The British were fighting the Boers in South Africa, a conflict that started with heavy losses for the Empire's forces. America came out as neutral at the outset but was facing accusations of pro-Boer bias when Merton made his offer. He had agreed to accommodate four wounded officers at the Royal Bath only days before, so the war was at the forefront of his mind. With its hint of amateur diplomacy, the gift received widespread publicity on both sides of the

47 The bust of George Washington given by Merton to the American people in 1900. Described in Home and Abroad *as 'modelled by the late Josiah Wedgwood', reports in the American press referred to it as a copy of the bust made in 1785 by Jean-Antoine Houdon (1741–1828).*[30] *Given the similarities between the two pieces, the latter is likely to be the more accurate description.* (From Home and Abroad)

Atlantic. The US Secretary of State recognised it as such and sent a letter of thanks for the spirit of goodwill. Placing the bust in the Senate, as Merton had wanted, proved impossible, and so it found a home in the Congressional Library instead.

Despite its subtle undertones, Merton's critics might still have cited the Washington bust as an example of his flamboyant style of giving. Indeed, even his journalist friend, William Pickford, called him a past master at gaining the ear of the press. Yet Pickford also saw a side of him that was hidden to most. 'Many a man owes him a debt of gratitude for kind deeds done with quiet tact,' he wrote. 'The balance sheet of his life, could it be published, would not err on the side of self.' [31] In writing these words, Pickford may have been thinking of Harutune Michaelyan (1875–1955), an ethnic Armenian who fled Turkey during the Ottoman massacres of the 1890s. These atrocities, an attempt at ethnic cleansing by the Sultan, led to the deaths of thousands of Armenian Christians. The slaughter had started soon after Merton and Annie called in at Constantinople on their way back from the Holy Land. The head of the local American Bible Mission kept them informed as events unfolded, and Merton later used his mayoral clout to highlight the situation in the press. As for Michaelyan, he was one of hundreds to flee to England, where he sought help from the YMCA in Bournemouth. This was one of the many charities supported by the couple, who took a personal interest in his plight. 'They helped me to gain a livelihood, they comforted me with their friendship,' their protégé explained many years afterwards.[32] He became a travelling salesman specialising in Middle-Eastern fabrics, a line of business in which Merton could at least advise him on the patter.

Michaelyan emigrated to America in the summer of 1901 and went on to make his fortune selling carpets. By the time he left England, his benefactors' new home was as good as finished. More than just a chalet, the completed house made an impact that amply justified five years of effort and expense. Before the decade was out, it would elevate Merton to a status he could only have dreamt of in his early days in Bournemouth. More than that, this grand villa on the East Cliff would erase South Road, and all other past controversies, from the town's collective memory.

Notes:

1. *The Star* (Guernsey) and *Congleton and Macclesfield Mercury*, 10 August 1895.
2. *Bournemouth Observer*, 4 September 1895.
3. *Cheltenham Chronicle*, 21 September 1895. In a letter to the *Bournemouth Guardian* on 11 November 1899, Merton said he received no remuneration of any kind during his mayoralty and covered all expenses out of his own pocket.
4. *Bournemouth Observer*, 7 September 1895 (edited). Lord Salisbury was the Prime

Minister at the time, while Arthur Balfour was the leader of the House of Commons.
5. *Home and Abroad*, p. 112.
6. ibid., p. 84.
7. ibid., p. 293. Alderman Charles Mate made these remarks in a speech in 1919. Mate wrote an important history of Bournemouth to mark the town's centenary in 1910, so was well placed to take an objective view of Merton's contribution.
8. *Wells Journal*, 14 November 1895.
9. Newlyn appointed Dr Hirons as his deputy – the man overlooked by Merton.
10. *Home and Abroad*, p. 347.
11. Merton refers to making regular purchases at the Walker Gallery's autumn exhibitions while visiting his brother, Alfred. However, as the gallery only opened in 1877, all bar one of these visits must have taken place after Alfred's death in 1878.
12. *Home and Abroad*, p. 688.
13. Merton lent paintings to the British section of the Chicago Exhibition in 1893, which was curated by Lord Frederic Leighton. Leighton approached the artists he wanted to exhibit, who then nominated their preferred pictures. The paintings loaned by Merton were *The Palm Offering* by Frederick Goodall, *King Ahab's Coveting* by Thomas Rooke, and *How Liza Loved The King* by Edmund Blair Leighton.
14. *Sheffield Daily Telegraph*, 5 May 1896. Merton's sixty paintings were displayed in a room next door to another loan collection, that of Frederick A. Kelley, a local brewer. By coincidence, Kelley was born in Wolverhampton and went to Tettenhall College.
15. The lease is dated 6 April 1898 but ran for 99 years from 24 June 1896, implying that the previous lease expired on the earlier date.
16. Annie's letter, dated 1 February 1898, is held by the Russell-Cotes Art Gallery and Museum (BORGM:2009.201). One intriguing passage reads: 'If I gave £55,000 [for both freeholds] it would leave £40,000 for the RBH.' The 'I' here may be a slip of the pen but could suggest that more of the couple's wealth was vested in Annie's name than might otherwise be apparent.
17. *Home and Abroad*, p. 217.
18. ibid.
19. Merton and Annie often visited Rothesay and usually stayed at the Glenburn, a hydropathic hotel overlooking the bay. Merton's sisters, Mary and Georgina, died in the town in 1901 and 1912 respectively.
20. Richard Drew, the said uncle, was originally from Christchurch and died in 1915 at Branksome Park with an estate valued at almost £200,000.
21. *Letters from Russia*, p. 14.
22. *Home and Abroad*, pp. 637–38.
23. *Letters from Russia*, p. 25.
24. ibid., p. 17.
25. *Home and Abroad*, p. 654.
26. ibid., p. 653. Sidney Cooper, the American consul in Gothenburg during the 1880s, recalled: 'I knew from inquiry of the obliging hotel porter, as well as by the absence of the royal standard on the palace flagstaff, that the King was absent

from the capital. When he is in Stockholm the palace gates are closed to travellers and to sightseers generally, but in his absence they are open to all, except the rabble and *canaille*, under the guidance and direction of one of the royal attendants.' (See *Rambles in Sweden*, pp. 110–11).
27. *Derby Mercury*, 12 October 1898.
28. *Home and Abroad*, pp. 733–34.
29. *Evening Mail*, 4 February 1828.
30. *Home and Abroad*, p. 563. Merton says that Choate saw the bust in the Russell-Cotes Art Gallery and Museum, but this must be a mistake, as the building was still some way from completion at the time of the ambassador's visit.
31. *Bournemouth Guardian*, 5 February 1921.
32. *Home and Abroad*, p. 993. Michaelyan sent his tribute in a letter congratulating Merton and Annie on their diamond wedding anniversary in 1920.

12

CRUSADER

Despite the earlier problems, Merton made only minor changes when submitting his final plans for the chalet. The council approved them in March 1899, well over two years on from their first rejection. Bert got married that same month, marking a watershed moment in his life, too. His bride, a vivacious singer called Edith Quarry (1872–1956), had recently toured America with the D'Oyly Carte Opera Company. As a keen amateur performer himself, it is easy to see how Bert fell for her. A loyal son and a qualified solicitor, his new wife embodied the glitz and glamour of a life beyond the hotel trade and the legal profession. Bert divided his time between the two but took on more of the burden of running the Royal Bath as his father's building project took shape next door.

Merton describes his new house as an attempt to combine 'the Renaissance with Italian and old Scottish baronial styles.' [1] The task of realising this eclectic mix fell to John F. Fogerty (1863–1938), an Irishman with an architectural practice in Bournemouth since 1893. Merton fails to mention Fogerty in *Home and Abroad*, an odd oversight given his role in the building's conception. If this suggests a strained relationship – and there are rumours of disputes over payments – Merton was happy to use him for later commissions. Not only that, but their dealings went beyond the bounds of professional services. A few months into the project, he bought a corn mill inherited by Fogerty in his home town of Limerick.[2] Although his motives are unclear, it was typical of Merton to seize the chance of a deal.

With the chalet plot only yards from the Royal Bath, Fogerty needed to minimise disturbance as the work progressed. That may explain why the building took more than two years to complete. Along with the nebulous brief, Fogerty faced the difficulties of a steep site and concerns about blocking the view of neighbouring properties. He solved these problems by making a deep cutting in the hillside aligned between the houses opposite. The chalet sat in this cutting, with only the top floor rising above the road to

48 The Bournemouth regatta in August 1900, with the chalet under construction on the overcliff. The proximity of the house to the hotel – partly visible on the far left – prompted the police to insist that a fence be erected between the two properties when the Royal Bath's licence came up for renewal the following month. (Bournemouth Library)

the rear. It looked drab when viewed from that side, with the cement rendering doing little to lift its appearance. Three floors faced out to sea on the other side, where a small garden separated the house from the footpath along the clifftop. Here, the building came into its own. Curves and turrets gave it a fairy-tale appearance, as much French chateau as Italian villa or Scottish castle. Even without these flourishes, its position on the East Cliff guaranteed that it would stand out.

According to most accounts, the house was finished ready for occupation in July 1901. 'When completed and furnished,' wrote Merton, 'I gave it to my wife as a birthday present, assigning to her the 99 years lease from Sir George Meyrick.' [3] He neglects to say in which year he made the gift, but the documentation reveals that he had transferred the lease to Annie back in June 1899. It was, then, no romantic birthday surprise. The structure may have been complete by the summer of 1901 – Merton appealed against its rating assessment the following spring – but they are unlikely to have moved straight in. Indeed, Annie's name does not appear on the electoral roll against the building until 1903.[4] Prior to that, there was furniture to buy, artworks to move and cabinets to fill. This fitting out appears to have spanned many months, so it is not clear when the couple first spent the night in their new home. Some of this confusion about dates is down to their decision to call the house East Cliff Hall. They moved out of the first building to bear that name – epicentre of the South Road debate – in 1897, when it became a lodging house under its former name of Rothesay. Merton sometimes gave his address as East Cliff Hall afterwards, implying that another building within the hotel complex had acquired that name. If so, then it prevented anyone else from purloining it during the chalet's construction.

Such a grand name demanded a grand residence, and Fogerty more than delivered. 'The fact was,' explained Merton, 'the house was specially constructed for the reception of art treasures.'[5] Whether he intended it as a *public* display space is another matter, but the layout suggests a hybrid of home and gallery. With the bottom floor devoted to guest rooms and the servants' quarters, the signs of the home-gallery compromise are in the upper storeys. Fogerty arranged the reception rooms around a double-height main hall, overlooked on all four sides by a balcony. Itself intended for paintings, this lofty vantage point offered an alternative aspect on the artworks planned for the hall beneath. In feel, if not in architectural detail, this arrangement may have been inspired by Merton and Annie's visit to Leighton House in London, the former home of the artist Lord Frederic Leighton (1830–1896). And yet, despite these distinctive design features, its conspicuous presence and a striking facade, East Cliff Hall took its place on Bournemouth seafront without fuss or fanfare.

The main entrance to the building faced the road on the north side, with visitors approaching directly from the street. After crossing a mosaic in the lobby bearing the monogram 'ARC' – Annie owned the house, after all – they reached a half-landing on the stairs between the top two floors. A stained-glass dome of stars, bats and comets lit the way down to the main hall, rewarding a few moments spent gazing upwards. Above the balcony, a skylight of suns, winds and signs of the zodiac added to the celestial scene, while the basin of a courtyard-style fountain in the hall mirrored the suns in mosaic. This dramatic descent into the heart of the building made for a stunning first impression, but the stairs also drew visitors towards the sea on the south side of the house. If anyone wondered how Merton came to be so captivated by Bournemouth all those years before, then the view from the terrace gave them the answer. Few places in England could match its breathtaking panorama of town, pier, beach and bay.

Although hard to distinguish Merton's input from Fogerty's in the building's layout, he left his distinctive stamp on the internal design. As with the Royal Bath, East Cliff Hall became not only a showcase for his art but an artwork in itself. He re-engaged John Thomas and his son, Oliver (1864–1941), to paint many of the interiors, often using designs copied from the hotel.[6] Commercial wall and ceiling coverings complemented their work, while liberal use of stained glass added further drama. Heraldry appeared throughout the house, with the arms of Cotes, Russell, Law and Clark coming together in the morning room fireplace. It created the illusion of Merton as

49 The main hall and balcony at East Cliff Hall, early 1900s. Sympathetic restoration in the 1990s, putting right decades of over-zealous redecoration, revived the period ambience and elegance evoked by this photograph. (From Home and Abroad)

a man of pedigree, with East Cliff Hall as his family seat. He had been using the arms of the Shropshire Coteses for several years, with the addition of his own punning motto *Je Défends Le Côté Faible* – 'I defend the weak side'. The Duke of Bedford's arms served for the Russell family – Lord John being of that ilk – while those of the extinct Lords of Ellenborough, whose surname was Law, did the honours for Merton's mother. The arms of a Perthshire clan represented the Clark family, and their hunting motto, 'Free for a Blast', featured in the stained glass in the main hall.

Merton put great effort into the landscaping, too. He always took pride in the Royal Bath's garden and bought mass-produced statuary to add interest to the planting. An occasional prize winner at shows, he once boasted of raising a six-pound cauliflower in the hotel's vegetable plot. His horticultural hero was Sir Joseph Paxton (1803–1865), who – as well as designing the Crystal Palace – was head gardener at Chatsworth House in his early career. Merton lists Paxton as an acquaintance, but he died more than thirty years earlier so had no direct influence on East Cliff Hall. A visit to Henley-on-Thames is a more likely source of inspiration. There, Merton toured the grounds of Friar Park, a gothic mansion owned by the eccentric lawyer Sir Frank Crisp (1843–1919).[7] On a vast scale compared to Merton's modest clifftop patch, the division of space into smaller, themed areas is common to both gardens. East Cliff Hall had no room for Crisp's alpine rockery with its twenty-foot high model of the Matterhorn, but Merton made best use of what he had. He squeezed in a Japanese garden – complete with teahouse – lawns, a grotto, a fountain, a pavilion and two summer houses.

50 East Cliff Hall, pictured here in the early 1900s, was at least the second building to bear that name. Rothesay was renamed as such before the South Road controversy, but Home and Abroad *also refers to a mysterious bungalow within the hotel complex. This, too, may have been known as East Cliff Hall, which would explain why Merton gave that as his address during the chalet building work. His granddaughter thought that the bungalow was demolished to make way for the chalet, but this is by no means certain.* (Bournemouth Library)

East Cliff Hall's mix of architectural and design styles reinforced Merton's image as a well-travelled man of culture. It was a potent display of wealth and status, a sort of miniaturised version of the grand residences built by the American robber barons. The house also showed that, despite being well into his sixties, Merton was still open to fresh ideas. It boasted electricity, secondary glazing and underfloor heating fed by boilers in the basement. The kitchen may have been small, but an electric buzzer underneath the dining table rang a bell in the Royal Bath's kitchen to summon its staff with ease. These comforts underline the fact that, for all its splendour, East Cliff Hall began life as a home to entertain friends and family. Merton and Annie were grandparents twice over now, thanks to the birth of Bert's first daughter in the autumn of 1900. Ella ended her long courtship by marrying Edward Stebbing a few months later and, after a brief stint in Hastings, returned to live in Bournemouth.[8] With Clarie and her daughter still based in the town, the couple had all their children and grandchildren close at hand for the time being.

Merton's reintegration into civic affairs in this period followed a similar pattern to the events of a decade earlier. Back then, world travels and business success helped him to bounce back from his troubles as a commissioner and make a pitch for the mayoralty. Now, acclaimed exhibitions and a new house laid the groundwork for a comeback from the South Road debacle. Nevertheless, another spell of ill-health prompted unfounded rumours of the Royal Bath merging with a London chain. Merton's plans for stepping back from his businesses meant a quieter reign, not an abdication. He reorganised the hotel into a family syndicate, with himself as chairman, Bert as deputy and Stebbing as the managing director. His son-in-law kept a low profile, leaving Bert to come to the fore as the public face of the hotel, albeit with a less dynamic style than his father's.

Merton used the time gained to indulge his other interests. His health and history precluded a return to the council, but he knew how to stay in the public eye. He wrote many letters to the press, airing his views on subjects as diverse as Russian icons and ladies' fashions. 'Some women are foolish enough to disfigure themselves and distort the natural formation of their bodies by tight lacing,' he grumbled to one newspaper.[9] Meanwhile, his loan collection continued its tour of the provinces, reaching Bath in the spring of 1902 and Oldham in the autumn of that year. The MP for the latter, an up-and-coming Conservative by the name of Winston Churchill (1874–1965), opened the exhibition. Merton was not there to hear his speech, but Churchill praised his generosity and hoped others would follow suit.

By the time the collection arrived in Burnley the following year, Churchill had joined the Liberals in a protest about free trade. Merton would not have approved. He was a long-standing member of the Primrose League, an organisation founded after Disraeli's death to promote Conservative values. In *Home and Abroad*, he describes the post-war coalition government as 'men out of work rejoicing in a sinecure' and yearned for a new Disraeli to save the nation.[10] Churchill, who rejoined the Tory ranks only after Merton's death, is unlikely to have qualified. Even so, their paths were to cross again before too long.

Regardless of the politics, praise from Churchill represented an endorsement from the establishment. Merton coveted rewards handed down from above and took immense satisfaction, to the point of obsession, with his F.R.G.S. In 1903, a fellowship awarded to Annie by the Royal Society of Literature gave her a set of letters to complement his own. Merton writes of the honour with pride, pointing out that Lord Halsbury (1823–1921) – the Society's president and the Lord High Chancellor – had a hand in awarding it.[11] This might surprise some readers of *Westward from the Golden Gate*, Annie's only published work up to this point. It has a similar feel to *Letters from Russia*, a book described by one reviewer as 'undemanding'.[12] To receive a fellowship for writing it only makes sense in the context of the Society's standing at the time. With lawyers and clergymen high up in its ranks, serious authors shunned it until a new ethos transformed its fortunes after 1910. Before that, the letters F.R.S.L. spoke less of the recipient's writing prowess and more about their social aspirations.

Always ardent joiners of clubs and subscribers to good causes, Merton and Annie's influence now spread in many directions. From the Bournemouth Horse Show to an appeal for victims of a fire at Ottawa, their names often appeared among lists of supporters. The Shaftesbury Society, a children's charity, was one of their favourites. In 1902, they gave a pulpit and communion table to the town's new Presbyterian church, gifts with a significance beyond their face value.[13] Merton had worshipped at St Peter's, Bournemouth's main Anglican church, until 1880, when he joined others in objecting to the appointment of a reformist vicar. Opposed to Sunday train services and secular music on the Sabbath, he decided that Annie's church was more to his liking. 'I am a member of the Established Church of Scotland,' he wrote, 'which in every way is on all fours with the Established Church of England. The real nonconformists are those who call themselves members of the Church of England and who flout its Protestant creed and laws.' [14] His views chimed with those of John Kensit (1853–1902), whose Protestant Truth Society fought against what he saw as creeping Catholicism in the Anglican church. Merton later served as the Society's president and sat on the council of the Church Association, an evangelical body with similar aims. When Kensit died as a result of a blow from a flying chisel after a rowdy meeting in Birkenhead, Merton mourned him as a martyr to the cause.

While always on the lookout for new outlets for his energies, the Royal Bath remained close to Merton's heart. He objected to the council's plans to run a tramway past the hotel, an idea intended to ferry day trippers from the station to the pier. A heated debate about the proposed route touched the nerve of Bournemouth's dilemma. Trams rolling down Bath Hill meant progress for some, but others thought it would upset the town's wealthier clientele. Merton wrote to a local newspaper to complain about the scheme. 'If a tram is absolutely necessary to the pier,' he asked, 'why not run it along Exeter Lane from the Square at little or no expense?' [15] This would have meant running the tracks past the Royal Exeter Hotel, but a wave of protests ensured that no trams ever troubled either establishment.

This intervention saw Merton finding his voice again on civic matters. Little had happened on the undercliff drive since his mayoralty to justify continued silence. Archibald Beckett (1841–1904) – councillor, hotelier and Boscombe property tycoon – had come closest to breaking the deadlock with plans that first appeared in the late 1890s.[16] Beckett foresaw villas, hotels, promenade trams and a cliff railway as part of a grand scheme stretching the full distance between the two piers. Sir George Meyrick offered him a lease of the seafront as an incentive to progress these ideas, hoping that a commercial scheme would prevent the costs from falling on the ratepayers. Merton was horrified at the prospect and, behind closed doors, threatened to sell up should the plans come to fruition. 'I love Bournemouth and detest the people,' he wrote in a letter to Meyrick's solicitors. 'At the same time, I have lived on this spot so long that I certainly ought to know what is likely to be for its benefit and what is not.' [17] The council, faced with the town's prized asset falling into private hands, took out the lease itself. That said, the deal came with a proviso that the seafront would revert to the freeholder if the council failed to build a drive within ten years. Meyrick, whose priority was to protect his property, could then proceed as he saw fit.

Municipal control of the seafront staved off the threat of overdevelopment but came with a sting in the tail. The council also wanted to build a drive along the overcliff, a much less controversial idea than the undercliff version. For Merton, however, the scheme raised the prospect of the clifftop path in front of the Royal Bath being widened to take vehicles. In a series of panicked letters, he urged Meyrick's solicitors to block that part of the plan: 'We are entitled to ask Sir George to give us a guarantee that under no circumstances will the cliff frontage of our property be interfered with, as it would simply mean ruin to us.' [18] Meyrick's lawyers could offer no such promise but assured him of a right to compensation in the unlikely event of the drive passing that way. Merton replied by saying that only the outright purchase of the Royal Bath, East Cliff Hall, Rothesay, Kildare and Lynwood would be adequate in those circumstances. His frustration is evident in the tone of the correspondence. 'What can you expect of a pig but a grunt?' he wrote in exasperation of the council.

As it transpired, the route along the clifftop avoided Merton's frontage when the council revealed its plans in 1903. With the project underway, attention turned back to the much thornier issue of the undercliff drive. That September, a group of councillors embarked on a tour of other seaside towns

51 The East Cliff, c. 1900. This photograph highlights how Bournemouth's geology makes it susceptible to landslips. Cliff erosion, and not sewerage or tourism, is what focused the undercliff drive debate in the end. The problem persists to this day, and a major collapse occurred not far from the Russell-Cotes Art Gallery and Museum in 2016. (Bournemouth Library)

THE ART OF A SALESMAN

to inspect their promenades at close quarters. Dubbed the 'Flying Squadron', they came back in favour not only of a drive below the cliffs but also of a pavilion near the pier. Old objections resurfaced as soon as the verdict was announced. The cost, the environment, the geology – all were thrust forward in an effort to block the plans. Another landslide near the Royal Bath failed to sway the argument, as everyone accepted the need to protect the cliffs. The point at issue was how to go about it. When one councillor warned of fatalities if they failed to act, another suggested sending the Flying Squadron to see the promenade at Lowestoft. 'All washed away,' he added, amid laughter.[19] There were lessons to be learned closer to home, too. Southbourne's drive, the object of envy for so long, had succumbed to a storm two years earlier.[20] That, depending on one's point of view, was either down to its poor construction or the inevitable result of wind and waves.

Merton chose this point to re-enter the debate with a vengeance. He adopted the undercliff drive and pavilion as personal crusades, documenting their progress in a new scrapbook of press cuttings. These included his own letters to the newspapers, many of them prodigious in length and forensic in argument. The *Bournemouth Graphic* remarked: 'If the undercliff drive is not carried out, it will not be the fault of Mr Merton Russell Cotes, proprietor of the Royal Bath Hotel, Bournemouth. I trust that many years will elapse before his post-mortem biography will be published but, even if such a book is written, it will be quite incomplete if his recent literary efforts respecting the undertaking in question are omitted from it.'[21]

As a war of words broke out in the press, many of Merton's adversaries preferred to remain anonymous. One local solicitor had no such qualms. J. Ralph Smythe (1857–1930) stepped forward as the mouthpiece of the Residents' Association, a body vehemently opposed to the undercliff drive. Smythe scorned it as a needless drain on the rates that would do nothing to protect the cliffs. He drew on evidence from an erosion specialist, who claimed a drive in Bournemouth would go the same way as Lowestoft's. Merton dismissed this expert – wrongly as it turned out – as a 'simple schoolmaster' and 'amateur geologist'.[22] He harked back to the 1870s and his 'intimate relations' with Messrs Bazalgette and Creeke, whose opinions he preferred to trust.

As a torrent of letters engulfed the town's newspaper editors, the name of East Cliff Hall – the source of so many of them – became bound up with the undercliff drive. The row went on for months. When Smythe published his expert's credentials, Merton belittled his opinions. 'Geologists find difficulties,' he observed, 'engineers overcome them.'[23] He went on to accuse Bournemouth's retirees of ignoring the town's traders, who could see 'bankruptcy stalking in their midst'. Smythe hit back with a raft of scientific detail, but Merton stood firm. 'I give the ratepayers of Bournemouth too much common sense than to swallow the pabulum and twaddle that he provides for them weekly.' [24] Smythe upped the ante by giving an interview to the *Bournemouth Graphic*, in which he said the only drive worth having was the one on the overcliff. He claimed that no one would use 'a straight road, with a cliff blocking all view on one side, and a grey, monotonous sea without pleasure craft, or any other sign of life, on the other.' [25] Merton seized on this latest salvo: 'First one bogey has been brought forward in the shape of an "eminent geologist", then we have Mr Smythe stigmatising our beautiful and picturesque bay.' [26]

The arguments raged on. If Smythe complained about the cost, Merton spoke of investment. When Merton talked of protecting the cliffs, Smythe said they could be stabilised from above. Where Smythe foretold of disaster if they went ahead, Merton predicted stagnation if they delayed. Why, he asked, should the council defer to those who were 'terrified out of their wits lest they should have to pay an extra penny or tuppence in the pound on their rental?' [27] He suggested building a trial section of drive from the pier westward to Durley Chine – about a third of the distance of the eastward route to Boscombe. In doing so, he avoided accusations of self-interest, as it missed out the shoreline below the Royal Bath.

Although public support for the drive was growing, Merton had seen too many false dawns to believe that letters alone could sweep away the protests. Powerful and well-known voices spoke for the opposition, including Joseph Cutler, Thomas Hankinson and Henry Newlyn. Pro-drive campaigners needed to be better organised to break down that level of resistance. To get things started, Merton joined forces with Frank Wareham (1852–1916), a respected local caterer with a reputation for straight dealing. They issued a joint circular to rally support, their objective being to cooperate with the council on any project 'for the betterment and prosperity of the borough as a first-class seaside health resort.' [28]

This plea attracted a raft of local heavyweights. Meeting for the first time in April 1904, the men agreed to form a progressive alliance in direct opposition to the Residents' Association. Vice-presidents and committee members were appointed by the dozen, including John Elmes Beale, the proprietor of the well-known shop. Beale, who was midway through the second of three successive terms as mayor, had found the drive as frustrating and infuriating as his predecessors. Six former mayors also pledged their support, as did Bert Cotes, who joined the committee. As for the presidency, Merton stood aside in favour of his old friend, Dr Roberts Thomson, and took on the role of co-treasurer instead. Together, this august body of men came up with an imposing name for themselves: The Undercliff Drive, Promenade and Pavilion League.

Press sympathy was vital in the League's battle for hearts and minds. William Pickford of the *Bournemouth Guardian* joined the committee, a man well used to Merton's powers of persuasion. 'There have been occasions,' he

THE ART OF A SALESMAN

later recalled, 'when I could have hung up my telephone receiver and let him go on talking to empty air.'[29] Yet Pickford also knew how to make a deal with him. Merton always wanted his quid pro quo, Pickford expected that, but the quo never failed to materialise. Soon after the League's formation, Merton lent a 100-guinea trophy to the Hampshire Football Association, despite having no interest in sport. Pickford, on the other hand, loved football so much that he served as the Hampshire FA's secretary. Quo or not, the trophy made the newspaper man far less likely to put the phone down when he received a demand for publicity.[30]

Merton soon came to the fore as the League's prime mover. He tried to link the pavilion to the undercliff drive, arguing that the profits from one would pay for the upkeep of the other. The idea proved hard to sell. To overcome the problems experienced by the Winter Gardens, the pavilion needed to be in the heart of town. The League backed a proposal to buy the Belle Vue Hotel and knock it down to make way for the new building. This was the same hotel that Merton tried to buy in the 1890s, raising an intriguing question about what would have happened if he had succeeded. The Belle Vue was in the hands of William Dore (1844–1912), who also owned The Imperial, one of the Royal Bath's main rivals. Dore wanted £65,000 for the site, more than four times the amount Merton had refused to pay. Many in the town baulked at such a large sum. Over and over again, the council discussed reports about the drive and the pavilion, each time referring them back for more discussion in committee. Summer turned to autumn turned to winter with no sign of meaningful progress.

At the end of 1904, the *Bournemouth Guardian* looked back on the year's events. It noted the death of Archibald Beckett, the transfer of Boscombe pier to the council, and a missed opportunity for the borough to buy a natural history collection from a private museum in Christchurch. In politics, it recalled how the voters of Boscombe East chose Mr Alfred Giles (1864–1919) to represent them, thus becoming the town's first Labour councillor. Less alarming for Merton, but far more frustrating, was the paper's verdict on the progress of the League's priorities: 'No steps have been made in the serious direction of an undercliff drive and shore pavilion.'[31] In truth, the League had already achieved its aims simply by baring its teeth. Three more years would need to pass, but fate decreed that the undercliff drive and East Cliff Hall would come together in one audacious triumph.

Notes:

1. *Home and Abroad*, p. 217.
2. The Limerick property was called Bannatyne Mills. Merton paid off several mortgages when he bought it.

3. *Home and Abroad*, p. 217.
4. Single women ratepayers had been allowed to vote in local elections since 1869. This was extended to married women in 1894, so Annie qualified as the ratepayer on the house.
5. *Home and Abroad*, p. 235.
6. Although John Thomas's influence is apparent at East Cliff Hall, it is not clear how much of it he painted himself. He appears to be absent from the 1901 census, so may have died before then. His three other sons were also decorative artists, one of whom – Arthur – moved to Bournemouth around the time East Cliff Hall was built. He may have helped his brother to apply their father's designs.
7. In 1970, Friar Park was bought by George Harrison, who restored the garden. The house inspired several of the ex-Beatle's songs, notably *The Ballad of Sir Frankie Crisp*.
8. According to Ella's daughter, Phyllis Lee-Duncan, her parents married when Stebbing retired from his job with the Union Castle Line.
9. *Bournemouth Daily Echo*, 4 December 1903.
10. *Home and Abroad*, p. 921.
11. The version of Annie's fellowship certificate shown in *Home and Abroad* is dated 1903 and names 'Lady Russell-Cotes' – the title she took in 1909. Some reports say she was one of only two female fellows at the time, but around a dozen had been awarded by 1903. Merton became a member of the Society, although not a fellow, in 1919.
12. Cross, *In the Lands of the Romanovs*, p. 322.
13. The Presbyterian Church was on Bath Road, between the Royal Bath Hotel and the Lansdowne. It later became the Christadelphian Church but was demolished in 2013.
14. *Bournemouth Daily Echo*, 21 January 1909.
15. ibid., 4 October 1902.
16. As a councillor, Beckett seconded the proposal to appoint Merton as mayor.
17. The quoted letter is one of several relating to seafront matters held by the Russell-Cotes Art Gallery and Museum (BORGM:2009.201).
18. Taken from the seafront letters held by the Russell-Cotes Art Gallery and Museum.
19. *Bournemouth Daily Echo*, 10 September 1903.
20. Southbourne pier was destroyed by the same storm, which raged either side of the new year in 1900/1. Unconnected to these events, Southbourne was incorporated into the borough of Bournemouth a few months later.
21. *Bournemouth Graphic*, 17 March 1904.
22. *Bournemouth Guardian*, 14 November 1903.
23. *Bournemouth Daily Echo*, 24 December 1903.
24. ibid., 12 February 1904.
25. *Bournemouth Graphic*, 28 January 1904.
26. *Bournemouth Daily Echo*, 4 March 1904.
27. ibid., 12 February 1904.
28. Taken from Merton's undercliff drive scrapbook.
29. *Bournemouth Guardian*, 5 February 1921.

THE ART OF A SALESMAN

30. In his book, *A Few Recollections of Sport*, Pickford recalls that Merton asked for the trophy back in 1908. He then lent it to the Royal Victoria Hospital but returned it to the Hampshire FA in 1919, this time as a permanent gift. The county's non-league teams still compete for the Russell-Cotes Cup today.
31. *Bournemouth Guardian*, 31 December 1904.

13

DONOR

The undercliff drive and pavilion made little headway for the most part of 1905. Debate continued in the council chamber, where those hostile to the cause joined forces to thwart progress. Arguments about the drive at first centred on the science of the weather and the sea, then moved on to the question of cost. As for the pavilion, a restrictive covenant discovered in the lease of the Belle Vue Hotel brought discussions to a halt. After the sale of the freehold fell through in 1898, Sir George Meyrick had granted a revised lease preventing the erection of any building in the vicinity over twenty feet in height. It added a legal complexity to the high price demanded for the site by William Dore. John Elmes Beale, nearing the end of his final term as mayor, looked to be heading for disappointment.

With the League watching developments from the sidelines, Merton could again focus on his own affairs. Life was anything but quiet as he approached the age of seventy. His loan collection came to the end of its travels after a long stay in Burnley and, with space at East Cliff Hall already at a premium, he decided upon a cull. More than 150 paintings went under the hammer at Christie's in March 1905 – a big enough sale to make the London art world take notice. *The Times* reported on the auction at length, describing the collection as made with 'exceedingly good taste.' [1] The *Bournemouth Graphic* called it the first successful auction of its kind 'since the serious fall in prices of modern British pictures a few years ago.' [2] When it came to financial matters, Merton's timing was seldom awry. He blamed the sale on a lack of hanging space and the effort involved in the exhibitions, but economics also played a part. The pictures raised almost £9,000 – about half the cost of building East Cliff Hall.[3] Moreover, the previous autumn he had acquired the lease of a private hotel in Dover Street, Mayfair, for an undisclosed sum. Known as Baldwin's after a previous owner, it was within easy reach of the Royal Academy. Indeed, the Arts Club – patronised by many Academy members – was only a few doors down the road. Even better, it served as a

London pied-à-terre just around the corner from Sir Henry Irving's home in Grafton Street. Merton, showing continued faith in Clarie, put his younger daughter in charge of this new business.

Despite the sale of his loan paintings, Merton retained a large collection in Bournemouth and remained a big player in the art market. East Cliff Hall, as perhaps intended from the outset, began to take on the mantle of a private gallery and museum. Its doors were open only to a select few at this stage, such as Sir Henry Irving and fellow thespian Sarah Bernhardt. They were both guests at the Royal Bath while performing at the Boscombe Hippodrome in 1905. Irving turned on the water of a new fountain in the hotel grounds during this latest stay, but it proved to be his final visit.[4] Still working at a frenetic pace in his late sixties, poor health had forced him to give notice of his retirement. Merton says he often urged the actor to quit the stage and blamed Bram Stoker, Irving's business manager, for overworking him. In October, nearing the end of his farewell tour, Irving fell ill after a performance of *Becket* in Bradford. One of his most acclaimed roles, it ends with the words 'Into Thy Hands, O Lord! Into Thy Hands.' He died that same evening in the lobby of his hotel.

The country reacted to the actor's passing with an outpouring of grief. Merton ordered the flags of the Royal Bath to be flown at half-mast when the news reached Bournemouth. An iconic figure, Irving was one of those rare individuals who transcend their sphere to find a place in the national psyche. Merton travelled to London to pay his last respects and file past a coffin containing the cremation urn. 'I cannot help but feel,' he wrote, 'that no one among the vast number bemourned his death more than myself and my wife.'[5] He recalls standing shoulder to shoulder with Bram Stoker beside the tomb in Westminster Abbey, where the actor's ashes were interred.

Merton was still mourning his 'dearest and most loved friend on earth' when he started to write *Home and Abroad* more than a decade after Irving's death. The chapter dedicated to the actor is an extended eulogy, more than 15,000 words of devotion and worship. It is a patchwork piece, stitched together from his own memories, several biographies and Stoker's *Personal Reminiscences*. While none of Irving's biographers mentions their friendship, Merton borrows from these other works in abundance. Sometimes he makes this clear, more often not, resulting in a confusing jumble of anecdotes.[6] In a section lifted almost verbatim from one book, he includes a tale told to 'me' – i.e. the biographer – by the doctor of Alfred Lord Tennyson. In another, he refers to an incident in 1865 – 'when I knew him first in Manchester' – culled from the same book. All this makes it difficult to assess the closeness of their relationship. Merton says that Irving often sent telegrams begging him to meet up. Once, while on holiday in Warwick, a message arrived inviting him to a performance of *Becket* in Birmingham. Backstage, the actor stayed in character to give a blessing to the thrilled Merton. 'I would rather

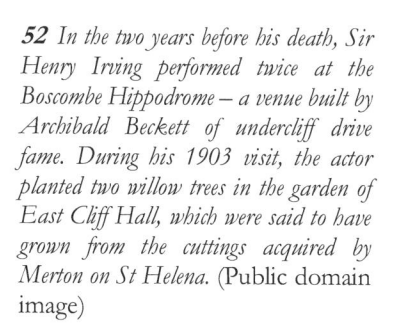

52 In the two years before his death, Sir Henry Irving performed twice at the Boscombe Hippodrome – a venue built by Archibald Beckett of undercliff drive fame. During his 1903 visit, the actor planted two willow trees in the garden of East Cliff Hall, which were said to have grown from the cuttings acquired by Merton on St Helena. (Public domain image)

be blessed by you than any man on earth,' he told Irving, 'even the Archbishop of Canterbury or the Pope of Rome!' [7]

Merton's reverence spilled over into a desire to add to his existing collection of Irving memorabilia. In December 1905, Christie's auctioned off the actor's theatrical effects in a vast sale spread over five days. Merton acquired an array of items, ranging from props and scripts to pictures and furniture. They formed the nucleus of a museum created in an upstairs room of East Cliff Hall. The Irving Room, as it came to be known, took on the air of a shrine.[8] Prized items included a landscape by the American actor Joseph Jefferson (1829–1905) – a keen amateur painter – which Merton had once varnished and cleaned for Irving with his own fair hands. Another was a painting of an orchard by Frank Richards (1863–1935), an artist with a studio in Boscombe. Much admired by Irving, Merton later commissioned Richards to paint portraits of his mother and father-in-law from photographs.

The hullabaloo surrounding Irving's death was not to everyone's taste. Marie Corelli (1855–1924), one of the most popular authors of the day, called it a 'pompous burial' and asked why the Dean of Westminster Abbey failed to question the actor's morals. She was alluding to Irving's long estrangement from his wife, and a relationship with Ellen Terry that is said to have gone beyond professional boundaries.[9] Although Corelli directed her remarks more at the Church than the actor, Merton felt compelled to rush to his defence. He wrote to assure her that 'no man on earth possessed a purer heart, or a nobler one, than my late dear and beloved friend.' [10] As for Irving's

THE ART OF A SALESMAN

estranged wife, Merton teased Corelli by claiming to know the inside story. The author was intrigued enough to meet him, and they became firm friends.

Corelli – real name Mary Mackay – shared Merton's instinct for publicity. Both sensed an opportunity when Mark Twain – real name Samuel Clemens (1835–1910) – came to England to receive a doctorate from Oxford University. Twain had met Corelli some years earlier and had taken an instant dislike to her. Unaware of this, she bombarded him with letters as soon as he arrived in London, pleading with him to visit her home in Stratford-upon-Avon. Worn down by the assault, Twain reluctantly agreed. The visit was a disaster, as Corelli basked in her guest's reflected glory in a sequence of stage-managed events. It was, Twain wrote in his diary, 'the most hateful day my seventy-two years have ever known.' [11] A few days later, Merton wrote to 'Dr Clemens', as he was by then, inviting him to the Royal Bath and admitting to wheedling his address from 'our mutual friend', Marie Corelli. Twain, who resisted the urge to destroy the letter, chose not to accept the invitation.[12]

In the period from Irving's passing in October 1905 to Twain's doctorate in June 1907, the long battle between the Residents' Association and the Undercliff Drive, Promenade and Pavilion League stumbled towards a conclusion. In the month of Irving's death, a report came before the council proposing a way forward. It recommended building a pavilion on the Belle Vue Hotel site and constructing a half-mile trial section of the drive to the

53 A view of the East Cliff taken from the pier in the early 1900s, with the undercliff drive still conspicuously absent. The building on the far left (with the tower) is Bournemouth's public baths, opened in 1864 and demolished in 1935. The site was later used for a controversial cinema that, because of its impact on the sea view, was reputed to be Britain's most hated building. (Bournemouth Library)

east of the pier. It needed Beale's casting vote, one of the last acts of his mayoralty, for the proposal to pass. Cracks began to appear in the opposition ranks from that point onwards. The death of Thomas Hankinson in December deprived the Residents' Association of its president, leaving Henry Newlyn to take his place. Days later, one prominent anti-drive man stood before a stunned members' meeting to confess to a complete change of heart.

Things came to a head in the early months of 1906. The Association triumphed on the pavilion front when a poll of ratepayers rejected the purchase of the Belle Vue. In lambasting the outcome, the *Bournemouth Guardian* pointed to a low turnout and an ill-framed question. On the undercliff drive, the League claimed victory in the council chamber. Having secured Sir George Meyrick's approval for the construction, the council asked the government for the borrowing powers to pay for it. This was *the* pivotal moment. After thirty years of haggling, Bournemouth at last stood on the banks of the Rubicon.

What followed was pure civic theatre. The Local Government Board insisted on a public inquiry chaired by one of its inspectors, giving both sides a chance to put their case. Two separate opposition bodies sent legal counsel to fight their cause. The Residents' Association led the charge, with Roland Vaughan Williams (1866–1949) – son of an appeal court judge and a cousin of the composer – speaking on their behalf. The town clerk, George Bailey (1863–1926), sat in the pro-drive corner. He was left to represent the council, the League and the rest of the drive's supporters entirely on his own. Bailey, though, had a few tricks up his sleeve. One of these turned out to be an eccentric turn from Merton.

On the first day of the inquiry, Bailey summarised the drive's long and turbulent history, a tale familiar to all those waiting to give evidence.[13] He then brought in the borough surveyor and other expert witnesses to speak in favour of the scheme. Vaughan Williams attacked them from all sides, presenting the drive as an enterprise championed by the town's trading community. Ordinary folk were against it, he claimed, pointing to a petition of 4,000 names compiled on behalf of the Residents' Association. Bailey countered that by calling upon a former councillor to testify that a certain class of resident always objected to the council's views. Vaughan Williams demanded to know who they were. 'I'm afraid,' said Bailey, 'they are the people represented by you.'

Bailey pulled off a neat move by bringing in Thomas Compton (1838–1925), the doctor responsible for the now ruined promenade at Southbourne. Compton spoke up in favour of a drive at Bournemouth and said his own scheme failed only because of its exposed position and a lack of funds for repairs. Bailey also called upon William Pickford, John Elmes Beale, the London and South Western Railway, and many others to speak up in support. As the weight of evidence threatened to overwhelm the opposition, Henry

Newlyn was one of the few to fight back. He admitted to supporting the drive at one time but argued that carriages were going out of fashion. Besides, he said, few of the Royal Exeter's distinguished guests had expressed much interest in the idea.

Merton's turn in the witness box came in the middle of all this. He began by referring to cliff falls in front of the Royal Bath, which led him to carry out his own protection work with hundreds of tons of soil. His point was that the town, not the hotel, would suffer if they failed to secure the cliffs. Moving on to the economic arguments, he cited the case of the late Sir William Jenner (1815–1898), formerly the Queen's physician. Jenner had once said he would have left his carriage and horses at home if he had known that Bournemouth lacked an undercliff drive. 'Did he tell *you* that he would not have brought his carriage and horses?' asked the inspector. 'No', replied Merton, who explained that he was only trying to cut a long story short. 'The reason given,' he went on, 'was that we were a stupid lot and that Bournemouth did not possess what he had come here for.' Vaughan Williams suggested that Jenner meant only that he was not comfortable in the town. 'Bournemouth is always comfortable,' retorted Merton, 'but the shore is not at all comfortable.'

After this awkward round of jousting, Vaughan Williams seemed uncertain how to handle him. Merton talked of the immense good a drive would do for the town. 'But has not Bournemouth gone ahead tremendously without this indispensable undercliff drive?' asked the counsel. 'The question answers itself,' said Merton. 'Yes, but answer my question,' Vaughan Williams persisted. 'Well, I will say yes to please you,' Merton replied, before turning his gaze on the second opposition counsel. 'Now, sir, have you got anything to say to that?' The gentleman answered in the negative. 'You have nothing to say,' Merton concluded. 'Thank you, I am delighted.'

According to the *Bournemouth Graphic*, this off-the-wall performance 'quite brought the house down'.[14] But it was Bailey who delivered the fatal blow by picking away at the methods used to gather signatures for the petition. One woman admitted to receiving a halfpenny for every one of the thousand names she had collected. Another witness spoke of canvassers signing names themselves and of scaremongering on the doorstep. Some residents had been told that a drive would put sixpence a week on their rent. When Bailey tried to call the culprits to give evidence, the opposing counsel was forced to admit they had gone to ground. These exchanges laid bare the bitterness of the debate. Vaughan Williams likened the atmosphere to a criminal trial, but Bailey kept up the attack. He accused the scheme's detractors of trying to win the day with misrepresentation and misconception. When he summed up his case at the end of the inquiry, the result looked to be a foregone conclusion. While the inspector gave nothing away, he took the evidence back to London and promised a swift verdict.

Although the undercliff drive was the main thrust of the inquiry, it was not the only matter under consideration. An application by the council to borrow money to set up a museum came a distant second on the agenda. The first attempt to create one dated back three years, when an appeal for funds to buy the collection of Edward Hart (1847–1928), a natural historian from Christchurch, had fallen on deaf ears. This time, they hoped to use a gift from the Scottish-American philanthropist Andrew Carnegie (1835–1919) to set up a museum and library at Horseshoe Common, near the town centre. Carnegie was giving away money for new libraries all over the country, and Bournemouth wanted its share of the cash. The Horseshoe Common plan came to nothing in the end, but it showed the appetite for a cultural attraction in the town.[15] It gave Merton food for thought, too. He had visited Sir John Soane's museum in London and the Poldi Pezzoli in Milan, two art collections housed in the former homes of their benefactors. These institutions offered a sort of immortality to those concerned. If that prospect failed to stir Merton's philanthropic senses, then an event in Bournemouth soon after the undercliff drive inquiry may have caused him to reconsider. John Elmes Beale received the freedom of the borough, thus becoming the second person to be accorded the honour. The first, Field-Marshal Lord Roberts (1832–1914), had led the British forces during the Boer War, but Beale was the first to be recognised solely for his services to Bournemouth. Although Merton missed the ceremony at the Winter Gardens, he would have heard about the illuminated address presented to Beale in a silver casket. This was the reward for selfless and conspicuous public service.

In October 1906, four months after the inquiry closed, the Local Government Board sanctioned the borrowing powers needed to build the trial section of drive. With the resistance beaten out of the opposition, the council acted with speed. The contract went out to tender in November, just after Bert Cotes was returned unopposed for the East Cliff ward in the local elections. He helped to keep up the momentum.[16] Construction began in January 1907 and went ahead at a blistering pace. This was in stark contrast to the marine drive at Scarborough, where North Sea weather meant that work was still going on a decade after it started. Bournemouth hoped to be finished by the autumn.

The drive's march along the beach epitomised the town's progress. In less than seventy years, an area of wild heathland, pine woods and deserted shores had become a bustling resort of 70,000 souls. The work of many people went into making it so, even if some were keener than others to highlight their contribution. Joseph Cutler, that seasoned anti-drive campaigner, chose this moment to publish his updated memoirs. A pocket-sized version came with it, described as an 'after spasm' by the *Bournemouth Graphic*. 'It becomes apparent to the reader,' said the newspaper, 'as he wades through this 8-page account of Mr Cutler's magnificent and glorious prowess that, but for this

54 *The building of the undercliff drive, 1907. Having been at the centre of bitter debate for over thirty years, construction of the first section from the pier to Meyrick Road took just ten months to complete.* (Bournemouth Library)

gentleman, Bournemouth would never have existed.' [17] If his half-baked legacy and over-egged claims risked ridicule, Cutler was in his late seventies and desperate to leave a mark. Merton, while of a similar mind, was not about to make the same misjudgement. With completion of the drive looming, he and Annie decided that, when it comes to legacy, bricks and mortar speak far more loudly than fine words and hot air.

Although autumn storms hampered construction work, the undercliff drive came through its first real test unscathed. Far from being washed away, promenaders were able to try it out in advance of the official opening. The formal ceremony took place in the first week of November 1907, when a civic party walked the full length of the drive. At the eastern end, the mayor laid the last stone at the head of a flight of steps. The mayoress christened it the 'East Cliff Undercliff Drive and Promenade' – a wordy mouthful few bothered to use again. It was a day to put aside old rivalries, as the likes of Joseph Cutler and Henry Newlyn mingled with Bert Cotes and William Pickford. Merton and Annie were in the front rank of the guests, standing alongside the mayor as he ended thirty years of argument with a few taps of a silver trowel. The couple's presence there, ahead of the chairman of the Undercliff Drive Committee in the pecking order, gave a hint of what was to come.

The civic party took lunch at the Royal Bath, where members of the municipal orchestra played selections from *The Merry Widow* and *Carmen*. A large contingent from the national press helped to swell the throng, including men from *The Times*, the *Daily Telegraph* and the *Daily Mirror*. Along with the usual toasts and speeches, the mayor regaled the assembled dignitaries with statistics about Bournemouth's housing stock and rateable value. Afterwards, Merton came forward to present a set of gold medals he had commissioned to commemorate the event. Featuring the drive on one side and the borough arms on the other, they went to around a dozen of the scheme's most prominent supporters – Bert Cotes among them. Yet gold medals were as nothing compared to what happened next.

The mayor again rose to his feet. To gasps, which turned to applause and then to loud cheers, he gave the men of the press a real story to enliven their columns: 'I have the authority of Mr and Mrs Merton Russell Cotes to tell you that, subject to the arrangement of certain details, for which I suggest we will have to appoint a committee, they jointly and severally offer as a free gift to the town their private house known as East Cliff Hall.' [18] This, the mayor added, included their collection of artworks, bringing the total value of the gift to around £40,000. The couple also planned to donate 'certain freehold property in Ireland' – meaning the corn mill once owned by John F. Fogerty – to provide for the upkeep of the building. Their only proviso was that they reserved the right to live in the house for the rest of their lives. In lavishing praise upon the donors, the mayor held a little back for their children. They were now disinherited to an extent, he said, but he assured those present of their willing support.[19]

The gift was beyond generous, its timing brilliant. Some would come to

55 Merton walking alongside the mayor, John Aldridge Parsons, at the opening of the undercliff drive, 6th November 1907. Parsons left office a few days later and died the following year. Merton's granddaughter, Edith Cotes – daughter of Bert – married George Parsons, the ex-mayor's nephew, in 1931. (From Home and Abroad)

question the couple's motives in the days ahead, but Merton dismisses any suggestion of a grander purpose. He and Annie 'had no earthly motive whatever in the world in making that gift beyond their earnest desire to preserve their regard for their fellow townspeople. They hoped the gift would be appreciated purely upon its merits, for it was offered with no view to this or that object.' [20] As for the timing, his special regard for the outgoing mayor had convinced him that the completion of the undercliff drive was the 'psychological moment'.[21]

If, before that day, anyone doubted Merton's contribution to the completion of the drive, then his name would be forever associated with its opening. That placed even more importance on the scheme's success. He and Annie were parting with East Cliff Hall come what may, but a failed drive would undermine the gift's foundations.

Notes:

1. *The Times*, 13 March 1905.
2. *Bournemouth Graphic*, 16 March 1905. Merton bought back at least one of the paintings sold at the auction – *Always Welcome* by Lady Alma-Tadema.
3. The construction cost of East Cliff Hall is given as £18,000 on p. 281 of *Home and Abroad*.
4. Irving laid the foundation stone of the same fountain while staying at the Royal Bath over Christmas and New Year in 1904/5.
5. *Home and Abroad*, p. 801.
6. Stoker aside, extracts from at least three biographies are included in *Home and Abroad*: Fitzgerald's *Sir Henry Irving, A Biography* (1906), Menpes' *Henry Irving* (1906) and Brereton's *Life of Henry Irving* (1908). Stoker's book lists almost 1,000 guests at Irving's hospitality events, although Merton's name is not among them.
7. *Home and Abroad*, p. 782.
8. An article in *The Stage* on 18 November 1920 refers to a 'new' Irving Room in the Russell-Cotes Art Gallery and Museum, but the *Bournemouth Graphic* mentioned it in its edition of 29 March 1906.
9. The 'pompous burial' quote first appeared in *Cassell's Magazine* and was widely reported. After Irving's first big triumph in *The Bells* in 1871, his wife, Florence, is reputed to have asked him: 'Are you going on making a fool of yourself like this all your life?' Irving is said to have stopped the carriage and stepped out into the night, never to speak to her again.
10. *Home and Abroad*, p. 866.
11. *Autobiography of Mark Twain*, Volume 3, 16 August 1907.
12. Merton's letter is held by the Mark Twain Project at the University of California.
13. The account of the public inquiry, including the quotations, comes from reports in the *Bournemouth Guardian* of 5 May, 26 May and 2 June 1906. The hearings were spread over several weeks.
14. *Bournemouth Graphic*, 31 May 1906.
15. Carnegie gave money for numerous British libraries, leading many councils to

grant him the freedom of their boroughs. Critics denounced him for cynical self-promotion – an occupational hazard for any philanthropist. In 1903, he offered £10,000 for branch libraries in Bournemouth, but concerns about the conditions attached to the gift delayed the project for several years.
16. Bert already had experience of local government, as he had been elected to the Christchurch Board of Guardians in 1904.
17. *Bournemouth Graphic*, 13 June 1907.
18. *Bournemouth Guardian*, 9 November 1907.
19. The mayor's speech mentions only Bert and Ella. Clarie was running Baldwin's hotel at this point. A few months before the drive's opening, Annie settled the premises of G. Lane & Co. (the wine merchants in the town centre) on Ella. Merton and Arthur Painter were the partners in the business at the time.
20. *Home and Abroad*, p. 236.
21. ibid.

14

RECIPIENT

A month after the drive's inauguration, the *Daily Mirror* broke the news that formed the stuff of Merton's nightmares: 'At Bournemouth, the new undercliff drive, only opened a few weeks ago, has been practically destroyed.' [1] A photograph appeared alongside the article, showing great slabs of kerbing strewn all over the beach. Here was a story to gladden the hearts of the I-told-you-so party. After all the fine talk by its supporters at the public inquiry, this much-heralded saviour of the cliffs had surrendered to the first gale of the winter. Or so it appeared to anyone who relied on the London press for their information. In Bournemouth, most residents read the report with consternation. They knew the storm had disturbed a layer of gravel and buffeted a few stones waiting to be laid, but that was about the extent of it.

Suspicion soon grew about the source of the story. Days before it broke, the secretary of the Residents' Association had sent a letter to the *Bournemouth Guardian* complaining about 'the Sub-Marine Drive'.[2] He refused to believe assurances about earlier storm damage and claimed that costs were running out of control. The council, he said, had built a pointless path near the electric lift and wasted money on 'massive stone erections' – meaning the toilets near the pier. The newspaper, knowing where to point the finger, sent a man down to canvas opinion on the seafront. 'It was a delightful, almost summerlike day,' he reported back. 'A host of happy residents, including lots of members of the Residents' Association (not on the committee) were enjoying the promenade.' [3] As for the *Daily Mirror*, it blundered again when printing a retraction. The storm had not destroyed the drive after all, it admitted, and just fifty pounds would set it to rights. 'This beautiful drive,' it went on, 'the gift to the town of Mr Russell Cotes, will therefore be available for the enjoyment of the inhabitants of Bournemouth and visitors without interruption.' [4]

Most newspapers correctly reported Merton and Annie's gift, but even the mayor was forced to revise part of his original announcement. It comprised *a collection* of works of art, he was obliged to say, and not *the collection*, as first stated. Moreover, the couple had yet to confirm the inclusion of the Irish property in the gift. Although mere quibbles, these details highlight the complexities of the transaction. Merton sought to dispel any lingering doubts about their intentions by inviting members of the council to see East Cliff Hall for themselves. Only then did the scale of the couple's generosity become clear. The mayor described the place as 'overloaded', with the main hall and balcony alone crammed with enough treasures to fill the house.[5] The visit also allayed fears about the building's suitability for public use, with the mayor even raising the possibility of extending it.

While *Home and Abroad* offers few clues about the couple's motives for giving away so much, the council's inspection delivered one instant by-product: Merton regained control of his own narrative. No one was carping about blocked roads, Square clocks or children's carnivals anymore. The council acknowledged the gift without reservation and with well-deserved plaudits. It is surprising, then, to read in *Home and Abroad* that the couple's first thought was to leave the house to the town only after their deaths. They gained enormous satisfaction from their philanthropy, a pleasure that a posthumous gift would have denied them. If that induced a change of heart, then a planned move to the suburbs of Poole may also have influenced the

56 Storm damage on the undercliff drive, 1907. The drive was not tarmacked at first, giving rise to dire warnings when December gales disturbed the loose surface. 'If pessimism is an art,' wrote the Bournemouth Guardian, *'the committee of the Bournemouth Residents' Association possesses it in full measure and overflowing.'*[6] (Bournemouth Library)

decision to act when they did. As early as 1905, a friend had tried to persuade them to build a house next to his own in Parkstone, an idea very much on their minds when they gave away East Cliff Hall. The timing of the gift makes more sense when viewed in that light, with the life tenancy providing a useful backstop in case the move to Poole fell through.

The couple signed the deed of gift on 1st February 1908, their forty-eighth wedding anniversary. It transferred East Cliff Hall to the council with immediate effect. Henceforth, the building would be called 'The Russell Cotes Art Gallery and Museum' and run by a committee.[7] More than 250 items, over a third of them paintings, are listed in the schedule of art and artefacts, but this tells only part of the story. Many are cabinets and display tables, each of which contained a host of ceramics or curiosities. Also of interest are the comments added by Merton to highlight the things he valued most. The Buddhist shrine bought in Japan and a lacquered table used by Disraeli are among the items to include a few words about their provenance. There are some surprises in the document, too. The Eugénie cabinet is listed, but the entry says nothing about the Empress, let alone her swoon. *Girl Combing Her Hair*, Merton's first painting, is not mentioned at all, implying that the couple intended to leave the more personal items to the family. The Irving relics are also excluded, but Merton later changed his mind about those.

Although the deed of gift transferred the ownership of East Cliff Hall to the council, Merton and Annie needed to give their permission for its public use while they were still in residence. When they agreed to hold an open day for ratepayers in April 1908, more than a thousand people flocked to see the house. This enthusiasm fulfilled the prediction made by the curator of the

57 Girl Combing Her Hair *by the Scottish artist James Giles. Also known as* The Toilet, *Merton named the work as his first art purchase in an interview with the* Bournemouth Guardian *in 1917. Giles was a member of the Royal Scottish Academy and spent much of his life in Aberdeen, where Merton bought the painting.* (Russell-Cotes Art Gallery and Museum)

Glasgow Corporation Art Gallery soon after the gift was announced. 'I am sure it will be well appreciated by inhabitants and visitors to your lovely and salubrious town,' he wrote to Merton. 'We may hope also that it will be recognised in a tangible manner in the highest circle.' [8] Recognition and gratitude were, of course, bound to follow such a remarkable act of generosity. For its part, the council wasted no time in doing the right thing. With the ink barely dry on the deed of gift, they voted unanimously to confer the freedom of the borough on the beneficent couple. At the same meeting, the council agreed to make an offer of £40,000 for the Belle Vue Hotel – the long-awaited first step towards building a pavilion. What with that, and a growing clamour for the extension of the undercliff drive, Merton was gaining a reputation as the town's benefactor, sage and venerated elder statesman.

On 15th July 1908, the council summoned a glittering array of lords, knights and MPs to Bournemouth to honour their new freemen. Lord and Lady Wimborne sent their apologies, as did Herbert Asquith (1852–1928), the Prime Minister. It was almost thirteen years to the day since Merton had refused to call a public meeting about South Road. On her seventy-third birthday, Annie joined her husband on the stage of the Winter Gardens in readiness to be inducted as the town's first female freeman. Some reports claimed she was the first woman in the country to be granted the distinction, thus overlooking at least one recent recipient. Dorothea Beale (1831–1906) – no relation to the Bournemouth shopkeeper – received the freedom of Cheltenham in 1901 for her work with the Ladies' College. A champion of feminist causes, Beale stood at the other end of the spectrum to Annie, who sat on the committee of the local branch of the Anti-Suffrage League. Merton, who served alongside her, described militant suffragettes as 'demented, insane and absolute lunatics.' [9]

Like John Elmes Beale, the couple received their freedom scroll in a silver-gilt casket. Its design, the result of a competition between local art students, featured East Cliff Hall, the undercliff drive and the arms of the Shropshire Coteses. The mayor's speech catalogued Merton's contributions to the town, including the pier opening, the mace and badge, the BMA conference, Prince Henry of Battenberg, et al. In stressing the importance of these events to Bournemouth's development, the mayor also acknowledged the boost they gave to the Royal Bath. This, however, was as close as he came to dredging up past controversies. His précis of Merton's mayoralty dwelt only on the positives and steered well clear of South Road. By doing so, he placed the gift of East Cliff Hall against a backdrop of unblemished public service. In response, Merton focused on his obsession for art, but stressed that he and Annie were not millionaires, despite rumours to the contrary. He urged wealthy citizens to help the museum to expand and assured them of a happier mind if they chose not to hoard their money. By way of

58 Merton depicted in a cartoon by Eustace Nash (1886–1969), a regular contributor to the Bournemouth Graphic. *Merton and Annie were the third and fourth freemen of the town. The twenty-eighth and last – the final decision made by Bournemouth Borough Council before it merged with Christchurch and Poole in 2019 – was Eddie Howe, manager of AFC Bournemouth.* (Bournemouth Library)

encouragement, he announced that Bert would be donating his personal collection of Irving relics to the museum.

Praise for the new freemen flooded in from all quarters. While the *Glasgow Herald* confined itself to Annie's links to the city and her occasional literary efforts, Ayrshire's *Carrick Courier* could barely contain its excitement. The honour would 'redound to the glory of Girvan,' it enthused, 'the little town kissed by the waters of the Firth of Clyde and fanned by the ozone-laden winds of the North Atlantic.' The paper's pride ended on a note of frustration that the couple had chosen not to make their home in the town. 'We must concede,' it went on, 'that the same opportunities could not have been furnished here of attaining such high social distinction.' [10]

Girvan, with or without Merton and Annie, could never have rivalled Bournemouth's rate of expansion. The weather almost guaranteed that. The two towns were of a similar size when the couple took over at the Bath Hotel, but Bournemouth had grown ten-fold since then. Merton, who had achieved so much off the back of that growth, could be forgiven for resting on the casket of his newly acquired honour. But that was never in his nature. On the contrary, he used the freedom of the borough to lobby even harder for his pet projects. When he heard of plans to feature seaside resorts at an exhibition in London, he implored the council to seize its chance. They should make a model of the borough in stucco, he suggested, and display plans for the pavilion. He even came up with ideas for Bournemouth-themed products – photograph albums, decorated china and pine-scented soap. The new freeman also threw his weight behind the mayor's personal efforts to promote the resort. In a letter to the press, he urged the town's shopkeepers to show the same level of commitment as its hotels: 'I may add that for thirty-three years, during which time I have been connected with the Royal Bath Hotel, the account for its advertising has varied from about £400 to between £600 and £700 per annum.' [11] This was the feisty and opinionated Merton familiar to all, the difference being that people were now taking more notice. When he presented a bust of Christopher Creeke to adorn the council chamber, no one complained or tried to have it put somewhere else. The council not only agreed to accept the gift but received a bust of Merton into the bargain, donated and unveiled by Annie.

The freedom of the borough also gave Merton certain liberties outside Bournemouth. Later that year, he used his clout to secure an audience with Jack Pease (1860–1943), the Chief Whip in Asquith's Liberal government. The reason for the meeting is uncertain, but the mere fact that Pease agreed to see him speaks volumes. Merton may have been there to discuss the Licensing Bill, a contentious plan to curb excessive drinking by culling the number of licensed premises. He wanted hotels exempted from a proposed compensation levy as they were not the cause of the problem the Bill sought to address. As it turned out, the House of Lords threw out the proposals on the day of the planned meeting, so it may not have gone ahead anyway. Merton, though, was riding the wave of self-confidence that came with being a man of importance.

While entitled to remain at East Cliff Hall for the rest of their days, Merton and Annie hankered after a more secluded retirement. They still favoured a move to Parkstone, where Horace Dobell, Merton's former doctor, owned a bungalow. Having been convinced by Dobell of the charms of the place, Merton decided not to hold back. Towards the end of 1908, he bought forty acres of land from Lord Wimborne in an area known as Constitution Hill. The estate lay about a mile from the centre of Poole and came with fine views across the harbour towards the Isle of Purbeck. As keen as ever to put his ideas into action, Merton commissioned the local architect Harry Hawker (1855–1926) to design a two-storey house for the site.[12] It marks the start of a puzzling sequence of events that drew Merton into the murky world of political favours and the vagaries of party funding.

The immediate sequel to the Parkstone purchase was an appointment with Winston Churchill at his office in Westminster. Churchill, who was Lady Wimborne's nephew, held a cabinet seat as president of the Board of Trade. As such, the undercliff drive extension, the pavilion or the resort exhibition in London are the most likely topics Merton wanted to discuss. The purpose of the meeting is, however, less important than the fact it took place. He went to London armed with a letter of introduction from Lady Wimborne, who also wrote a private letter to her nephew with some background about the Bournemouth hotelier. She mentioned the Royal Bath, the gift of East Cliff

Hall, the Parkstone estate purchase and Merton's aspirations to become what she called 'an influential country gentleman.' All this served as a preamble to the main point of her letter: a plea to Churchill to make a fuss of his visitor in the hope that he might declare himself in favour of the Liberals. While admitting ignorance of Merton's political allegiances, she believed that a man of such wealth and influence would be a great asset to the cash-strapped party.[13]

Churchill had never met Merton but should have been aware of him. The Wimbornes owned an estate at Branksome Dene, to the west of Bournemouth, which Churchill often visited in his youth. He came close to death there in his teens when he tried to jump from a bridge into a pine tree and fell thirty feet onto hard ground. If the owner of the Royal Bath failed to come to his notice during these visits, then the two men also shared the connection of the Oldham art exhibition. Lady Wimborne drew attention to the fact by enclosing an extract from a press report with her letter.[14] In a further twist to the tale, Merton's autobiography reveals that, in 1905, the Conservatives invited him to stand for parliament in the Oldham seat at the next general election. His loan collection put him in the frame when Churchill left to join the Liberals. Merton thought little of the politicians of the day, believing that the country would be best run by 'thoroughly capable, travelled men of business.'[15] If that made him well qualified, then an exchange of letters with Central Office suggests he took some time to make up his mind. He declined on health grounds in the end, but the story highlights the rich vein of Conservatism running throughout *Home and Abroad.*

Despite his Conservative leanings, Merton was not one to allow politics to get in the way of business. When it came to the museum, he reserved a place on the management committee for the local MP, regardless of who they, or their party, happened to be. It was Arthur Acland Allen (1868–1939), the Liberal member for Christchurch, at the time of his meeting with Churchill. Allen held regular meetings in Bournemouth, none of which Merton is known to have attended until he went to a gathering at Westbourne in January 1909. Captain Freddie Guest (1875–1937) – the Liberal candidate for East Dorset and a son of Lady Wimborne – gave a speech at the same meeting. Guest was then Churchill's private secretary but went on to become the Liberal Chief Whip during and after the Great War. In that role, he worked hard to plug the hole in the party's coffers by creating a fixed-price menu for peerages, baronetcies and knighthoods.[16] While things had yet to reach that stage in 1909, the Liberals had been playing the honours game since the mid-1890s. While there is little to suggest that Merton chose to join in, his untimely trip to Westbourne might well have surprised anyone familiar with his politics. As unfortunate as that might seem, these events are less a reflection on him than they are an indictment of a broken honours system. Regardless of his motives, only a harsh critic would deny that Merton paid his dues to the common good when he gave up his home and art collection.

As 1909 rolled on, plans for the Parkstone estate appeared to be heading towards a conclusion. Rumours surfaced of an imminent departure from East Cliff Hall, prompting hopes of a quick handover of the museum to the council. The sale of Merton's Mayfair hotel at around the same time suggests there was an element of substance to this gossip. Yet there was no hint of such a move when the Lord Mayor of London, Sir George Truscott (1857– 1941), visited the town in June of that year. He came to cut the ribbon on an extension to the pier opened by his father some twenty-nine years earlier. The day's schedule allowed for a tour of East Cliff Hall, enabling Merton to make much of the link between the father, the son, the pier and himself. He presented his guest with an album of photographs, including one captioned 'Mr and Mrs Russell Cotes at home'.[17] Truscott and his two sheriffs returned the compliment by posing for a snapshot with their host and the mayor of Bournemouth. Four of these five gentlemen were to appear on the King's birthday honours list published later that month. The two sheriffs received knighthoods, while Truscott was elevated to the baronetage. One of the two local men also received some good news.

Three weeks after the Lord Mayor's visit, the people of Bournemouth opened their newspapers to read the glad tidings. The King had raised Merton to the rank of knight bachelor – a non-hereditary title that made him a 'Sir' and Annie a 'Lady'. Mr and Mrs Russell Cotes, it could be said, were no longer at home. The sober-minded *Bournemouth Guardian* presented the plain facts of the case: 'Our old friend and townsman, who has been so prominently connected with Bournemouth for so many years, has fairly won his spurs.'[18] The more playful *Bournemouth Graphic* preferred to rejoice in verse:

> *All honour to those to whom due*
> *Is an axiom both good and true*
> *And Sir M. Russell Cotes*
> *Every burgess now votes*
> *None worthier of knighthood than you.*[19]

In the national press, *The Times*, while hailing him as a good citizen and generous benefactor, listed Merton under a general heading in its roll call of honours. It would have been more natural to place him under 'Philanthropy' or 'Art, Science and Letters'. Their citation includes the gift of East Cliff Hall and the travelling loan collection, and yet 'Governor of the Royal Victoria Hospital' appears first among his achievements. This was a minor thing compared to the rest, as a governorship was an honorary position given to those making generous contributions to the hospital's funds. There is little doubt, however, that East Cliff Hall won Merton his knighthood, irrespective

THE ART OF A SALESMAN

of any influence brought to bear by the Liberal Party. The result was the same in any event: Bournemouth gained a house crammed with art and artefacts, while the bagman's boy from Wolverhampton joined the establishment he had esteemed for so long. Nevertheless, the new title caused confusion in some quarters, with one newspaper dubbing him 'Sir Russell' in the immediate aftermath of the announcement. Introducing a hyphen between his middle and last names eventually dealt with that confusion, although a subsequent upgrade of Cotes to Côtes may have had more to do with aesthetics.

Merton went to the Palace on 22nd July 1909 to be knighted by King Edward VII. Among others invested that day were the dramatist Arthur Pinero (1855–1934) and the actor Herbert Beerbohm Tree (1852–1917). As the men waited nervously in the ballroom, military officers in dazzling uniforms stood on the other side of a rope partition. When it came to his turn, Merton revelled in those few precious moments spent with his sovereign. To his astonishment, as he struggled to rise from his knees, the King took his hand and helped him up. 'Is it to be wondered at,' he wrote, 'that this great-hearted man was universally loved and called "The Prince of Peacemakers"?' [20]

At the other end of the kingdom, Girvan passed a resolution in council to congratulate the new knight and his lady. Bournemouth did likewise, amid continuing rumours of the couple's impending move to Poole. They proved unfounded. Whether a straightforward change of mind, or a dream tainted

59 Merton in a photograph to mark his knighthood in July 1909. Herbert Beerbohm Tree, who was knighted on the same day, was the father of the film director Carol Reed and grandfather of the actor Oliver Reed. Also honoured that day was Mark Oldroyd, a woollen manufacturer and resident of Batley – a town familiar to Merton from his days as a commercial traveller. (From *Home and Abroad*)

by political intrigue, the planned house in Parkstone never came to fruition. The forty acres of land at Constitution Hill lay untouched for a decade until a final burst of philanthropy saw the entire estate given away to good causes. Merton chose not to consummate his flirtation with the Liberals and, if anything, his politics shifted to the right as time went on. Regardless of what happened in the months leading up to it, he was determined to enjoy his hard-won knighthood.

Notes:

1. Quoted in the *Bournemouth Guardian*, 21 December 1907.
2. *Bournemouth Guardian*, 14 December 1907.
3. ibid., 21 December 1907.
4. *Daily Mirror*, 19 December 1907, taken from Merton's undercliff drive scrapbook.
5. *Bournemouth Guardian*, 7 December 1907.
6. ibid., 21 December 1907.
7. The deed names the committee as follows: the mayor, the deputy mayor, two aldermen (chosen annually), the Lord Lieutenant of the County of Southampton, Sir George Meyrick (or his successor), the MP for the borough (meaning the MP for Christchurch at the time) and the trustees of Merton's will. Two discretionary members were also named, Sir Charles Scotter and Alfred Trapnell, who could be replaced at the committee's discretion. Trapnell was a porcelain collector based in Boscombe.
8. *Home and Abroad*, p. 233.
9. Taken from Merton's scrapbooks.
10. ibid.
11. ibid.
12. The plans are dated February 1909. Why Merton favoured Hawker over Fogerty for this commission is not known. Hawker also designed The Imperial in Bournemouth and was responsible for the extension of the Royal Exeter Hotel in the 1880s.
13. The letters referred to are held by the Churchill College Archives, Cambridge (CHAR2/36, 21 to 24).
14. Merton must have supplied the extract, because the quotation on pp. 696–97 of *Home and Abroad* is identical to that given in Lady Wimborne's letter.
15. *Home and Abroad*, p. 922.
16. The Honours (Prevention of Abuses) Act of 1925 outlawed such practices.
17. *Bournemouth Guardian*, 12 June 1909.
18. ibid., 26 June 1909.
19. *Bournemouth Graphic*, 1 July 1909.
20. *Home and Abroad*, p. 269.

15

KNIGHT

Merton and Annie repaid Girvan's compliment by making it their first port of call as a titled couple. They cut short their visit to attend a function arranged by Marie Corelli in Stratford-upon-Avon, where they made their public debut as Sir Merton and Lady Annie Russell Cotes. This was a big moment for them and for the publicity-conscious writer. A firm believer in preserving Stratford's old buildings, Corelli had persuaded a Chicago businessman to buy a house once owned by the grandfather of the founder of Harvard University. Built during Shakespeare's lifetime, but with no other connection to the playwright, she hoped it would become a place of pilgrimage for the bard's American fans. Merton found himself named alongside Sir Thomas Lipton at the top of the guest list for the grand opening of the restored house.

Corelli's invitation shows how hard Merton worked to maintain his social network. Not content with relying on friends to read the newspapers, he sent press cuttings far and wide to apprise them of his doings. Corelli was one of those who received a missive with news of the gift of East Cliff Hall, and she vowed to see it at the earliest opportunity. It took until after Merton's knighthood to make good on the promise, perhaps being less inclined to head south after the *Bournemouth Graphic* dismissed her latest novel as '500 pages of twaddle'.[1] When she did finally visit, Merton invited their old vicar from Altrincham to come and meet her. The two men had kept in touch for forty years. 'It pleases me greatly,' wrote the clergyman, 'that I am thought to be still one of your circle by the fact that the Bournemouth newspapers are sent to me whenever something special is happening there. And these special events are not rare in a community so spirited as yours.'[2]

Merton's enthusiasm for nurturing his contacts showed no sign of diminishing with age. His knighthood placed him in a position of patronage, giving him the same power of conferring favours that he had so often sought from others. Whichever side of that transaction he found himself on, he liked to think of it as more than a matter of expediency. The frequency with which he refers to people as 'my dear old friend' and 'an intimate friend' suggests that he took a broad view of these phrases. One of his most intriguing post-knighthood friendships was with the children of Edward Kenealy (1819–1880), a maverick lawyer who represented the defendant in one of the most infamous trials of the nineteenth century. The case concerned the apparent return from the dead of the son of a baronet. Assumed drowned after a shipwreck in 1854, a man claiming to be Sir Roger Tichborne (b. 1829) surfaced more than a decade later in the guise of a butcher from Wagga Wagga. A civil case concluded he was an imposter, leading to a criminal trial for perjury, a prison sentence and Kenealy's disbarment for misconduct.

Merton considered the Tichborne case to be a gross miscarriage of justice and was not shy of saying so. This helps to explain the dedication that appears in a book about the trial written by Maurice Kenealy (1858–1921), the lawyer's son. It reads: 'To my good friend, Sir Merton Russell-Cotes, J.P., F.R.G.S., Member of the Council of the Church Association, and President of the Protestant Truth Society, as an appreciation of his love of justice and sense of public responsibility, I dedicate this book.' [3] The high-minded principles so admired here sprang from the same source as the obstinate high-handedness derided by others in the past.

Maurice Kenealy was one of many friends and associates who came to Bournemouth in 1910 to celebrate Merton and Annie's golden wedding. The couple chose to wait until the summer to mark the occasion, as it allowed them to round off the town's centenary festivities with their own celebrations. The council had arranged a programme of fetes, carnivals and balls to honour the moment when Lewis Tregonwell first set eyes on the Bourne stream. These events demanded largesse, prompting the press to publish the names of those who made a contribution. If the sum given is a guide to status, then Merton's £250 put him in the same league as Lady Wimborne and the local MP. An air show at Southbourne provided the main attraction, drawing in crowds to watch aviators compete for height, speed and precision of landing. This last contest saw Britain's first fatal accident in a powered aircraft when Charles Rolls (1877–1910), co-founder of Rolls-Royce, crashed his biplane in front of the grandstand. Sir Thomas Lipton took on the grim task of breaking the news to his parents when they arrived in Bournemouth.

By holding their party at the end of the centenary, Merton and Annie gave their guests another reason to make the journey. Lipton himself was invited but was too busy with the social whirl leading up to Cowes Week to attend.[4] Instead, Sir George Meyrick and Sir Charles Scotter headed the guest list for the garden party at East Cliff Hall. Meyrick presented the couple with a gift from their friends – a silver-gilt punch bowl made by Garrard, the crown jewellers. A gold bonbon spoon, a gold cigar cutter, a gold pencil case and a gold coffee bean featured among the smaller presents. In the evening, Merton paid tribute to the woman he loved during a dinner at the Royal Bath. 'After fifty years, one has found out whether one's wife or husband is companionable,' he said. 'I have found out that there is only one woman in the world for whom I would die and that is my wife.' [5]

In the autumn, the couple embarked on their last long holiday abroad – to southern Spain and the French Riviera. Bert, who was nearing the end of a difficult year, went with them for the first part of the trip. He had resigned from the council in February, citing overwork caused by his burgeoning business commitments. Among them was the chairmanship of a speculative mining venture in Mexico, to where he had set sail soon after his resignation. On returning to England in April, his ship struck rocks in a thick fog as it passed the Isles of Scilly, fortunately without loss of life. Bert kept his business affairs closer to home after that. His trip to Spain presented its own problems, as his mother twice required the services of a doctor during their visit to Gibraltar. The early signs of heart problems, Annie's condition warranted an extended stay in Cannes to recuperate. Merton was worried enough to wire home asking Ella to join them. The couple returned to Bournemouth in the spring, a few days before Bert's wife delivered the last of their six grandchildren.

With Annie's health now a constant concern, Merton settled into a different pattern of life. His status as the oracle of seaside progressiveness was now assured, and his title brought gravitas to many a prize-giving, flower show and charity event. The council made him an honoured guest at the laying of the foundation stone of the undercliff drive extension in June 1911, but the lack of progress on the pavilion was now his biggest bugbear.[6] Interviewed by a local newspaper for a series entitled *Prominent People on Bournemouth's Future*, he thought it even more pressing than extending the drive. 'What we really need,' he said, 'is a pavilion that would put at the disposal of our visitors all the conveniences and comforts of a first-rate London club. It should contain reading rooms, conversation rooms, billiard rooms, ballrooms and the like.' [7]

Although the council had bought the Belle Vue site back in 1908, problems with the alcohol licence meant that not a brick had been laid since. The Local Government Board would only license the dining room, but the council wanted to include the whole building to make the venture pay. After repeated pleas failed to overturn the decision, the mayor asked Merton to make their case in person. He went to London to see John Burns MP (1858–1943), the board's president. A Liberal man by party but a trade unionist in deed, Burns – the son of a fitter and a washerwoman – was the first working-class man to serve in the cabinet. Merton's arguments failed to persuade him, but not for the reasons he might have expected. Burns knew Bournemouth as a high-class resort and believed it should stay as such, an opinion shared

60 John Burns MP was president of the Local Government Board from 1905 to 1914. A powerful orator, he received a six-week prison sentence in 1887 for defying a ban on public meetings in Trafalgar Square. He was also a puritanical teetotaller and held firm in the face of pressure to relax the licensing conditions for Bournemouth's planned pavilion. (Public domain image)

by them both. They differed in that Burns could see trouble ahead if he allowed the sale of strong drink in the pavilion basement – a part of the building intended for the hoi polloi. Merton went away disappointed, then grew ever more frustrated as the debate went endlessly round in circles. Letters to the press aside, his efforts to solve the impasse were his last significant foray into local politics. He devoted the best part of his time and energy to Annie and the museum thereafter.

By the end of 1911, almost four years on from its formal transfer to the council, East Cliff Hall had yet to open to the public other than for occasional one-off viewings. While this was inevitable after the couple shelved their move to Parkstone, the lapse of time meant that some people had all but forgotten about the place. At the annual meeting of the Bournemouth Arts Society that December, its chairman – a local magistrate, no less – called it a disgrace that the town had no art gallery. The council spent money on the drive and the pavilion, he complained, yet neglected to invest in high culture. This awkward state of affairs spurred Merton and the council into action. Less than a fortnight later, the mayor announced that the museum would open for two hours on the first Wednesday of every month. To manage the numbers, visitors were obliged to obtain a free ticket from the town clerk. Merton underlined the building's new status by asking John F. Fogerty to design a decorative panel over the main entrance. Several hundred people passed beneath it each month in the first year of opening.

With the Russell-Cotes Art Gallery and Museum now a functioning institution, Merton occupied a revered place in local life. One newspaper dubbed him the town's 'G.O.M.' (Grand Old Man), while another called him 'The Maker of Bournemouth'.[8] The latter might not have sat well with those who had crossed him in the past, but many of that old guard were no longer around to dispute the claim. Henry Newlyn died in March 1912, following

61 There is no clear point when Merton adopted the hyphen between 'Russell' and 'Cotes', although he uses it throughout Home and Abroad. *The improved entrance to East Cliff Hall (pictured here) includes one, whereas the 1908 deed of gift does not. Bert remained as plain Herbert V. M. Cotes while his father was alive but changed his surname by deed poll to 'Russell Cotes' – without the hyphen – in August 1921. (From* Home and Abroad*)*

Enoch White (1890), J. H. Moore (1898), Thomas Hankinson (1905) and Joseph Cutler (1910) into the silence of the grave. J. Ralph Smythe was still very much alive but had taken a promenade to Damascus in respect of the undercliff drive. While Newlyn's death brought the expected tributes, years of solid public service were not enough to make him stand out from his peers in the long run. Today, he is largely forgotten. Merton, who was prevented by illness from attending the funeral, lowered the flags of the Royal Bath out of respect to his old rival.

The part-time opening of East Cliff Hall did little to silence the debate about its future. While best known for its paintings and sculptures, the house was always intended to serve as a museum as well as an art gallery. The deed of gift said as much, but the building was already struggling to cope with what it had. This meant, for example, that a further gift by Merton and Annie of more than a hundred historic weapons – a mixture of swords, pistols and bows and arrows – came with the caveat that they remained in storage until the couple moved out. New acquisitions also swelled the museum's stock, while appeals from Merton for Irving memorabilia yielded results and the occasional rebuke. 'There is a man in Bournemouth I stand in dread of!' Ellen Terry complained in a letter to Annie. 'You know him!! In fact, you married him!!!'[9]

For the council, the crux of the matter was whether East Cliff Hall alone could serve as the town's museum. The question became more pressing when the Bournemouth Natural Science Society wanted a display space for its eclectic array of specimens.[10] Amid talk of setting up its own premises, some people pointed out the obvious: the Russell-Cotes Art Gallery and Museum would serve the purpose if the council exercised the right to extend it set out in the deed of gift. Merton and Annie urged them to do just that and offered to endow further property if the council bought the freehold. But with no money to spare in the borough coffers, and with Sir George Meyrick said to be against the idea, the first flush of enthusiasm soon faded. The Bournemouth Natural Science Society later set up a home for itself away from the town centre.

Although Merton failed to convince the council to expand the museum, his knighthood gave him far more influence than he had wielded in the past. In early 1914, he persuaded Lord Ribblesdale (1854–1925), a trustee of the National Gallery, to fill the vacancy on the museum's management committee caused by the death of Sir Charles Scotter.[11] Ribblesdale had recently visited Bournemouth to open a modern art exhibition, prompting him to tell a joke about a painting hanging upside down when he called at East Cliff Hall afterwards. Merton could have been describing himself when he says of Ribblesdale: 'He is a great enthusiast in British art but has a great contempt for the impressionist and cubist school.'[12] Royal Academy members still held sway in Merton's eyes, hence his delight when Sir Hubert von Herkomer (1849–1914) stayed at the Royal Bath soon after Ribblesdale's departure. Thanks to Merton and Annie's persuasion, Herkomer agreed to lend a selection of his works for an exhibition at the local art college. It

62 The Russell-Cotes family, c. 1913. Standing (L–R): Evelyn (Bert's daughter), Gwendoline (Clarie's daughter), Merton, Clarie, Anita (Bert's middle daughter) and Ella. Seated: Bert and Edith Cotes (with daughter Edith in arms), Annie, and Edward Stebbing. Edward and Phyllis (Ella's children) are sitting on the floor. (From *Home and Abroad*)

opened in May 1914 and ran until a few weeks before the outbreak of war.[13] Despite living in England for fifty years and bearing a British knighthood, Herkomer's roots would have proved awkward if the exhibition had run much longer. Later sensitivities around all things Germanic were such that Merton, writing towards the end of the war, describes the Bavarian-born artist as 'Anglo-Dutch' in *Home and Abroad*.

None of that mattered in the early months of 1914. More than 30,000 people paid to stroll on the pier over the Easter holidays, and all the hotels were packed to capacity. The undercliff drive extension opened in June, completing Sir Joseph Bazalgette's vision of an unbroken promenade between Bournemouth and Boscombe. Merton and Annie marked the event by endowing property to the museum, despite receiving no promises about its extension in return. They laid on a civic lunch at the King's Hall – the Royal Bath's cavernous new ballroom. Opened the previous December, it was one of John F. Fogerty's last commissions in Bournemouth before he emigrated to South Africa. Merton brought in Oliver Thomas to decorate the hall in his father's style, but events elsewhere meant that it would be several years before the work concluded.

Less than a month after the opening of the extended drive, a Bosnian-Serb radical shot dead an Austrian archduke in Sarajevo, triggering the chain of events that led to global catastrophe. Britain entered the war on 4th August 1914, the day after the summer bank holiday.[14] Bournemouth, already quieter than usual in the build-up, saw visitors drift away as soon as the news broke. There were fewer arrivals, too, as train companies suspended services in the initial confusion. Things settled down a little over the next few days as people took heed of reassurances that it would all be over by Christmas. The town clerk advised businesses to carry on regardless, a message Merton took up in a letter to the London press. The resort remained open to visitors, he pointed out, with the town's traders ready to receive them and the railways back to normal.

Some disruption was inevitable, of course. In mid-August, along with many other coastal towns, the government declared Bournemouth a prohibited area, meaning that German nationals needed a permit to remain. That same month, the council requisitioned the Queen of Sweden's former holiday home on the East Cliff as a hospital for the wounded. In September, reports emerged of a plan to billet up to 12,000 soldiers in the town in readiness for crossing the Channel. The pavilion project received the go-ahead in the middle of this upheaval, a change of heart that meant nothing in practice. With the war bringing all but essential building work to a halt, the scheme entered a long hiatus that continued until after Merton's death.[15]

Despite claims in the German press of the populace fleeing in panic, Bournemouth did its best to present a cheery face. The town's hotels tried to do likewise, if not always successfully. Local magistrates fined the Royal

Bath's manager for failing to inform the authorities about a German man working there, while new lighting regulations caused no end of trouble. With a blackout required for all rooms facing the sea, the hotel was left at the mercy of guests rearranging the blinds. It led to a succession of fines. Merton, meanwhile, stood accused of being too quick to protect the Royal Bath's interests. Those residents who hoped to earn extra cash to compensate for absent menfolk blamed him when fewer soldiers arrived in the town than expected. As rumours spread that Merton had asked the War Office to keep them away, he denied doing anything of the sort and offered a ten-guinea reward to unearth the source of the story. As proof of his good intentions, he made the King's Hall available free of charge to anyone raising money for the mayor's war fund and other good causes. The offer stood for the duration of the conflict, allowing whist drives, rousing lectures and toy sales by disabled soldiers to do their patriotic bit. Bert's wife even came out of retirement to sing in concerts, while Merton brought in even more cash for the mayor's war chest by charging sixpence to visit the museum.

Merton's approach was typical of how Bournemouth dealt with the dilemma facing any holiday resort in wartime. The town wanted to be more than just a haven for the wounded and the battle-weary. As hordes of young men signed up for active service, those left behind raised money, tended the injured, billeted soldiers and welcomed Belgian refugees. Bert Cotes, who was too old for active service at the outset, joined the local volunteer regiment. In his own unique contribution to the country's morale, he sent an acrostic to the *Daily Express* forming the word 'Justice' from the names of the allied countries.[16]

To outsiders, the town's hotels appeared to be carrying on as normal. 'At

63 Bert Cotes was forty-three at the outbreak of war, putting him over the age limit (forty-one) when the government brought in conscription in 1916. From the outset, he served in the Hampshire Volunteer Regiment, attached to the Royal Garrison Artillery. The conscription age was extended to fifty in April 1918, but Bert's business commitments may have exempted him from active service. (From *Home and Abroad*)

first sight,' wrote *The Times* in January 1915, 'the Bournemouth of this winter is precisely the same as the Bournemouth of last winter.' [17] A second glance would have revealed otherwise. The wealthy, prevented by the conflict from travelling to their favoured foreign resorts, shared the Royal Bath's dining room with army officers in search of respite. This new, often younger, clientele offered a fresh perspective on the hotel's much-praised style and ambience. One Canadian colonel, recalling a visit with his comrades, found the décor in the main lounge overpowering: 'It was a discordant orgy of decorative effects, and the result was unutterably depressing.' When one of their party tried to make a joke of it, another muttered: 'I feel that nobody ever laughed in this place.' [18] While some of this negativity is down to age and culture, the remarks suggest that the Royal Bath risked getting stuck in the past.

The hotel, although a limited company since 1913, remained under Merton's ultimate control. The investment in the King's Hall speaks of a man looking forward, but an old-fashioned taste in art reflected his struggle to adapt to changing times. There is bewilderment, verging on despair, when he rails against the modern world in *Home and Abroad*. The war made things far, far worse. He bemoans jangling telephones and blaring car horns, not so much for what they are as for what they represent. 'Science has attempted to rob us of everything that is worth possessing,' he wrote. 'The beautiful stories in the Bible have been held up to ridicule, even to the question as to the existence of the Almighty Creator.' [19] Merton saw men of science as thieves, because they took away faith and gave nothing in return but misery, destruction and death. Modern women also infuriated him. They smoked cigarettes, travelled alone on buses and rode astride horses. Worse, they bathed in skin-tight costumes alongside men in some other resorts. Many of these gripes are those of an old man in any era – moral decline, bad manners and a lack of respect for parents. Others show his Presbyterian work ethic at odds with the frivolity he saw in the working classes. He thought they frittered away their time in music halls and cinemas instead of striving – as he had done – to better themselves.

East Cliff Hall provided a sanctuary away from these irritants. No matter how chaotic things seemed in the war-torn world outside, a lifetime's collection of art treasures helped Merton to make sense of his own place in it. Now entering his eighties, and with Annie less able to take her place at his side, he acted on behalf of them both to secure their legacy. They paid £1,000 for the freehold of the museum in December 1915, overcoming Sir George Meyrick's preference for leases. The following summer, they engaged Harry Hawker to design three new galleries at a further cost of £5,000. The walls were in place by the end of September, but then – in what Merton calls a 'bolt from the blue' – the Ministry of Munitions put a stop to the work.[20] Major building projects needed a licence, and the museum had failed to apply for one. Merton wrote to Lord Ribblesdale, who suggested sending a deputation to London to plead their case. Then, just as the negotiations reached a conclusion, a long-expected family bereavement struck. Daughter Clarie died in November 1916 at her London home, leaving an infant grandson – Merton and Annie's first great-grandchild – behind her.[21] She was fifty-four and had been suffering from cancer. A good reason for anyone to reflect on life's journey, Merton worked even harder from then onwards to tie up the loose ends of his own.

Notes:

1. *Bournemouth Graphic*, 24 September 1908. Corelli visited Bournemouth in November 1911, when she was reported to have presented Merton with a poem called *England*. A letter on p. 867 of *Home and Abroad* refers to her sending him the same poem in December 1908, while a facsimile of the verse opposite p. 875 is dated April 1909.
2. *Home and Abroad*, p. 943.
3. Kenealy's book, called *The Tichborne Tragedy*, was published in 1913. The 'J.P.' mentioned in the dedication refers to the seat on the bench that came with Merton's freedom of the borough. There may be two reasons for his interest in the case: Tichborne was in Buenos Aires prior to his fateful voyage, overlapping with Merton's time there. Moreover, Henry Angel – who captained their ship to Australia in 1884 – was a witness at the trial. As the claimant left prison just days before they sailed, it must have been a talking point en route.
4. Lipton was the most unsuccessful challenger in the history of the America's Cup, failing to win the trophy five times between 1899 and 1930.
5. *Bournemouth Guardian*, 30 July 1910.
6. A separate, quarter-mile section of promenade was opened to the west of the pier in June 1910.
7. *Bournemouth Graphic*, 10 November 1911.
8. *Sporting Times*, 15 June 1912 and *Bournemouth Graphic*, 20 December 1912.
9. *Home and Abroad*, p. 915, with Terry's exclamation marks.
10. The Bournemouth Natural Science Society was established in 1903. Merton and Annie joined in 1914.
11. The vacancy existed for more than three years, as Scotter died in December 1910.
12. *Home and Abroad*, p. 315.
13. Herkomer, who had also stayed at the Royal Bath in 1892, died a few weeks after his 1914 visit. His wife gave her blessing for the exhibition to go ahead.
14. The August bank holiday was on the first Monday of the month until the 1960s.
15. The pavilion was opened on the Belle Vue Hotel site in 1929.
16. The acrostic read **J**apan, R**u**ssia, **S**erbia, Mon**t**enegro, Belg**i**um, Fran**ce**, **E**ngland.
17. *The Times*, 15 January 1915.
18. Nasmith, *On the Fringe of the Great Fight*, pp. 54–55.
19. *Home and Abroad*, p. 8.
20. ibid., p. 275. A plaque on the wall of the galleries states that they were presented

to the borough on 15th July 1916. This appears to mark the date, Annie's eighty-first birthday, when the couple agreed to fund the extension. No building work had started at that point.
21. Clarie's daughter, Gwendoline Drew, married Ronald Stanford in 1915. They had a son and a daughter in 1916 and 1917 – the only great-grandchildren born in Merton and Annie's lifetime.

16

PHILANTHROPIST

With winter on the way and no roof on the new galleries, Merton turned to another museum trustee for help. The local MP, Henry Page Croft (1881–1947), arranged for Harry Hawker and the town clerk to see the minister in charge of building licences. They agreed a compromise: East Cliff Hall could have its extension but must use only two skilled men over the age of sixty, plus one labourer. Construction proceeded apace despite this lack of manpower and the adverse time of year. Merton acquired a few war souvenirs as the work progressed – a German officer's helmet among them – as he sought to widen the museum's appeal. Visitors in this period included Sir George Cave (1856–1928), the Home Secretary, who was not the first to liken it to a miniature Wallace Collection. Bequeathed to the nation by the widow of Sir Richard Wallace (1818–1890), the museum in Marylebone is still housed, like the Russell-Cotes, in the former home of its founder.

The builders completed their work in time for Merton and Annie's wedding anniversary in February 1917. To celebrate, the mayor held a gathering of distinguished guests in the empty galleries before moving on to the King's Hall for a formal reception. Annie, as the owner of the East Cliff Hall freehold and the nominal sponsor of the building work, received an illuminated address of thanks. Merton, so familiar now with the rituals of these occasions, spoke of his wife with pride. There was something reassuring about the proceedings – a symbol of order and goodwill in a time of chaos and hostility. This was the Britain Merton knew and loved, not the one embroiled in a brutal war of attrition on the other side of the Channel.

Thoughts of the conflict were uppermost in his mind when he began his autobiography in the spring of that same year.[1] After wistful musings about Tettenhall in the opening paragraphs, he veers off into a jarring rant about the world's ills. War was once 'a chivalrous and noble achievement,' he wrote, into which 'men rode like valiant heroes.'[2] By using poisoned gas, liquid fire and the like, he believed that Germany was using science to dehumanise the ordinary soldier. 'To please the Prussian Kaiser and his hosts,' he went on, 'they have to burrow and bury themselves in holes in the earth and fight, not face to face, but on their bellies in the mud like wild beasts.'

Merton, like many others in the town, had once been eager to pay homage to Kaiser Wilhelm (1859–1941). When the German Emperor stayed at nearby Highcliffe Castle in 1907, thousands turned out to see him inspect the new undercliff drive during his brief visit to Bournemouth. The council passed a vote of thanks and hoped for his return, while Merton – who put up part of the Emperor's suite at the Royal Bath – sent him a set of photographs of East Cliff Hall. Annie later forwarded a copy of *Westward from the Golden Gate* to the German embassy in London. Roll forward ten years and Merton was blaming the Kaiser not only for the war in Europe but also for the Russian Revolution. Bolshevism, he wrote, was 'a pernicious plant of German origin, which is absolutely alien to the Russian character.'[3]

Soon after Merton began *Home and Abroad*, a new political movement emerged that echoed some of his views. The National Party sprang from a breakaway group of Conservative MPs, with Henry Page Croft as one of its key figures. A veteran of two years on the Western Front, Croft found it hard to stomach petty squabbling in the House of Commons after witnessing mass slaughter.[4] His new party wanted a government of national unity to deliver swift and total victory in the war. Its message was patriotic, anti-German and pro-Empire. Some accused it of xenophobia, but many saw it as a beacon of hope after three years of conflict. Merton pledged his support as soon as the party's manifesto became public. Although sharing Croft's vision for Britain, the two men did not always agree on how to go about it. Croft urged understanding between employers and their workers and toyed with joining forces with the Labour Party. Merton branded striking workers as traitors and wanted them imprisoned or sent to the front.

While *Home and Abroad* only hints at Merton's links to the National Party, and says nothing of his offerings to the Kaiser, it is not the sort of book to rummage in the author's closet. The narrative relies heavily on information already in the public domain, much of it transcribed from various scrapbooks by his secretary, Louisa Sherrard (1865–1948). According to Merton's granddaughter, Miss Sherrard found him difficult to work with, and only generous inducements persuaded her not to quit.[5] Part of the tension may have arisen from the fact that a continuing flow of philanthropy was creating new material as they went along. Annie's gift of two houses in Bournemouth to the Royal Victoria Hospital warrants a brief mention in the book, as does two other properties she gave to the Shaftesbury Society and £500 that went to Dr Barnado's. These were generous gifts in themselves, but it is the couple's frequent endowments to the museum that claims the most prominent place in *Home and Abroad*.

In the autumn of 1917, Annie gave the freehold of East Cliff Hall to the borough and, at the same time, Merton signed over almost everything in the building not already covered by their earlier donations. This prompted the council to rename the street alongside the museum to 'Russell Cotes Road' in their honour.[6] It took until well into 1918 to finalise the paperwork for these latest gifts, by which time the war had turned decisively in the Allies' favour. Annie was in marked decline by then. 'Very gradually,' wrote Merton, 'little acts of loving care for others had to be relinquished, as failing health made rest and quiet imperative.'[7] As infirmity forced her to retreat from the public eye, a full-time nurse was brought in to care for her. These were anxious times. The war in Europe may have been nearing its end, but the influenza pandemic that was killing millions around the world also claimed many lives locally. This may be why, at the height of the crisis, Merton asked the council to suspend public access to East Cliff Hall.

The end of the war triggered a general election, the first in which women – or some of them, at least – were allowed to vote. The National Party hoped to back up its patriotic message with success at the polls, but things failed to go as planned. Henry Page Croft, standing in the new constituency of Bournemouth, was one of only two of its candidates to win a seat at Westminster. Despite hailing his victory as the dawn of a new era, the party's brightest days were already behind it. Besides, Merton now had more pressing priorities than politics. With Annie's life nearing its end, he decided to place her at the heart of an extraordinary trilogy of philanthropy in the year ahead. It kept the couple in the public eye for most of 1919 and brought a succession of royal visitors to East Cliff Hall.

The first of these three events, the official opening of the museum's extension, had been in the offing for some while. Although the council celebrated the completion of the work in 1917, the three new galleries were empty shells at the time. Merton then took charge of their decoration, using a simpler, brighter design than the main house. These were functional rather than domestic spaces. Skylights flooded the rooms with natural light, allowing old favourites and new acquisitions to be shown off to best advantage. Pride of place went to a group of biblical scenes by Edwin Long, whose vast canvasses benefitted from the airy and well-lit surroundings. Merton, copying John Thomas's literary flourishes at the hotel, composed a series of maxims to adorn the archways connecting each gallery. 'The eye rejoices in the beautiful from hour to hour' is typical of these.

Merton wanted to hold a grand opening for the finished galleries and, at the same time, mark the formal handover of the museum's freehold to the council. Keen for a regal presence to add gloss, he sought advice from Sir Thomas Lipton about who best to invite. Lipton, whose yachting exploits made him a royal favourite, placed Princess Beatrice – the late Queen's youngest daughter – at the head of an all-female shortlist.[8] Almost a local, the Princess lived at Carisbrooke Castle on the Isle of Wight and, as the widow

64 Princess Beatrice (1857–1944) had stayed at the Royal Bath in 1911, but Merton missed her visit because of his trip to Spain and France. For the Princess to open the museum's new galleries was a great honour, as she scaled back her public engagements after the death of her son, Maurice, at Ypres in 1914. She relinquished the title 'Princess Henry of Battenberg' in 1917 when the family anglicised its surname to Mountbatten. (Library of Congress)

of Prince Henry of Battenberg, provided a link to Merton's mayoralty.

The Princess came to Bournemouth on 1st February 1919, Merton and Annie's fifty-ninth wedding anniversary. Merton marked the event by inscribing the date, and its personal significance, above the door separating the new galleries from the original house. His sister Clara had died a few days earlier, making him the last survivor of the ten children of Samuel and Elizabeth Coates.[9] One wonders what they would have made of their beknighted son showing the Queen's daughter around the Russell-Cotes Art Gallery and Museum. Annie kept to her room – she was now too frail to greet even a royal visitor – but Merton made sure she was not forgotten. Ella, standing in for her mother, handed over the deeds of the building to the Princess, who in turn passed them on to the mayor. Afterwards, Merton announced a further gift of £5,000 to the museum on behalf of the couple, which he hoped would provide enough income to employ a curator. He also handed over a portrait of Edward VII, the Princess's late brother, in honour of their royal guest's visit.

Lunch, in the now familiar fashion, was laid on at the Royal Bath to celebrate. The guests included the president of Dr Barnado's and the director of the Shaftesbury Society, whose presence that day pointed the way towards the second and third acts of Merton's charitable opus. He and Annie had agreed to give away the whole of their Parkstone estate to these two organisations. Most of it went to Dr Barnardo's as a site for a nautical school for boys, the rest to the Shaftesbury Society for a children's home. The land alone was said to be worth £20,000, but the giving did not stop there. To encourage others to donate to the school – a scheme costing £80,000 – the couple donated a tenth of that sum in Annie's name towards the cost of the building work. Their generosity allowed Dr Barnado's to press ahead with the project. The new institution was to be called 'The Russell-Cotes Nautical School', while its main building would be named 'Lady Russell-Cotes House'. It was not the charity's only establishment of this type, but it was the first to focus on the Merchant Service rather than the Royal Navy. As Henry Page Croft put it: 'No gift was more fitting or more opportune in that hour when they were dictating terms to their enemies.' It would, he said, 'give to the British Empire more of the men merchant-trained in the arts of the sea.' [10]

The laying of the school's foundation stone took place on 8th May 1919, Merton's eighty-fourth birthday. Prince Albert (1895–1952) – the future King George VI and a veteran of the naval action at Jutland – came to do the honours. Battling shyness and a stammer in a rare public speech, he paid tribute to the sacrifices made by the Merchant Service during the war. Merton was not strong enough to go to Parkstone to hear him, but the Prince called at East Cliff Hall to pose for a photograph in front of the portrait of Edward VII. Exhausted from giving a guided tour, Merton excused himself from the subsequent lunch at the Royal Bath.

Two months after Prince Albert's visit, Princess Marie Louise of Schleswig-Holstein (1872–1956) – a granddaughter of Queen Victoria – laid the foundation stone of the Russell-Cotes Home for Children at Parkstone. The event, arranged to coincide with Annie's birthday, brought the couple's benevolence to a climax. They gave £3,000 towards the cost of the main building, which was again to be called Lady Russell-Cotes House.[11] The Princess followed Prince Albert's lead in paying her respects at East Cliff Hall and taking the guided tour. 'Have you and Lady Russell-Cotes collected all

65 Prince Albert pictured at East Cliff Hall, 8th May 1919. Standing between Merton and Bert is Major Louis Greig (1880–1953), who partnered the future King George VI at the Wimbledon men's doubles in 1926. They lost 6–1, 6–3, 6–2 in the first round. Merton believed that the famously shy Prince made his first public speech at Parkstone, but he had spoken during the opening of a rifle range at the House of Lords in 1916. (From Home and Abroad)

these things yourselves?' she asked Merton in astonishment. 'It must have taken a long time.' [12]

Merton, as with the two previous royal visits, made sure no one forgot about Annie. She was bedridden now, her strength ebbing away in a sunny bedroom facing the sea in a tranquil corner of East Cliff Hall. 'Very precious are the memories of those last months,' he wrote. 'No word or sound of the world's unrest and strife was ever allowed to cross the threshold of the room which few were privileged to enter.' [13] Annie lived long enough to see in their diamond wedding anniversary in February 1920, but it was a quiet family affair spent at home. Letters of congratulation poured in from near and far, including from the National Party, the Church Association, Bournemouth Literature and Art Association, the Japan Society, the Royal Colonial Institute, the National Provincial Bank, the county magistrates and many, many more. Florence Laney (1870–1935), Bournemouth's first female councillor, wrote a warm tribute on behalf of the local Women's Suffrage Society.

A thirty-strong group of friends and associates formed a committee to buy a gift to mark this latest milestone. Its chairman, Sir Daniel Morris (1844–1933), was an eminent botanist who knew Merton through the Bournemouth Natural Science Society. Others on the committee included Field Marshall Lord Grenfell (1841–1925) – who owned a house in the town – Sir George Meyrick, Sir Thomas Lipton and Henry Page Croft. The role of secretary went to J. Ralph Smythe, who epitomised the seismic shift in the public perception of his old sparring partner. 'However I may have differed with you in the past on the subject of the undercliff drive,' he wrote to Merton, 'I am at one with you in admiration of that splendid promenade now.' [14] Smythe had his work cut out dealing with the letters sent in from all parts of the globe. He collected over £500 in donations, enough to commission a portrait of the couple from Frank Richards, the Boscombe artist. The plan was for the painting to be ready for Annie's birthday, but her rapid decline overtook its completion.

With her condition nearing its crisis, the committee arranged a belated anniversary celebration at East Cliff Hall in March 1920. Each guest received a souvenir brochure to remind them of the couple's contributions to the town. It was a rousing work compiled by the journalist Austin Brereton (1862–1922) – one of Sir Henry Irving's many biographers – who made much of Merton's dogged determination. 'Opposition flung against any well-considered project of his only made him more pertinacious,' he wrote. 'He knew he was right. And right always won. Even the most persistent in opposition to him would finally recognise that this far-sighted and calculating man was right.' Merton was keen to deflect the praise onto Annie when he thanked his guests. 'I may tell you,' he said, 'that every good work, every admirable deed which has been carried through by myself, has been at her

66 Lady Margaret Morris – wife of Sir Daniel – presenting Merton with an illuminated address in belated recognition of his and Annie's diamond wedding anniversary, 24th March 1920. The address was designed by Blanche Funnell, a former pupil at the Bournemouth Municipal School of Art. (From *Home and Abroad*)

inspiration and instigation. At the present moment she is lying in bed day after day for the last year or more with perfect patience and contentment, with not a word, not a syllable of complaint.' [15] Annie, dubbed 'The Queen of Bournemouth' by her grandchildren, was entering the final weeks of her reign.[16] One of her last acts was to insist on seeing the first intake of boys to the nautical school when they came to look round the museum. 'It was beautiful to see her tender concern for a boy's distress when calling her "Miss" instead of "My Lady",' wrote Merton.[17]

Annie died, aged eighty-four, in her room at East Cliff Hall on the evening of 17th April 1920. Tributes were generous, but Merton's personal loss far outweighed the formal expressions of sadness. 'The light of my life has gone out,' he wrote in an emotional epilogue to *Home and Abroad*. 'My soul yearns with inconceivable longing to meet my darling wife again.' [18] He had lost his rock, the calming influence on what had often been a turbulent life. William Pickford knew them as an affectionate couple, the one providing a shoulder for the other to lean on. 'Don't imagine,' he added, 'that he never vexed her with his masterfulness, or that she never irritated him by proposing domestic problems when his mind was in the clouds.' [19] They were a formidable partnership, that much is clear, whatever their differences in personality.

Annie was buried three days later, her coffin carried to its final resting place in a glass carriage escorted by boys from the nautical school. Merton was too unwell to attend and so missed the heartfelt eulogy delivered by their Presbyterian minister. He remembered a devout woman, sincere in her charity and with 'a buoyant, albeit a quiet temperament.'[20] She was interred in a grand mausoleum at the town's Wimborne Road cemetery. Bearing the arms of the Cotes family on the outside, and with busts of the devoted couple within, it was decorated in a style reminiscent of East Cliff Hall.[21]

A fortnight later, Merton reached his eighty-fifth birthday. Bert's eldest daughter, Evelyn, had chosen that day to get married, but she cancelled the reception and called in on her grandfather before going on honeymoon. Merton seldom left the house now. A ceremony planned for Annie's birthday to present him with the Frank Richards portrait had to be postponed, but he disliked the painting anyway. With the two subjects unavailable for sittings, Richards carried out his commission from a photograph. It shows Annie standing beside her seated husband, with the arms of the Cotes and Clark families on the wall behind them. Merton looks immaculate in a black suit, red cravat and white spats, his feet planted on a bearskin rug. He is holding what appears to be a pamphlet, with a discarded envelope on the floor at his side. The untidiness annoyed him, and he asked the artist to paint over the offending item. When Richards refused, Merton gave the picture to the council to hang in their gallery of mayoral portraits.

67 Annie's funeral cortege, 20th April 1920. 'Her public benefactions were many and generous,' ran the obituary in the Bournemouth Guardian. *'Indeed, we are informed that it was her desire to distribute all she possessed during her lifetime and that, prior to her last illness, she had accomplished this.'[22] Their information was, to all intents and purposes, correct: Annie's estate amounted to only £400. (From* Home and Abroad*)*

Bert handed over the painting in October 1920, along with a silver-gilt chalice, given in his mother's name, for ceremonial use by the council. Merton gave £2,000 in the same month towards a home for blind women in Bournemouth – his last big donation. His final public appearance came at the end of November, when he invited members of the local Primrose League to East Cliff Hall to present them with a banner in Annie's memory. Beside a bust of Disraeli garlanded with primroses, he made a speech in praise of the League's work that ended with a lament. The world was descending into anarchy, he said, the result of the loss of Christian influence on the human mind. The tone of these remarks echoes his downbeat assessment of the future in *Home and Abroad*. Desperate to finish the book before time ran out, he seems to have approached the end with his faith in mankind shattered.

Despite hundreds of acquaintances, Merton had to content himself with his own company for much of the time. William Pickford called in to see him over Christmas and came away with a deep sense of sorrow. Merton was, he felt, 'pathetically lonely in his great age amid all the treasures of East Cliff Hall.' [23] A lifetime's accumulation counted for little with the house bereft of the woman who made it a home. Pickford remembers him feeding the birds during a hard frost that winter, the sort of thing he left to Annie in former days. Still, he had enough energy for one last spat with the council. Eager to add a fourth gallery to the museum, he found his way blocked by, of all things, concerns about the stability of the cliffs.

The issue remained unresolved when, a few weeks after Christmas, Merton took to his bed after complaining of feeling unwell. Spared the long, slow decline so painful to witness in Annie, he died of heart failure on 27th January 1921. His funeral took place on 1st February – the couple's sixty-first wedding anniversary. Bert says this was a coincidence, as he realised the significance of the date only after making the arrangements. 'Thus it happens,' he wrote, 'that, so far as my knowledge goes, they have never spent a wedding day apart.' [24] Merton had an unshakeable confidence in the afterlife and never doubted that he and Annie would one day be reunited. Indeed, he quotes Sir Henry Irving in his closing lines to *Home and Abroad:* 'I believe in immortality, and my belief is strengthened with advancing years. Without faith in things spiritual, this life would indeed be a weary waste.' [25]

Merton was laid to rest after a simple Presbyterian service. Buglers from the nautical school played the Last Post as his coffin was placed in the mausoleum alongside Annie's. Local dignitaries and officials of their favoured organisations made up the greater part of the mourners. Sir Thomas Lipton headed the smaller list of personal friends. Merton had outlived many of those close to him, and yet this display of public homage was wholly apt. A man of grand gestures with a love of ceremonials, he would have approved of a solemn funeral that reflected his support for so many good causes. The Grand Old Man of Bournemouth was dead, but his legacy lived on.

Notes:

1. *Home and Abroad* opens with the line: 'On this, the 82nd anniversary of my natal day, I begin this review...' Merton contradicts this later by saying that he started work on his autobiography before the war. Bert's postscript supports the later date, so the earlier one may refer to preparatory work.
2. ibid., pp. 6–7.
3. ibid., p. 652.
4. Croft was a vehement critic of abuse of the honours system by political parties.
5. Phyllis Lee-Duncan recalls paying Miss Sherrard a pension of £300 per annum until her death in 1948.
6. The road name omits the hyphen. It was previously called Cliff Road.
7. *Home and Abroad*, p. 1016.
8. Lipton also suggested Princess Louise (another of Queen Victoria's daughters), Princess Patricia of Connaught (a granddaughter) and Princess Arthur of Connaught (a great-granddaughter).
9. Clara died in Birkenhead, where she spent the last few years of her life. She was ninety-one.
10. *Western Gazette*, 16 May 1919.
11. The Lady Russell-Cotes House built for the children's home no longer exists, as it has made way for housing. The building of the same name at the nautical school was taken over by the local college when the establishment closed in 1964. It is unoccupied at the time of writing.
12. *Home and Abroad,* pp. 370–71. Other people had given items to the museum by this time, a fact acknowledged by Merton in *Home and Abroad*.
13. ibid., p. 1016.
14. ibid., p. 1000.
15. *Bournemouth Guardian*, 27 March 1920.
16. *Home and Abroad*, p. 1016.
17. ibid., p. 1017.
18. ibid., p. 1015.
19. *Bournemouth Guardian*, 5 February 1921.
20. *Home and Abroad*, p. 1031.
21. Historic England attributes the mausoleum to John F. Fogerty, which dates its conception to no later than 1914, although discussions about the plot took place as early as 1903. The mausoleum's gates and bronze doors were stolen in 2010.
22. *Bournemouth Guardian*, 24 April 1920.
23. ibid., 5 February 1921.
24. *Home and Abroad*, p. 1039.
25. ibid., p. 1035.

17

BENEFACTOR

Among the many tributes paid to Merton in the days after his death, the two retrospectives published by the *Bournemouth Guardian* offer an intriguing contrast. Its formal obituary sticks to a well-told story, with only minor revelations about his expenditure during the pier opening and the visit of Prince Henry of Battenberg. While this says a lot about the information he shared with the press, it does nothing to chip away at his public persona. This is what makes the paper's second tribute so valuable. Written by its editor, William Pickford, it sheds more light on Merton's character than all the rehashed potted biographies put together. Pickford knew him better than most and regarded him as a friend. He provides a glimpse of Merton as a person, a unique insight into a man who knew a multitude of people but who rarely let his guard down. 'His was a complex character. In a way, he was a genius,' suggested Pickford in a piece that strikes the right balance between praise and appraisal.

Pickford had experienced both the best and the worst of Merton. He had often been left feeling irritated and exasperated by a telephone call demanding column inches in his newspaper. 'I have sometimes wished him to Halifax,' he wrote. 'A message delivered by a printer's devil at a particularly awkward moment has, ere this, made me have a deep sigh or worse.' While conceding that Merton was pushy, ambitious and obsessed with his title and a string of post-nominal letters, Pickford knew few better men of business. He could be difficult to deal with, as others knew only too well, but he always put his money where his mouth was. Pickford did not profess to know what drove him, nor could he make sense of his many contradictions. How, he wondered, could someone who spent so much money on civic entertainments take such an obstinate stance on South Road? This, in retrospect, is one of the easier questions to answer. Merton, who never compromised when it came to the Royal Bath, saw a threat and took firm action to put a stop to it.

68 William Pickford, Merton's obituarist, was not only a journalist but also a key figure in early football administration. As well as his involvement with the Hampshire Football Association, he served as president of the English FA from 1937 until his death a year later. In 1906, he published one of the first books about refereeing. (Author's collection)

Pickford avoided the clichés found in most other accounts of Merton's life. Words such as collector, traveller and mayor all have their place, but his story is far more nuanced and ambiguous than these over-used labels suggest. Indeed, if he had felt able to open up a little more about his background and setbacks in *Home and Abroad*, then his achievements would have come across as all the more remarkable. While not alone among his peers in wanting to trumpet his successes, he did himself a disservice by overdoing it. Pickford observed how his detractors often criticised him for putting on a 'good show', and yet this very thirst for publicity clouds so much of what Merton did. It brought accusations of self-interest in his early days in Bournemouth, a charge that dogged him as the South Road saga unfolded. A more benign figure might have got away with it, but he had upset too many people to expect his actions to be greeted with anything other than condemnation. It is an irony, then, that South Road was not only his biggest disaster but also the start of the rehabilitation that ultimately led to his knighthood. This transformation, driven to a large extent by philanthropy, allowed his own view of the world to prevail in a way that Joseph Cutler's never did. Both men longed to be recognised as one of the town's visionaries, but Merton underpinned his claim with a string of tangible legacies. As the council came together time and again to celebrate them, old disputes were glossed over and past contributions polished up so as to muddy the waters for later historians. Local newspapers reported these events in meticulous detail, and it is their words, not the author's, that account for much of *Home and Abroad*'s bulk. They form the backbone of the last act of self-promotion by a determined salesman who sold himself with gusto.

Merton made the final changes to his autobiography in the weeks before his death, and Bert published it privately later that year. He sent copies to libraries in Britain and America, but one wonders how many people have read it. Merton is not well known enough to attract the curious, and the two weighty volumes are heavy going for anyone who bothers. His travel writing is not as engaging as Richard Tangye's and, as a life story, the narrative is disjointed and sketchy. As local history, it is too one-sided to be of great value. Merton made an important contribution to Bournemouth's growth, there is no doubt about that, but he was a catalyst rather than an elemental force. The direct line and undercliff drive, although not his ideas, benefitted from his energetic support, while the money he spent on banquets, luncheons and garden parties helped to boost the town's profile. These things deserve credit, but to describe Bournemouth as 'his monument', as Austin Brereton did, is a step too far. Tregonwell, Gervis and Creeke have much stronger claims on that score. While they live on mainly in pub names and road signs, Merton's is a far more conspicuous and vibrant legacy. The gift of the museum inevitably enhanced his mixed reputation, but this exceptional largesse made it that much harder – and still does – to put his achievements into perspective. His travails as mayor and improvement commissioner suggest that he was ill-suited to the rough and tumble of civic affairs. While confident and opinionated, the stress caused by scrutiny and contradiction put paid to any hopes of making his mark in local politics. Instead, he revelled in his position as a man of wealth and influence in his adopted town. Poor health and long absences may explain why he never built an empire beyond Bournemouth, but the stream of eminent guests at the Royal Bath reflected the glory of a much bigger stage.

If mental strife and a chronic lung condition were his weakness, then Merton defied them both with a long and active life. Even so, his preoccupation with medical matters persisted to the very end. His will required two independent doctors to confirm his death before committing him for burial, an unusual request that raises another contradiction. He spent his final months yearning for a reunion with Annie, and yet here he seems to be clinging to the hope of delaying it for a while longer. Aside from this odd proviso, and a plea to his children and grandchildren to visit the graves of his family, Merton's will is a simple affair. He left all his worldly goods to Bert, and there are no specific bequests. The gross value of his estate came to £50,000 – enough to make him wealthy, if not fabulously so. Joseph Cutler and Enoch White, two moderately successful businessmen, amassed half that sum between them. Sir Thomas Lipton, the king of groceries, left ten times as much. What makes Merton's estate unusual is that its net value amounted to just £800. In other words, the bulk of his assets were spoken for either by debts or, more likely, outstanding gifts. It seems that, having worked so hard to amass their fortune, Merton and Annie almost succeeded in giving it all away.

69 The Russell-Cotes Art Gallery and Museum as it is today. (Russell-Cotes Art Gallery and Museum)

Cynics might say that Merton was no more than an adept salesman who bought his way to good favour, or that he bartered his house for a knighthood. While both may be true, the couple kept on giving long after achieving those things. It was as if philanthropy became a compulsion or an act of faith – a case of heeding the biblical warning about the rich man and the eye of the needle. The sincerity of their religious convictions is beyond doubt and may have been their primary motivation as they approached the end of their lives. Prestige, status, pride and duty also played a part, but Annie's role in their giving should not be underestimated. She never forgot her Girvan roots, where a humble childhood shaped her attitudes to wealth and developed a keen sense of duty to those less fortunate than herself. For Merton, money was always a tool, never an ornament, and he seldom failed to use it wisely. Regardless of their motives, the couple's rich and enduring cultural legacy secured their well-deserved place at the forefront of Bournemouth's history.

The Russell-Cotes Art Gallery and Museum officially opened in March 1922. Richard Quick (1860–1940), its first curator, was a veteran of museums in London and Bristol who knew Merton through the Japan Society. Ella and Bert continued to support their parents' legacy and were present at the opening of the fourth gallery in 1926. The Royal Bath, meanwhile, carried on under Bert's guidance. He tried to adapt to changing times, and the hotel's dance band and orchestra often appeared on the fledgling BBC. In general,

70 The main hall at the Russell-Cotes Art Gallery and Museum as it is today. (Russell-Cotes Art Gallery and Museum)

though, it fared less well than in his father's day. Its décor and ambience belonged to a bygone age, not the new era of post-war optimism. Phyllis Lee-Duncan, when interviewed in the 1990s, recalled challenging times, with Bert and his manager at loggerheads, the bank nervous, and personal issues making a difficult situation worse. The details are of no concern here, but there is little doubt that Bert was a troubled man. He was found dead in his bed in August 1932, having taken his own life at the age of sixty-one. His suicide note was not made public, apart from a few lines confirming his intentions.

After Bert's death, the Royal Bath passed via Ella Stebbing – the last survivor of Merton and Annie's children – into the hands of her daughter, the formidable Mrs Lee-Duncan. She played a big part in restoring the hotel's fortunes. By the time of her mother's death in 1954 at the age of ninety-three, it had once again acquired a five-star reputation. Its sale to the De Vere chain in 1963 ended a family connection stretching back almost ninety years.

SELECTED BIBLIOGRAPHY

Addison, Paul. (2004) 'Churchill, Sir Winston Leonard Spencer (1874–1965)'. In: *Oxford Dictionary of National Biography*. Oxford: Oxford University Press.

Beg, M. A. (1911) *The Guide to Lucknow*. Lucknow: M. A. Beg.

Bills, Mark, ed. (2001) *Art in the Age of Queen Victoria*. Bournemouth: Russell-Cotes Art Gallery and Museum.

Brereton, Austin. (1908) *The Life of Henry Irving, Volumes 1 and 2*. London: Longmans, Green and Co.

Brereton, Austin. (1920) *Sir Merton & Lady Russell-Cotes*. Bournemouth: Russell-Cotes Art Gallery and Museum.

Bridge, John. (1884) *A Visit to the Isle of Wight by Two Wights*. London: Wyman & Sons.

Brown, Kenneth D. (2004) 'Burns, John Elliott (1858–1943)'. In: *Oxford Dictionary of National Biography*. Oxford: Oxford University Press.

Capper, Alfred. (1915) *A Rambler's Recollections and Reflections*. London: George Allen and Unwin Ltd.

Carey, Agnes. (1920) *Empress Eugenie in Exile*. New York: The Century Co.

Challen, Peter and Whittaker, Ron. (2000) *Lives and Times of the Mayors of Bournemouth, 1890–2000*. Bournemouth: Bournemouth Borough Council.

Churchill, Winston. (1930) *A Roving Commission: My Early Life*. New York: Charles Scribner's Sons.

Cooke, Anthony. (2010) *The rise and fall of the Scottish cotton industry, 1778–1914: 'The secret spring'*. Manchester: Manchester University Press.

Cooper, Sidney W. (1884) *Rambles in Sweden: A series of letters from Sweden to a newspaper in America*. Gothenburg: s. n.

Crick, Throne. (1847) *Sketches from the Diary of a Commercial Traveller*. London: Joseph Masters.

Cross, Anthony. (2014) *In the Lands of the Romanovs: An Annotated Bibliography of First-hand English-language Accounts of The Russian Empire (1613–1917)*. Open Book Publishers.

Davey, Elizabeth. (2009) *Birkenhead: A History*. Chichester: Phillimore & Co. Ltd.

De-la-Noy, Michael. (1985) *The Honours System*. London: Allison & Busby Ltd.

Dodds, James. (1897) *Records of the Scottish Settlers in the River Plate and their Churches*. Buenos Aires: Grant and Sylvester.

Edgington, M. A. (1985) *Bournemouth and the First World War: The Evergreen Valley, 1914 to 1919*. Bournemouth: Bournemouth Local Studies Publications.

Edwards, Jackie. (2010) *A Bed By The Sea: A History of Bournemouth's Hotels*. Christchurch: Natula Publications.

Edwards, Lee MacCormick. (2004) 'Herkomer, Sir Hubert von Herkomer (1849–1914)'. In: *Oxford Dictionary of National Biography*. Oxford: Oxford University Press.

Fitzgerald, Percy. (1906) *Sir Henry Irving, A Biography*. Philadelphia: George W. Jacobs & Co.

French, Michael. (2010) On the road: travelling salesmen and experiences of mobility before 1939. *Journal of Transport History*. 31(2). pp. 133–50.

Furniss, Harry. (1892) *Flying Visits*. New York: United States Book Company.

Garner, Shaun. (1992) *The Motives for the foundation of a museum in Bournemouth by Merton and Annie Russell-Cotes at the turn of the century*. Unpublished Master's thesis.

Gilbert and Sullivan Archive. *Who was who in the D'Oyly Carte Opera Company (1875–1982)*. www.gsarchive.net.

Granville, A. B. (1841) *Spas of England and Principal Sea-Bathing Places: Southern Spas*. London: Henry Colburn.

Greenslade, M. W., Johnson, D.A. and Tringham, N. J. (1988) *A History of Tettenhall*. Wolverhampton: Staffordshire Libraries, Arts and Archives.

Grimsditch, H. B. (2004) 'Solomon, Solomon Joseph (1860–1927)'. In: *Oxford Dictionary of National Biography*. Oxford: Oxford University Press.

Hancock, Geoffrey. (1991) *A Tettenhall History*. Tettenhall: Broadside.

Hart-Davis, Rupert, ed. (1962) *The Letters of Oscar Wilde*. New York: Harcourt, Brace & World, Inc.

Hazlehurst, Cameron and Woodland, Christine, eds. (1994) *A Liberal Chronicle: Journals and Papers of J. A. Pease, 1st Lord Gainford, 1908–1910*. London: The Historians' Press.

Jacobs, Arthur. (1984) *Arthur Sullivan: A Victorian Musician*. Oxford: Oxford University Press.

James, Jude. (2012) *Treacle Mines, Tragedies and Triumph: The Building of the Bournemouth Direct Line 1883–88*. Christchurch: Natula Publications.

Jenkins, Carl. (1965) *Jenkins & Sons Builders, A History*. Privately published.

Kenealy, Maurice Edward. (1913) *The Tichborne Tragedy*. London: Francis Griffiths.

Ledbetter, Kathryn. (2012) *Victorian Needlework*. Santa Barbara, CA: Praeger.

Lester, V. Markham. (1995) *Victorian Insolvency: Bankruptcy, Imprisonment for Debt, and Company Winding-up in Nineteenth-Century England*. Oxford: Clarendon Press.

Liddell, T. Hodgson. (1910) *China: Its Marvel and Mystery*. London: George Allen & Sons.

Lipton, Thomas. (c. 1932) *Leaves from the Lipton Logs*. London: Hutchinson & Co. (Publishers) Ltd.

Llorca, Manuel. (2008) *British Textile Exports to the Southern Cone During the First Half of the Nineteenth Century: Growth, Structure and the Marketing Chain*. PhD thesis, University of Leicester.

Mackay, James. (1998) *The Man Who Invented Himself: A Life of Sir Thomas Lipton*. Edinburgh: Mainstream Publishing.

BIBLIOGRAPHY

Malchow, H. L. (1992) *Gentlemen Capitalists: The Social and Political World of the Victorian Businessman*. Stanford, CA: Stanford University Press.

Maskelyne, Jasper. (n.d.) *White Magic: The Story of Maskelynes*. London: Stanley Paul & Co. Ltd.

Mate, Chas H. and Riddle, Chas. (1910) *Bournemouth: 1810–1910: The History of a Modern Health and Pleasure Resort*. Bournemouth: W. Mate and Sons Ltd.

Matthew, H. C. G. (2004) 'George VI (1895–1952)'. In: *Oxford Dictionary of National Biography*. Oxford: Oxford University Press.

May, Vincent and Marsh, Jan, eds. (2010) *Bournemouth 1810–2010: From Smugglers to Surfers*. Wimborne: Dovecote Press.

McWilliam, Rohan. (2004) 'Tichborne claimant (d. 1898)'. In: *Oxford Dictionary of National Biography*. Oxford: Oxford University Press.

Menpes, Mortimer. (1906) *Henry Irving*. London: Adam and Charles Black.

Millais, John Guille. (1899) *The Life and Letters of Sir John Everett Millais, President of the Royal Academy*. London: Methuen & Co.

Moscucci, Ornella. (2004) 'Granville, Augustus Bozzi (1783–1872)'. In: *Oxford Dictionary of National Biography*. Oxford: Oxford University Press.

Mulhall, M. G. & E. T. (1869) *Handbook of the River Plate*. Buenos Aires: Standard Printing Office.

Mullin, Katherine. (2004) 'Mackay, Mary [pseud. Marie Corelli] (1855–1924).' In: *Oxford Dictionary of National Biography*. Oxford: Oxford University Press.

Nasmith, George C. (1917) *On the Fringe of the Great Fight*. Toronto: McClelland, Goodchild and Stewart.

Norman, Andrew. (2010) *Bournemouth's Founders and Famous Visitors*. Stroud: The History Press.

Olding, Simon and Garner, Shaun. (1997) *So Fair a House: The Story of the Russell-Cotes Art Gallery and Museum*. Bournemouth: Russell-Cotes Art Gallery and Museum.

Olding, Simon, Waterfield, Giles and Bills, Mark. (1999) *A Victorian Salon: Paintings from the Russell-Cotes Art Gallery and Museum*. London: Lund Humphries Publishers.

Owen, Mrs Henry. (1847) *The Illuminated Book of Needlework, comprising knitting, netting, crochet and embroidery*. London: Henry G. Bohn.

Pickford, William. (n.d.) *A Few Recollections of Sport*. s.l: s.n.

Pilbeam, Pamela. (2006) 'Eugénie (1826–1920).' In: *Oxford Dictionary of National Biography*. Oxford: Oxford University Press.

Popp, Andrew. (2007) Building the Market: John Shaw of Wolverhampton and commercial travelling in early nineteenth-century England. *Business History*. 49:3. pp. 321–47.

Popp, Andrew. (2012) *Entrepreneurial Families: Business, Marriage and Life in the Early Nineteenth Century*. London: Pickering & Chatto (Publishers) Ltd.

Postle, Martin. (2004) 'Cotes, Francis (1726–1770).' In: *Oxford Dictionary of National Biography*. Oxford: Oxford University Press.

Pugh, Peter. (1988) *The Royal Bath*. Cambridge: Cambridge Business Publishing.

Purdue, A.R. (2004) 'Beatrice, Princess (1857–1944).' In: *Oxford Dictionary of National Biography*. Oxford: Oxford University Press.

Quigly, Isabel. (2000) *The Royal Society of Literature: A Portrait*. London: Royal Society of Literature.

Reber, Vera Blinn. (1979) *British Mercantile Houses in Buenos Aires, 1810–1880*. Cambridge, MA: Harvard University Press.

Roberts, David. (1982) 'Leasehold estates and municipal enterprise: landowners, local government and the development of Bournemouth, c. 1850 to 1914.' In: Cannadine, David, ed. *Patricians, power and politics in nineteenth-century towns*. Leicester: Leicester University Press.

Russell-Cotes, Annie. (n.d.) *Letters from Russia*. s.l.: s.n.

Russell-Cotes, Annie. (n.d.) *Westward from the Golden Gate*. s.l.: s.n.

Russell-Cotes, Merton. (1921) *Home and Abroad: An Autobiography of an Octogenarian*. Bournemouth: Herbert Russell-Cotes.

Russell-Cotes Art Gallery and Museum. (2017) *Guide Book* (with text by Helen Ivaldi and Duncan Walker). Bournemouth: Russell-Cotes Art Gallery and Museum.

Searle, G. R. (2004) 'Guest, Frederick Edward (1875–1937)'. In: *Oxford Dictionary of National Biography*. Oxford: Oxford University Press.

Stoker, Bram. (1906) *Personal Reminiscences of Henry Irving*. Two volumes. London: William Heinemann.

Tangye, Richard. (1883) *Reminiscences of Travel in Australia, America and Egypt*. London: Sampson Low, Marston, Searle and Rivington.

Tangye, Richard. (1886) *Notes of My Fourth Voyage to the Australian Colonies*. Birmingham: White and Pike.

Thompson, Andrew S. (2004) 'Croft, Henry Page, first Baron Croft (1881–1947)'. In: *Oxford Dictionary of National Biography*. Oxford: Oxford University Press.

Trollope, Anthony. (1873) *Australia and New Zealand*. London: Chapman and Hall.

Tschudi, Clara (Cope, E. M. Translator). (1901) *Elizabeth, Empress of Austria and Queen of Hungary*. London: Swan Sonnenschein & Co.

Twain, Mark. (2015) *Autobiography of Mark Twain, Volume 3*. Berkeley, California: The Mark Twain Project.

Union Steam Ship Company of New Zealand. (1884) *Maoriland: An Illustrated Handbook to New Zealand*. Melbourne, Sydney, Adelaide and Brisbane: George Robertson and Co.

Upton, Chris. (1998) *A History of Wolverhampton*. Chichester: Phillimore & Co Ltd.

Wellings, Martin. (2004) 'Kensit, John (1853–1902)'. In: *Oxford Dictionary of National Biography*. Oxford: Oxford University Press.

INDEX

Aden – see Travels
Albany, Duchess of 93–94, 99, 101
Albert Edward, Prince of Wales – see Edward VII
Albert, Prince (consort of Queen Victoria) 9, 131
Albert, Prince (later King George VI) 187
Alexandra, Princess (consort of Prince of Wales) 98
Alexandra, Tsarina 131
Allen, Arthur Acland 168
Alma-Tadema, Lady 160
Altrincham – see Places of residence
Anderson, Robert 87
Angel, Henry 77–78, 181
Anti-Suffrage League – see Membership of organisations
Argentina
    British trade links 11
    Mercantile houses 11, 14–15
    MRC in Buenos Aires 11–17, 181
    St Andrew's Presbyterian Church and School 15–16
Argyll, Duke of 45, 53, 96
Art Manufacture Association 22
Art Treasures Exhibition (Old Trafford) 18
Art Union of London – see Membership of organisations
Arts Club (Mayfair) 151
Asquith, Herbert 165, 167
Australia – see Travels
Austria, Empress of 94

Bailey, Emma 53

Bailey, George 155–56
Baldwin's hotel – see Russell-Cotes, Merton
Balfour, Arthur 126, 136
Bath – see Loan collection
Bath Hotel – see Royal Bath Hotel
Batley – see Employers
Battenberg, Prince Henry of 121–22, 128, 165, 186, 193
Bazalgette, Joseph 46–48, 54, 90, 105, 146, 178
Beaconsfield, Lord – see Disraeli, Benjamin
Beale, Dorothea 165
Beale, John Elmes 57, 147, 151, 155, 157, 165
Beatrice, Princess 121, 185–86
Beckett, Archibald 144, 148, 153
Beechey, Thomas 69, 96, 103
Belgium, Prince Albert of 108
Belle Vue Hotel 54, 100, 116, 129, 148, 151, 154–55, 165, 174, 181
Bernhardt, Sarah 108, 152
Bethnal Green – see Places of residence
Billings, Josh 84
Birkenhead – see Places of residence
Blair, John & Co. – see Employers
Blomfield, Charles 81
Boer War 134, 157
Bonaparte, Napoleon I 48, 95–96, 100, 132
Bonaparte, Napoleon III 32, 75
Bonaparte, Prince Louis Lucien 48
Boscombe
    Library 119
    Pier 90, 96, 148

Regatta 126
Sewage problems 47–48, 54, 67
Boscombe Chine Hotel 88, 94
Boscombe Hippodrome 152–53
Bourbon-Parma, Prince Henry of 33–34
Bournemouth
   Before MRC's arrival 42–44
   Centenary 136, 173
   Commissioner elections 47–48, 58–67, 72, 76
   Council elections 103, 109, 114, 148, 157
   Great War (impact of) 178–80
   Improvement Act (1856) 46, 54
   Improvement commissioners 46–48, 50–51, 54–55, 58–76, 90–91, 96–98, 100, 102–3
   Incorporation 62, 68, 70, 89, 96, 102–6, 109
   King's Park 75
   Libraries 119, 124, 157, 160–61
   Margate (comparison to) 93, 110
   Meyrick Park 69, 116
   Museums 148, 157, 175–77
   Orchestra 108, 112
   Overcliff drive 111, 145, 147
   Pavilion 69, 108–11, 146–48, 151, 154–55, 165–67, 174–75, 178, 181
   Pier 46–53, 57–59, 61, 69–70, 96, 99, 111, 114, 127, 144, 165, 169, 193
   Pier extension (1909) 169
   Pier opening (1880) 50–53, 57
   Prince of Wales visit (1890) 96–99, 102–3, 112
   Railways – see Direct Line
   Regatta 96, 116, 139
   Residents' Association 62, 65, 146–47, 154–55, 162–63
   Sewage problems 46–48, 59, 67
   Town's Interest Committee 50–51, 61, 123
   Undercliff drive – see main heading
   Visitors' opinions 1, 12, 42, 57–58, 94, 114, 179–80
   Winter Gardens 45, 108, 119–20, 148, 157, 165
Bournemouth Arts Society 175
Bournemouth Literature and Art Association – see Membership of organisations
Bournemouth Municipal School of Art 189
Bournemouth Natural Science Society 176–77, 181, 188
Bournemouth School of Science and Art 124
Bournemouth, Swanage and Poole Steam Packet Company 70–71, 96
Bowdon – see Places of residence
Branksome Park – see Places of residence
Brearley, Robert & Sons – see Employers
Brereton, Austin 160, 188, 195
Briant, Arthur 38–41, 43–44, 53
Brierley & Cotes – see Employers
British Medical Association 105–6, 114–15, 120, 165
Buenos Aires – see Argentina
Burma – see Travels
Burnley – see Loan collection
Burns, John 174–75
Bute, Marquess of 115

Campbell, George – see Argyll, Duke of
Canada – see Travels
Canary Islands – see Travels
Capper, Alfred 106
Caribbean – see Travels
Carnegie, Andrew 157, 160–61
Cave, George 183
Ceylon – see Travels
Charles X of France 33
Chicago Exhibition – see Loan collection
Children (of MRC and ARC)
   Anita 26–27, 29, 31, 36
   Bert (Herbert) 32, 79, 95, 101, 105–6, 123, 129, 131, 138, 142–43, 147, 157–59, 161, 166, 174, 176–77, 179, 187, 190–92, 195–97
   Clarie (Clara) 25, 79, 95, 99, 105, 107, 112–13, 131, 142, 152, 161, 177, 181–82
   Ella 24, 37, 41, 56, 79, 90, 95, 106, 123, 131–32, 142, 149, 161, 174, 177, 186, 196–97
   Lottie (Charlotte) 26, 29, 36
China – see Travels
Choate, Joseph 134, 137
Christchurch 59, 62–63, 110, 148, 157, 166, 168, 171
Church Association – see Membership of organisations
Churchill, Randolph 98
Churchill, Winston 143, 167–68
Clark, Annie – see Russell-Cotes, Annie

INDEX

Clark, John King 19–23, 28, 36
Cleghorn, Archibald 81, 83
Clemens, Samuel – see Twain, Mark
Coates – see Cotes
Commercial travelling – see Russell-Cotes, Merton
Compton, Thomas 155
Connaught, Duke of 50
Conservative Party 44, 50, 64, 70, 92, 109, 143, 168, 184
Constable, John 134
Cook, James 82
Cooper, Sidney 50
Corelli, Marie 153–54, 172, 181
Cotes/Coates
    Alfred – see Siblings
    Anita (b. 1866) – see Children
    Anita (b. 1906) – see Grandchildren
    Ann – see Siblings
    Annie – see Russell-Cotes, Annie
    Benjamin 3–4, 7, 12, 17, 21
    Bert – see Children
    Charles 105, 111–12
    Charles Cecil 29, 111
    Charlotte – see Siblings
    Clara – see Siblings
    Clarie – see Children
    Edith – see Grandchildren
    Edward 12
    Elizabeth – see Law, Elizabeth
    Ella – see Children
    Emily – see Siblings
    Evelyn – see Grandchildren
    Francis 8, 12
    Frederick Merton 12
    Georgina – see Siblings
    Henrietta – see Siblings
    Laura 112
    Lottie – see Children
    Mary – see Siblings
    Merton – see Russell-Cotes, Merton
    Samuel (b. 1796) 3–7, 12, 37, 186
    Samuel (b. 1823) – see Siblings
    Shropshire family 2, 12, 21, 29, 105, 111, 141, 165
    W. Eastwick 111
Creeke, Christopher 45, 47, 53, 64, 66–70, 73, 75, 89–90, 146, 167, 195
Crisp, Frank 141, 149
Croft, Henry Page 183–85, 187–88, 192
Crome, John 18
Cutler, Joseph 59–62, 67–72, 96–97, 100, 103, 109, 119, 123–24, 147, 157–58, 176, 194–95

Derby – see Loan collection
Dickens, Charles 35, 40, 119
Direct Line (London to Bournemouth) 59–66, 68, 74, 89, 92–93, 99–100, 114, 195
Disraeli, Benjamin 44, 50, 75, 143, 164, 191
Dobell, Horace 74, 167
Dore, William 148, 151
Drew, Clarie – see Children
Drew, Gwendoline – see Grandchildren
Drew, Joseph 107, 131
Drew, Richard 136
Druitt, James 117
Dublin
    See Employers
    See Places of Residence

East Cliff Hall
    As private museum 152
    Construction 138–40, 151, 160
    Description 140–42
    Early designs (chalet) 129–131, 138
    Endowments (by MRC and ARC) 159, 164, 166, 176, 178, 183, 185–86
    Extensions 163, 178, 180–83, 185–86, 191, 196
    Freehold 177, 180, 184–85
    Garden 141
    Gift to the council 159–65
    Irving Collection/Room 153, 160, 164, 166, 176
    Land purchase 129
    Lease 129, 139
    Naming 139–40
    Opening to the public 164–65, 175, 179, 185
    Prince Albert visit (1919) 187
    Princess Beatrice visit (1919) 185–86
    Princess Marie Louise of Schleswig-Holstein visit (1919) 187–88
    Rothesay (named as East Cliff Hall) 117–18, 125–26, 139–40, 142
    Russell-Cotes Art Gallery and Museum 12, 56, 137, 160, 164, 175–76, 186, 196–97
    Trustees of museum 171
    Use for other collections 176–77
Edinburgh – see Hanover Hotel (Edinburgh)

Edward VII
  As King 170, 186–87
  As Prince of Wales 44–46, 50, 96–99, 102–3, 112, 118
Edwards, Henry 7–9, 15, 20, 37
Egypt – see Travels
Ellenborough, Lords of 141
Elwes, Captain 63
Employers (of MRC)
  Blair, John & Co. (Glasgow and Dublin) 24–25
  Brearley, Robert & Sons/Brierley & Cotes (Batley) 26, 30, 105
  Gifford Brothers (Buenos Aires) 14, 16
  Scott, Peter & Co. (Glasgow) 22, 25
  Scottish Amicable Society (apocryphal, Dublin) 17–19, 25–26, 28, 76, 105
Etty, William 132–33
Eugénie, Empress 32, 55–57, 59, 93–94, 164

Fernyhough, William 12
Ferrey, Benjamin 42
Fiji – see Travels
Fogerty, John 138, 140, 159, 171, 175, 178, 192
Formes, Karl 34, 84
France – see Travels
Funnell, Blanche 189
Furniss, Harry 1, 12

Garibaldi, Giuseppe 26
George, Prince (later King George V) 98
George VI, King – see Albert, Prince
Germany – see Travels
Gervis, George 42, 53, 98, 195
Gibraltar – see Travels
Gibson, Walter 81–82
Gifford Brothers – see Employers
Giles, Alfred 148
Giles, James 22, 164
Girl Combing Her Hair (painting) 22, 164
Girvan – see Russell-Cotes, Annie
Glasgow
  See Employers
  See Hanover Hotel (Glasgow)
  See Loan collection
  See Places of residence
  See Russell-Cotes, Annie
Glasgow University 8–11, 19
Godfrey, Dan 112

Goodall, Frederick 136
Grandchildren (of MRC and ARC)
  Cotes, Anita 177
  Cotes, Evelyn 142, 177, 190
  Cotes/Parsons, Edith 159, 174, 177
  Drew/Stanford, Gwendoline 113, 177, 182
  Stebbing, Edward 177
  Stebbing/Lee-Duncan, Phyllis 43, 100, 142, 149, 177, 184, 192, 197
Granville, Augustus 42–44
Greig, Louis 187
Grenfell, Lord 188
Griffiths, Elizabeth 48–49
Grover, Henry 75
Guest, Arthur 99
Guest, Freddie 168
Guest, Ivor – see Wimborne, Lord

Hallé, Charles 108
Halsbury, Lord 143
Hampshire Football Association – see Philanthropy
Hankinson, Thomas 61, 96, 100, 103–4, 147, 155, 176
Hanover Hotel (Edinburgh) 31–34, 39–41
Hanover Hotel (Glasgow) 31–41, 46, 48–49
Hargreaves, Fred 77
Harrison, Benjamin 102
Hart, Edward 157
Hawaii, King of 82–83
Hawaiian Islands – see Travels
Hawker, Harry 167, 171, 180, 183
Heenan, John 23–24
Herkomer, Hubert von 177–78, 181
Highcliffe Mansions hotel 50–51, 106
Highgate School 95
Hinton Admiral 63
Hirons, George 111, 116, 119–20, 136
Holder, Thomas 28
Holder, William 15–17, 28
Holloway, Thomas 53
Holman Hunt, William 123
Holy Land – see Travels
Hong Kong – see Travels
Houdon, Jean-Antoine 134
Hugo, Victor 32–33

Imperial hotel 90, 92, 99–100, 148, 171
Improvement commissioner (MRC as)
  Candidature 47–48, 58–66

INDEX

Chawbacons row 71–72
Commissioner 66–76
Direct Line – see main heading
Lamp post affair 69–71, 73
Resignation 73–75
Retrospective view 104, 115–16, 142, 195
Sanitary/Fever hospital 66–69, 73, 89, 116
India – see Travels
Irving, Henry 26, 108, 112, 120, 124, 132, 134, 152–54, 160, 164, 166, 176, 188, 191
Irving Room – see East Cliff Hall

Japan – see Travels
Japan Society – see Membership of organisations
Japanese Drawing Room – see Royal Bath Hotel
Jefferson, Joseph 153
Jenkins, Nelson 109, 112
Jenner, William 156

Kenealy, Edward 173
Kenealy, Maurice 173, 181
Kensit, John 144
Kilauea – see Travels, Hawaiian Islands
Kildare – see Rothesay, Kildare and Lynwood
King, Isabella 28
Kuntze, Franz 92, 95

Labour Party 148, 184
Lampard, James 43
Lanciarez, Eugenio-Martin 88
Lane, G. & Co. 73–74, 161
Lane, Gustavus 73–74
Laney, Florence 188
Lankester, Phebe 112
Law, Elizabeth 4, 6–9, 20, 37, 141, 153, 186
Law, Richard 41
Lawrence, Thomas 27
Leeds – see Loan collection
Lee-Duncan, Phyllis – see Grandchildren
Leighton, Edmund Blair 136
Leighton, Frederic 136, 140
Leopold, Prince 93
Letters from Russia – see Russell-Cotes, Annie
Liberal Party 109, 143, 167–68, 170–71, 174

Lipton, Thomas 32, 56, 172–73, 181, 185, 188, 191–92, 195
Lister, Joseph 10
Liverpool
See Loan collection
See Places of residence
See Russell-Cotes, Annie
Lloyd family – see Russell-Cotes, Annie
Loan collection (of MRC)
Bath 143
Burnley 143, 151
Chicago Exhibition 136
Derby 131–32
Glasgow 133
Hull 131
Knighthood citation 169
Leeds 128
Liverpool (Walker Gallery) 128, 136
Oldham 143, 168
Sale of 151–52
Sheffield (Mappin Gallery) 128, 133, 136
London and North Western Railway 8, 10, 18, 92
London and South Western Railway 59–66, 79, 92–93, 99, 104, 106, 114, 155
London, Lord Mayor of – see Truscott
Long, Edwin 133, 185
Lynwood – see Rothesay, Kildare and Lynwood

MacEwan, Clara – see Siblings
MacEwan, James 8–11, 15, 18–19, 21, 28, 30
Mackay, Mary – see Corelli, Marie
MacLeod, Norman 28
Malta – see Travels
Manchester – see Places of residence
Mappin Gallery – see Loan collection
Markham, Clements 99
Martin, Mary 53
Maskelyne, John 12–13
Mate, Charles 136
Mathews, Charles 39, 41
Mauritius – see Travels
Mayoralty (of MRC)
Appointment 109, 111, 114–16
Children's carnival affair 119–20, 127–28, 163
South Road affair 117–120, 122–23, 125–127, 129–30, 134–35, 140, 142, 163, 165, 193

207

Tenure 116–127
McWilliam, James 62
Membership of organisations (of MRC)
   Anti-Suffrage League 165
   Art Union of London 41
   Bournemouth Literature and Art Association 188
   Bournemouth Natural Science Society 181
   Church Association 144, 173, 188
   Japan Society (M.J.S.) 107, 112, 188, 196
   Primrose League 143, 191
   Protestant Truth Society 144, 173
   Royal Colonial Institute 188
   Royal Geographical Society (F.R.G.S.) 89, 91, 93, 99, 101–2, 106, 143, 173
   Royal Society of Literature 149
Meyrick, George (b. 1827) 43, 53–54, 63, 69, 76, 92, 107, 110–11, 114, 116, 118–120, 122–23, 125, 127, 129
Meyrick, George (b. 1855) 129–30, 139, 144–45, 151, 155, 171, 173, 177, 180, 188
Michaelyan, Haratune 135, 137
Millais, John Everett 108
Mont Dore hotel 57, 66, 74, 90–91, 93, 106
Moore, Henry 134
Moore, J. H. 103, 122, 176
Morris, Daniel 188–89
Morris, Margaret 189
Muirhead, James/John 28
Munck, Ebba 93

Nankivell, Herbert 63
Napoleon – see Bonaparte
National Gallery 177
National Party 184–85, 188
National Provincial Bank 188
Nelson, Ann 19
Nelson, James 41
New Zealand – see Travels
Newlyn, Henry 69–70, 90–91, 94, 96, 98, 102–3, 109–11, 116, 120, 122–23, 127, 136, 147, 155–56, 158, 175–76
Nicholas, Tsar 131
North British Railway Company 37, 39–40
Northcote, Stafford 64

Oldham – see Loan collection
Oldroyd, Mark 170
Oscar, Prince of Sweden 93

Painter, Arthur 75–76, 95, 100, 161
Panama – see Travels
Parkstone estate purchase – see Russell-Cotes, Merton
Parsons, George 159
Parsons, John Aldridge 159
Paterson, James 33–34, 48
Pattison, Godfrey & Co. 28
Paxton, Joseph 141
Pease, Jack 167
Philanthropy (of MRC and ARC)
   BMA conference 106
   Bournemouth centenary 173
   Clock/fountain (aborted gift) 130
   Dr Barnado's 184, 186–87
   East Cliff Hall – see main heading
   Hampshire Football Association 148, 150
   Mace and badge 103–5, 110, 165
   Other philanthropy 64, 126, 143–44, 167, 190–91
   Royal Victoria Hospital 96–97, 126, 169, 184
   Russell-Cotes Cup (football) 150
   Russell-Cotes Home for Children 186–88, 192
   Russell-Cotes Nautical School 186–87, 189–92
   Shaftesbury Society 143–44, 184, 186–87
   Washington bust 134–35, 137
   YMCA 135
Pickford, William 38, 41, 44, 53, 135, 147–48, 150, 155, 158, 189, 191, 193–94
Pinna, Joseph de 21, 28
Places of residence (of MRC)
   Altrincham/Bowdon 25–27, 30–31, 36, 99, 172
   Bethnal Green, London 9
   Bournemouth 42, *et seq.*
   Branksome Park, Dorset 89–90
   Dublin 25
   Glasgow 8–10, 13, 19, 21–25, 28, 31–41
   Manchester 18, 21, 28
   Merseyside (Birkenhead/Liverpool) 7–11, 15
   Wolverhampton 2, 4–7

INDEX

Poldi Pezzoli museum 157
Poole – see Russell-Cotes, Merton (Parkstone estate purchase)
Portal, Wyndham 59–63, 99, 114
Portarlington, Earl of 104
Primrose League – see Membership of organisations
Prince of Wales – see Edward VII
Promenade – see Undercliff drive
Protestant Truth Society – see Membership of organisations
Pullman, George 102

Quarry, Edith 138, 174, 177, 179
Quick, Richard 196

Rebbeck, Edward 70–71
Reingpach, Charles 75, 92
Rhodes, Cecil 95
Ribblesdale, Lord 177, 181
Richards, Frank 153, 188, 190
Ristori, Adelaide 34
Roberts, Field-Marshal 157
Rolls, Charles 173
Rooke, Thomas 136
Rothesay (Isle of Bute) 40, 118, 130, 136
Rothesay, Kildare and Lynwood (properties owned by MRC) 117–18, 145
Royal Academy 8, 50, 108, 151, 177
Royal Aquarium 35–36
Royal Bath Hotel
    After death of MRC 196–97
    BMA conference (1891) 106–7
    Early history 42–44
    Eminent guests 1, 42, 44, 47–48, 51–53, 55–57, 59, 64, 93–94, 99, 104, 107–8, 112, 119–21, 134, 152, 160, 177, 181, 186–87
    Foundation stone 58–59
    Freehold 129
    Great War (impact of) 178–80
    Guests' opinions 52, 57–58, 60, 114, 180
    Improvements by MRC 45, 48–50, 57, 69, 89–92, 94, 112, 178
    Japanese Drawing Room 57, 83, 85, 91–93, 99
    King's Hall 178–80, 183
    Lease 43, 129
    Managers 53, 68, 75, 92, 95, 179, 197
    Pier opening (1880) 51–53, 57, 61
    Prince of Wales visit (1890) 96–99
    Promotion by MRC 1–2, 44–46, 51–53, 57–58, 61, 64, 96, 102, 114, 154, 165, 167
    Purchase by MRC 38–41, 43–44
    Reported sale 127, 142
    'Royal' prefix 45–46, 54
Royal Colonial Institute – see Membership of organisations
Royal Counties Agricultural Society 120–22
Royal Exeter Hotel 70, 90–91, 94, 108, 110, 144, 156, 171
Royal Geographical Society – see Membership of organisations
Royal Hanover Hotel – see Hanover Hotel (Glasgow)
Royal Society of Literature
    See Membership of organisations
    See Russell-Cotes, Annie
Royal Victoria Hospital 96–99, 126, 150, 169, 184
Rôze, Marie 34
Russell, Lord John 5, 42, 53, 79, 141
Russell-Cotes, Annie
    Children – see main heading
    Children's carnival 119, 128
    Cotton connections 19
    Death/funeral 189–90
    Diamond wedding 28, 137, 188–90
    East Cliff Hall – see main heading
    Education 9–10, 15, 20–21
    Family background 10, 12, 19–21, 23, 28, 36, 41
    Father – see Clark, John King
    First meeting with MRC 9–11, 15, 21
    Freedom of the borough 165–66
    Girvan connections 19–21, 36, 41, 87, 123, 166, 170, 172, 196
    Glasgow connections 9, 19–21, 23–25, 88, 166
    Golden wedding 173–74
    Grandchildren – see main heading
    Great-grandchildren 181–82
    Health issues 101, 174, 185–86, 188–89
    Letters from Russia 131–32, 143
    Liverpool connections 9, 15, 20–21
    Lloyd family 9–10, 15, 20–21, 28
    Marriage 23
    Mother – see Nelson, Ann
    Philanthropy – see main heading
    Property ownership 74, 76, 101, 136, 139–40, 149, 161, 184

Religious views 15, 144, 190, 196
Royal Bath Hotel 44, 49
Royal Society of Literature (F.R.S.L) 143, 149
Support for MRC 27, 44, 67, 174, 188–89, 196
Travels – see main heading
Westward from the Golden Gate 77, 84–88, 100, 143, 184
Women's suffrage (attitude to) 165
Russell-Cotes Art Gallery and Museum – see East Cliff Hall
Russell-Cotes Cup – see Philanthropy
Russell-Cotes Home for Children – see Philanthropy
Russell-Cotes, Merton
 Art (love of) 1–2, 8, 17, 22, 27, 35–36, 49–51, 57, 80, 82, 85, 91, 107–8, 128–29, 132–34, 140, 151–52, 164–65, 177, 180
 Baldwin's hotel 151–52, 161, 169
 Belle Vue Hotel (attempted purchase) 129, 148
 Bournemouth (first visit) 38, 41
 Bournemouth (legacy to) 2, 102, 158, 175, 194–96
 Bournemouth (promotion of) 45, 53, 90, 95, 102, 109–10, 114–15, 127, 144, 166–67, 174
 Bournemouth (threat to leave) 127–28
 Business interests beyond hotels 33, 49, 70, 73
 Children – see main heading
 Commercial travelling 24–27, 30–31, 170
 Death/funeral 191
 Diamond wedding 28, 137, 188–90
 East Cliff Hall – see main heading
 Education 8–11, 15, 105
 Employers – see main heading
 Family background 2–11
 Father – see Cotes/Coates, Samuel (b. 1796)
 Freedom of the borough 165–67
 Golden wedding 173–74
 Grandchildren – see main heading
 Great War (views on) 180, 183–84
 Great-grandchildren 181–82
 Hanover Hotel – see main heading
 Health issues 11, 17, 36–37, 68, 73–74, 78, 101, 104, 115–16, 124, 127, 132, 142, 168, 195

 Home and Abroad (writing of) 183–84, 192, 194
 Horses (love of) 75, 143
 Improvement commissioner – see main heading
 Investment (attitude to) 17, 27, 30, 49, 110, 147, 180
 Knighthood 169–73
 Licensing Bill (objections to) 167
 Loan collection – see main heading
 Marriage 23
 Mayoralty – see main heading
 Medical studies 8–11, 105
 Membership of organisations – see main heading
 Mother – see Law, Elizabeth
 Naming styles 4–5, 21, 89, 170, 176
 Obituaries 193–94
 Parkstone estate purchase 164, 167–69, 171, 175, 186
 Philanthropy – see main heading
 Places of residence – see main heading
 Political views 44, 50, 64, 70, 109, 143, 168, 184–85, 188
 Property ownership beyond hotels 49, 54, 57, 89, 99, 167
 Religious views 23, 25, 27–28, 84, 86, 95, 109, 113, 144, 173, 180, 191, 196
 Royal Bath Hotel – see main heading
 Siblings – see main heading
 Stepfather – see Edwards, Henry
 Tettenhall connections 2–3, 5–7, 12, 89, 99, 136, 183
 Travels – see main heading
 Undercliff drive – see main heading
 Will 195
 Women's suffrage (attitude to) 165
Russell-Cotes Nautical School – see Philanthropy
Russia – see Travels

St Andrew's Presbyterian Church and School – see Argentina
St Helena – see Travels
Sala, George Augustus 1–2, 81, 86
Salisbury, Lord 92, 126, 135
Samoa – see Travels
Sanitary/Fever hospital – see Improvement commissioner
Saunders, Joseph 12
Sayers, Tom 23–24

INDEX

Schleswig-Holstein, Princess Marie Louise of 187–88
Scott, Peter & Co. – see Employers
Scott, Walter 49, 119
Scotter, Charles 27, 99, 104, 119, 171, 173, 177, 181
Scottish Amicable Society – see Employers
Shaftesbury Society – see Philanthropy
Shaw, John 12
Sheffield – see Loan collection
Sherrard, Louisa 184, 192
Shropshire Coteses – see Cotes, Shropshire family
Siblings (of MRC)
    Alfred 4, 6, 8–11, 18, 48–49, 92, 136
    Ann 4
    Charlotte 4, 6
    Clara (MacEwan) 4, 8–10, 18–19, 26, 30–34, 39–41, 43, 49, 107, 130, 186, 192
    Emily 4
    Georgina 4, 6, 31, 130, 136
    Henrietta 6
    Mary 4, 7, 29, 31, 130, 136
    Samuel 4, 6–8, 12, 18, 21, 25, 107, 112, 117
Singapore – see Travels
Smythe, J. Ralph 146–47, 176, 188
Soane, John 157
Solomon, Solomon J. 129
South Africa – see Travels
South Road affair – see Mayoralty
Southbourne-on-Sea 90, 146, 149, 155, 173
Spain – see Travels
Spens, William (junior) 76
Spens, William (senior) 17–18, 76
Spreckels, Claus 83–84
Stanford, Ronald 182
Stanley, Henry Morton 102
Stebbing, Edward (junior) – see Grandchildren
Stebbing, Edward (senior) 95, 142–43, 149, 177
Stebbing, Ella – see Children
Stebbing/Lee-Duncan, Phyllis – see Grandchildren
Stevenson, Robert Louis 74
Stoker, Bram 91, 107, 152, 160
Sullivan, Arthur 35–36
Sweden – see Travels
Sweden, King of 57, 93, 132, 136

Sweden, Queen of 55, 57, 93, 132, 178
Switzerland – see Travels

Tangye, Richard 77, 80, 82–83, 89, 195
Tapps, George 53
Tapps-Gervis – see Gervis
Tapps-Gervis-Meyrick – see Meyrick
Tavernier, Jules 82, 87
Tennyson, Alfred 152
Terry, Ellen 27, 108, 153, 176
Tettenhall – see Russell-Cotes, Merton
Thomas, Arthur 149
Thomas, John 57, 91, 100, 140, 149, 178, 185
Thomas, Oliver 140, 149, 178
Thomson, Alexander 'Greek' 24
Thomson, J. Roberts 38, 147
Thorneycroft, Florence 12
Thorneycroft, George 104
Thorneycroft, Thomas 5, 12, 104
Thrustance, Appolina 12
Thrustance, Charlotte 12
Tichborne, Roger 173, 181
Toomer, Mary 53
Trapnell, Alfred 171
Travels (of MRC and ARC)
    Aden 87
    Argentina (MRC solo) – see main heading
    Australia 77–79, 181
    Burma 87
    Canada 102
    Canary Islands 127–28
    Caribbean 108
    Ceylon 86
    China 85
    Egypt 87, 113
    Fiji 81
    France 174, 186
    Germany 120
    Gibraltar 87, 174
    Hawaiian Islands 79, 81–84, 88
    Holy Land 113–14, 123, 135
    Hong Kong 85
    India 1, 86–87
    Italy 109, 120
    Japan 83–85, 88, 91–92, 164
    Malta 87
    Mauritius 17 (MRC solo)
    New Zealand 77, 79–81
    Panama 101
    Russia 131–32
    St Helena 95–96, 153

Samoa 81
Singapore 85
South Africa 95
Spain 174, 186
Sweden 131–32
Switzerland 109
Turkey 114, 135
United States of America 79, 83–84, 101–2
Tree, Herbert Beerbohm 170
Tregonwell, Lewis 42, 90, 173, 195
Trollope, Anthony 77, 80–81
Truscott, Francis (Lord Mayor of London 1880) 50–53, 57–58, 60–62, 103, 115, 169
Truscott, George (Lord Mayor of London 1909) 169
Turkey – see Travels
Turner, J. M. W. 18–19, 27
Twain, Mark 84, 154

Undercliff drive
    Construction 157–58
    Early proposals 47–48, 74, 90, 95–96, 105–6, 108–11, 114, 116–17, 119–20, 127, 144–47
    Extension 165, 167, 174, 178
    Opening 158–60
    Public inquiry 155–57
    Storm damage 162–63
    Undercliff Drive, Promenade and Pavilion League 147–48, 151, 154–55
United States of America – see Travels

Vaughan Williams, Roland 155–56
Victoria, Queen 9, 23, 42, 50, 55, 93–94, 96, 102, 121–22, 130–31, 156, 185–87, 192
Vogel, Julius 80

Walker Gallery – see Loan collection
Wallace, Richard/Wallace Collection 183
Wareham, Frank 147
Warwick, Earl of 115
Washington bust – see Philanthropy
Watchers Asleep, The (painting) 35, 50, 124
Watkins, William 13
Wedgwood, Josiah 134
Westbourne 68, 74, 100, 168
Westward from the Golden Gate – see Russell-Cotes, Annie
White, Enoch 59–62, 67–73, 75–76, 97–98, 100, 176, 195
Wilde, Oscar 1, 75, 108, 112
Wilhelm II, Kaiser 184
Wimborne, Lady 97–99, 165, 167–68, 171, 173
Wimborne, Lord 97, 99, 165, 167–68
Winterhalter, Franz 56
Wolverhampton – see Places of residence
Wyndham, Charles 26, 41

YMCA – see Philanthropy
Young, Charles Baring 89

ABOUT THE AUTHOR

Paul Whittaker spent most of his childhood in the Southampton area, where he began his working life in the finance industry. A career change into IT took him to Bournemouth in the late 1980s, and he has lived in the town ever since. After becoming a volunteer at the Russell-Cotes Art Gallery and Museum in 2011, an interest in the founders' family history led him to embark on a master's degree in genealogy with the University of Strathclyde. His thesis examined the value of autobiographies as representative life stories, focusing on Sir Merton Russell-Cotes and five of his contemporaries. *The Art of a Salesman* – Paul's first book – builds on the results of that research. His other interests are running, indoor bowls, travel and the occasional quiz. He was runner-up on BBC *Mastermind* in 2012–13.

Printed in Great Britain
by Amazon